An Introduction to Persian

Thurs. May 17?
203
Sever Hall 9:15

Sepideh
628-4810

(chala — Çağla)
876·4339

chala@mit.edu

Tara
·493·8427

Michael office 4 copy of test
495 2355

Finals
tuesday
23rd — 9:15 am
Emerson 108

-end of the year final
17 May, 9:15 @
203 Sever Hall

An Introduction to
Persian
Revised Third Edition

Wheeler M. Thackston

IBEX Publishers
Bethesda, Maryland

An Introduction to Persian
Revised Third Edition
by Wheeler M. Thackston

Manufactured in the United States of America

The paper used in this book meets the minimum requirements
of the American National Standard for Information Services—
Permanence of Paper for Printed Library Materials, ANSI
Z39.48-1984

Audio cassette set of the Persian sections
of the book is available (isbn 0-936347-30-9)

IBEX Publishers / Iranbooks
Post Office Box 30087
Bethesda, Maryland 20824 U.S.A.
Telephone: 301-718-8188
Facsimile: 301-907-8707
www.ibexpub.com

Library of Congress Cataloging-in-Publication Data

Thackston, W.M. (Wheeler McIntosh), 1944-
An introduction to Persian / W. M. Thackston. -- Rev. ed.
p. cm.
Includes index.
ISBN 0-936347-29-5 (pbk.)
1. Persian language--Grammar. I. Title.
PK6235.T47   1993
491'.5582421--dc20   92-35714
CIP

3   5   7   9   8   6   4

Contents

INTRODUCTION: PHONOLOGY AND SCRIPT

PART ONE: THE GRAMMAR OF MODERN PERSIAN

Lesson One   1

§1 Word order. §2 Stress. §3 Gender. §4 State of the noun. §5 Orthography of the indefinite enclitic. §6 Adjectival order. §7 The plural. §8 The non-specific plural.

Lesson Two   6

§9 Demonstrative adjectives and pronouns. §10 Verbal agreement with the plural. §11 Co-ordination. §12 Adverbs. §13 Interrogative sentences. Supplementary Vocabulary: Courtesy Phrases.

Lesson Three   12

§14 The *ezâfe*. §15 The noun in the predicate position.

Preface

THIS BOOK IS intended to serve as an introduction on the elementary level to the modern Persian language.

A member of the Indo-Iranian branch of the Indo-European family, this language is called New Persian to distinguish it from Old Persian, the language of the Achaemenid Empire (6th–4th centuries B.C.), and from Middle Persian, the language of the Sassanians (3rd–7th centuries A.D.). In its present form Persian emerged during the tenth century of our era and, with the exception of certain items of vocabulary and a very few features of grammar and syntax, has changed remarkably little since the tenth and eleventh centuries. In its classical form, Persian became the language par excellence of poetry and mystical expression and, especially after the Mongol invasion of the thirteenth century, was the medium of culture and literature throughout the non-Arab Islamic world. From Constantinople to Bengal and from Central Asia to the south of India, Persian reigned for centuries as the language of high culture and belles-lettres.

At present Persian is the official language of Iran, and, although there are large areas of Iran where Persian is not the mother tongue (Azerbaijan, Kurdistan, Luristan, e.g.), it is spoken by almost everyone. In Afghanistan, where it is often called Dari, it enjoys official status along with Pashto and is spoken by all educated persons. Called Tajiki, it is the language of Tajikistan, where until recently it was written in the Cyrillic alphabet.

Persian is remarkably simple in terms of formal grammar: no gender, no noun inflection, no adjectival agreement, and no irregularities in verbal conjugation. However—and rather like English in this respect—what it lacks in inflection it more than makes up for in syntactic and idiomatic complexity; and it is to the syntax and idiom of Persian that the student's attention should be turned from the very beginning. The importance of understanding the proper relationships among the various members of a Persian sentence cannot be overstated (especially in view of the fact that the most important indicator of syntactic relationships is not usually indicated in the writing system), for even the simplest expression is liable to misunderstanding if the syntax is disregarded. It should also be kept in mind that simple, straightforward prose is relatively rare in Persian.

A second major hurdle in learning a language like Persian is the acquisition of vocabulary. Since there are no cognates to speak of between English and Persian, the English-speaking student starts from zero—quite unlike learning French or German, where, whether one is aware of it or not, one already "knows" a great many words that are shared or cognate. This problem is only compounded by the high proportion of borrowed Arabic vocabulary in Persian, not unlike English with our Latin, Greek and Norman French derivatives. The vocabulary lists at the end of each lesson are intended for active acquisition: these words should be learned not only for recognition within a Persian context but also for proper use in composition and conversation. Specialized supplementary vocabulary lists are also scattered throughout the book, and these should be studied for passive recognition. As the supplementary vocabularies consist of concrete, everyday items, which tend on the whole to be easier to remember, they can be learned according to the student's desire and/or need.

Each lesson is provided with specific exercises and drills for the major grammatical and syntactical points introduced therein. It is a good idea to begin each lesson by familiarizing oneself with the new vocabulary for that lesson, since the examples for the grammatical points usually contain some of those words.

Part Two of the grammar, in which the outstanding differences between modern and classical usage are given, should be studied carefully before attempting the classical prose selections.

In Part Three the distinguishing features of ordinary colloquial Persian are given. According to the wishes of the instructor, these sections may be presented at any time after the written form has been mastered, since the colloquial form can almost always be predicted from the written—but not vice-versa.

Introduction مقدمه

Phonology and تلفظ و خط
Script

THE PHONOLOGY OF PERSIAN

Vowels and Glides.

i	*u*	
e	*o*	*ay*
a	*â*	*aw*

i   is a high front open vowel [i], like the "ea" in 'please' but without the "y"-glide characteristic of English. Contrast *si* with "sea."

e   is a middle front open vowel [ɛ], like the "e" in "bet." This vowel is in fairly free variation with [ɪ], like the "i" in "sit"; word-finally, however, it is always realized as [ɛ]. Compare *shen* with "shin."

a   is a low front open vowel [æ], like the "a" in "cat" but slightly lower. Word-finally this phoneme is always realized as [ɛ] in modern Iranian pronunciation, which will be reflected in the transcription employed here. Compare *bad* with "bad."

â   is a low back open vowel between the "a" of "father" and "bald" but without the lip-rounding of English. Compare *bâl* with "ball," *bâm* with "balm."

o   is a middle to high middle back rounded vowel [o] with the quality of the "o" in "coped" but considerably shorter and without the "w" off-glide that accompanies most American pronunciations of "o." This vowel is also realized in free variation as [ʊ], like the "oo" of "book." Compare *kot* with "coat" and *por* with "pour."

u   is a high back rounded vowel [u], like the "oo" of "moon" but without the off-glide characteristic of English. Compare *nun* with "noon" and *sud* with "sued."

ay   is a glide very close to the "a" in "wade." Compare *may* and "may," *pay* and "pay."

aw   is a "w"-glide like the "o" in "bone." Compare *raw* and "row," *gawd* and "goad," *jaw* and "Joe."

Speakers of English must exercise particular care to distinguish *a* from *â*, especially before *r*. Contrast the following:

rast he escaped	*râst* straight
dar in	*dâr* gibbet
bar over	*bâr* load
tar wet	*târ* string
dasht wasteland	*dâsht* he had

Similarly, *e–ay* and *o–aw* must be distinguished. Contrast the following:

dor pearl	*dawr* around
do two	*daw* run
joz except	*jawz* walnut
ke that	*kay* when?
serr mystery	*sayr* travel
sel tuberculosis	*sayl* torrent

When followed in the same syllable by a consonant cluster, the "short" vowels *a, e* and *o* are considerably lengthened. Contrast the vowel lengths in the following:

shah king	*shahr* city
var and if	*varz* exercise
meh mist	*mehr* affection
por full	*pors* ask

Vowels in Persian are **never** reduced. All vowels, even in unstressed syllables, are given their full quality—unlike English, where many unstressed vowels tend to be "slurred over" with an "uh" sound. The sound "uh" [ə] does not exist in educated Iranian speech.

Consonants.

Stops					
voiceless	*p*	*t*	*k*		'
voiced	*b*	*d*	*g*	*q*	
Fricatives					
voiceless	*f*	*s*	*sh*	*kh*	*h*
voiced	*v*	*z*	*zh*		
Affricates					
voiceless			*ch*		
voiced			*j*		
Nasals	*m*	*n*			
Lateral		*l*			
Flap		*r*			
Semivowel			*y*		

The stops *p, b, t* and *d* are realized similarly to their English counterparts; *p* and *t,* however, are heavily aspirated in all environments. Contrast *aspân* with "Aspen" and *bâstân* with "Boston."

k and *g* are pronounced like English "k" and "hard g" as in "go." When syllable-final, however, *k* and *g* are heavily palatalized, i.e., a "y" sound is heard after the *k* and *g*, much like the English "cute." Practice the following words with your instructor: *pâk, doktor, sag, sang.*

q is normally a back velar or front uvular stop and is generally accompanied by a slight trace of voicing. It is pronounced similarly to *k* but farther back in the throat. When *q* occurs intervocalically, it tends toward a uvular fricative [γ]; the two allophones are in fairly free variation, however.

' is the glottal stop. This sound occurs in English between the syllables of "uh-oh" and in dialect pronunciations of "bottle" and "little" as "bo'l" and "li'l." Syllable-final as well as doubled glottal stop is alien to English and must be practiced carefully. Contrast the following:

mani egotism	*mani'* impregnable
man I	*man'* prevention
jam Jamshid	*jam'* collection
so'âl question	*moqa''ar* concave
sho'â' ray	*ashe''e* rays

v has two conditioned allophones, [v] and [w]. In prevocalic and post-consonantal positions it is realized as [v]. Following *a* in the same syllable, *v* becomes the semi-vowel [w] in the glide *aw;* it remains [v] after all other vowels and consonants, as *div, dâvtalab* and *jozv.*

f is like the "f" in "fish."

s is like the "s" in "say."

sh is like the "sh" in "shine."

zh is like the "g" in "beige."

kh is like the "ch" in German *Bach* or Scottish *loch.* It is a scraping sound produced against the velar ridge [x].

h is like the English "h." Intervocalic *h* is, as in English, a breathy vibration of the vocal cords. The Persian *h* occurs in environments unfamiliar to English, such as syllable- and word-final. It also occurs in clusters alien to English. Practice pronouncing the following words:

fahmid	*sohbat*	*koh*	*mehr*
shâh	*sehhat*	*boht*	*sharh*
kuh	*beh*	*fahm*	*shahr*
bahs	*shabih*	*dahr*	*sath*

ch is like the "ch" in "church."

j is like the "j" in "judge."

m is like the "m" in "moon."

n is like the "n" in "noon." Before *b, n* is always pronounced [m], as *tanbal,* pronounced *tambal.*

l is liquid in all environments, never the dull "l" of English. Contrast *âl* with "all," *lâ* with "law," *fil* with "feel."

r is a flap as in Spanish or Italian, never the constriction of American English. Doubled *rr* is trilled as in Spanish. Contrast *dare* and *dar rah, pâru* and *porru.*

y is like the "y" in "yes."

SYLLABIFICATION

For the purposes of syllabification, remember that the Persian sounds represented by two English letters *(ch, kh, zh, sh)* are counted as **one** consonant.

All syllables in Persian contain one and only one vowel or glide. There are thus as many syllables in a word as there are vowels or glides. The first syllable in a word may begin with a vowel *(ân, in, oftâd),* but all subsequent syllables begin with one and only one consonant. No internal syllable may begin with a vowel. Syllables may end in (1) a vowel *(khâ•ne, â•ma•de),* (2) one consonant *(fah•mid, of•tâd),* or (3) two consonants *(shahr•bân, torsh•ru).* The syllabic division falls therefore between the two consonants of a two-consonant cluster and between the second and third consonants of a three-consonant cluster.

For determining syllabification, the hyphens that indicate enclitics should be ignored *(pedar-am = pe•da•ram, ketâb-i-râ-ke = ke•tâ•bi•râ•ke).*

These rules of syllabification apply to modern Persian as it is spoken in Iran. They do not apply to the scansion of classical Persian poetry or to Persian as it is spoken outside of Iran.

STRESS

The stress patterns of nouns, adjectives and prepositions.

All nouns, adjectives and prepositions in Persian are stressed on the last syllable, e.g.: *khâné, pedár, barâdár, keshvár, dâneshjú.*

When enclitics are added, stress remains where it was, e.g.: *khâné-i, pedár-am, barâdár-râ, keshvár-e, dâneshjú-i-râ-ke.*

When suffixes are added, stress is moved to the final syllable of the suffix: *khânehâ´, pedarâné, barâdarâ´n, dâneshjuí.*

The stress patterns of verbs.

The stress patterns of verbs will be taken up along with the various tenses and moods.

THE PERSIAN ALPHABET

Persian is written in a slightly modified form of the Arabic alphabet. This alphabet, written from right to left, has a total of thirty-two characters, all but one of which represent consonants. The Arabic alphabet does not normally represent the "short" vowels *a, e* and *o;* only the "long" vowels *â, i* and *u* and the glides *ay* and *aw* have graphic representations.

The alphabet is a "script" in that most letters must be connected one to another. There are no separate letter forms corresponding to Latin-alphabet printing. All letters have at least two forms and at most four.

Those letters that connect on both sides have four forms: (1) the initial form, used when the letter is the first letter of a word and followed by another letter, or when the letter is preceded by a non-connecting letter and followed by another letter; (2) the medial form, used when the letter is both preceded and followed by connecting letters; (3) the final form, used when it is the last letter in a word and is preceded by a connecting letter; and (4) the alone form, used when it is the last letter in the word and preceded by a non-connecting letter.

The seven letters that do not connect forward, i.e., to the next letter to the left, have only two forms, (1) the initial-alone form and (2) the medial-final form. All non-connecting letters must be followed by initial (or alone) forms.

There are three varieties of the Arabic script in common use in Iran today. The first, *naskh,* is the base for type fonts and the typewriter; it should not be taken as the model for handwriting. The second style, *nasta'liq,* is the basic cursive script and is the model for good handwriting. The third variety, actually a variant of *nasta'liq,* is called *shekaste.* In this style many orthographic "breaks" that are mandatory in *naskh* and *nasta'liq* are bridged, certain letters have wildly divergent forms, and "shorthand" ligatures abound.

The Alphabet

NAME LETTER SOUND GROUP

NAME	LETTER	SOUND	GROUP	NAME	LETTER	SOUND	GROUP
alef	ا	—	1	*sin*	س	s	6
be	ب	b	2	*shin*	ش	sh	6
pe	پ	p	2	*sâd*	ص	s	7
te	ت	t	2	*zâd*	ض	z	7
se	ث	s	2	*tâ, tayn*	ط	t	8
jim	ج	j	3	*zâ*	ظ	z	8
che	چ	ch	3	*ayn*	ع	'	9
he-jimi	ح	h	3	*qayn*	غ	q	9
khe	خ	kh	3	*fe*	ف	f	10
dâl	د	d	4	*qâf*	ق	q	10
zâl	ذ	z	4	*kâf*	ك	k	11
re	ر	r	5	*gâf*	گ	g	11
ze	ز	z	5	*lâm*	ل	l	12
zhe	ژ	zh	5	*mim*	م	m	13

| nun | ن | n | 2 | he | ه | h | 15 |
| vâv | و | v | 14 | ye | ى | y | 2 |

Additional signs.

lâm-alef	ﻻ	lâ
alef-madde	آ	â
te-tammat	ة	-atan
alef-tanvin	اً	-an
hamze	ء	'
tashdid	ّ	(doubling)

Group by group, the letters of the alphabet will be given in their printed and handwritten forms.

Group 1

This group contains only *alef,* a non-connecting letter that stands initially for all initial vowels. Following consonants, *alef* stands for the vowel *â.* Other uses of *alef* will be treated under the vowels and other signs.

Initial/alone   ا   *ا*   Medial/final   ا   ـا···

Group 2

This group consists of *be, pe, te, se, nun* and *ye.* It is a connecting shape. *Nun* and *ye* differ slightly in their final- and alone-forms from the others. The basic shapes are:

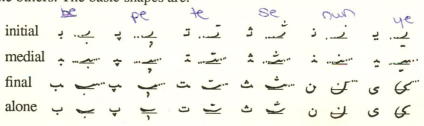

	be	pe	te	se	nun	ye
initial	...	...	...	...	...	...
medial	...	...	...	...	...	...
final	...	...	...	...	...	...
alone	...	...	...	...	...	...

Ye loses its dots in its final- and alone-forms. An initial form of this group followed by final *ye* is written ﮑﻰ, not ﯩ. Also, final *nun* and *ye* and Group 5 come directly off the top of the "teeth" characteristic of this group; thus, سِیـن *b-y-n,* not مِیـن , and بِیـنـی *b-y-n-y,* not بِینی .

The letter *se* stands for "th" as in "thing" in Arabic and is usually transliterated *th;* it is the least common of the three letters for *s* in Persian.

Group 3

This connecting shape consists of *jim, che, he-jimi* and *khe.* This *he* is called *he-jimi* or *he-hotti* to distinguish it from the other *he (he-havvaz,* Group 15). In Arabic the pronunciation of these two h's is quite distinct, but in Persian they are identical. In transliteration *he-jimi* is represented by *ḥ.*

	jim		che		he-jimi		khe	
Initial	جـ	جـ	چـ	چـ	حـ	حـ	خـ	خـ
Medial	ـجـ	ـجـ	ـچـ	ـچـ	ـحـ	ـحـ	ـخـ	ـخـ
Final	ـج	ـج	ـچ	ـچ	ـح	ـح	ـخ	ـخ
Alone	ج	ج	چ	چ	ح	ح	خ	خ

Before the "descenders," given below, the initial form of this group changes to the following "rounded" shape in handwriting:

Initial (before "descenders"):

The "descenders" are: Group 3 final, as in حج hajj

Group 3, medial, as in حجت hojjat

Group 5, medial/final, as in جز joz

Group 13, final, as in خم kham

Group 13, medial, as in حمال hammâl

Group 2, final *ye* only, as in چی chi

Group 4

This non-connecting shape consists of *dâl* and *zâl*.

		dal		zal
Initial/alone	د	ـد	ذ	ـذ
Medial/final	ـد	ـد	ذ	ـذ

Zâl occurs, with only a few exceptions, in words of Arabic origin and is usually transliterated *dh*. It is one of the least common of the letters for *z*.

Group 5

This non-connecting shape includes *re*, *ze* and *zhe*.

		re		ze		zhe
Initial/alone	ر	ـر	ز	ـز	ژ	ـژ
Medial/final	ر	ـر	ز	ـز	ژ	ـژ

A "tooth" preceding this shape loses its "tooth" quality in handwriting and becomes a "hump," as in ـر *babr*, not ـبر, and ـچ *chiz*, not ـچیز.

Group 6

This connecting shape includes *sin* and *shin*. Note that in all forms this shape may be written either with three "teeth" or with an extended line.

		sin				shin	
Initial	ـس	...ـس	ـس		ش	...ـش	ـش
Medial	ـس	...ـس	ـس		ش	...ـش	ـش
Final	س	ـس	ـس		ش	ـش	ـش
Alone	س	ـس	ـس		ش	ـش	ـش

Always before the "descenders" and usually before *vâv*, the three "teeth" are obligatory. Thus, ـس *sahar*, not ـس; similarly, ـس *su*, not ـس. Elsewhere either form may be used.

Final *nun* and *ye* come directly off the top of the final "tooth" of this group, as ‏ـسن‎ *senn* and ‏سی‎ *si*, not ‏سن‎ or ‏سی‎ .

Group 7

A connecting shape, this group includes *sâd* and *zâd*, both of which occur exclusively in Arabic words and are transliterated as *ṣ* and *ḍ*.

Initial	‏صـ‎	‏صـ‎	‏ضـ‎	‏ضـ‎
Medial	‏ـصـ‎	‏ـصـ‎	‏ـضـ‎	‏ـضـ‎
Final	‏ـص‎	‏ـص‎	‏ض‎	‏ـض‎
Alone	‏ص‎	‏ص‎	‏ض‎	‏ض‎

Final *nun* and *ye* come directly off the top of the final "tooth" of this group, as ‏صن‎ *s-n* and ‏صی‎ *s-y*, not ‏صن‎ or ‏صی‎ .

Group 8

This is a connecting shape and includes *tâ (tayn)* and *zâ*, again letters that occur mainly in Arabic words and are transliterated *ṭ* and *ẓ*.

Initial	‏طـ‎	‏طـ‎	‏ظـ‎	‏ظـ‎
Medial	‏ـطـ‎	‏ـطـ‎	‏ـظـ‎	‏ـظـ‎
Final	‏ـط‎	‏ـط‎	‏ـظ‎	‏ـظ‎
Alone	‏ط‎	‏ط‎	‏ظ‎	‏ظ‎

This shape requires two strokes of the pen. It should never be made in one stroke. The vertical is placed at the same time as the dots, i.e., after completion of the word or graphic unit.

Group 9

A connecting shape, *ayn* (transliterated as ‘) occurs only in Arabic words. *Qayn* (transliterated *gh*) occurs mainly in Arabic but also in some Persian and Turkish words.

ayn   *qayn*

Initial	ع	...عـ	غ	...غـ
Medial	ـعـ	...ـعـ	ـغـ	...ـغـ
Final	ع	ـع	غ	ـغ
Alone	ع	ع	غ	غ

Group 10

A connecting shape. The final and alone forms differ slightly one from the other. *Qâf* is usually transliterated as *q*. Both *fe* and *qâf* are round shapes; medial *fe* (ـفـ) especially must be distinguished from medial *qayn* (ـغـ).

fe   *qâf*

Initial	ف	...فـ	ق	...قـ
Medial	ـفـ	...ـفـ	ـقـ	...ـقـ
Final	ف	ـف	ق	ـق
Alone	ف	ف	ق	ق

Group 11

Kâf and *gâf* are connective. The top strokes of these letters are put on from up to down after the word or graphic unit is completed; they are never made in one stroke.

kaf   *gaf*

Initial	ک	...کـ	گ	...گـ
Medial	ـکـ	...ـکـ...	ـگـ	...ـگـ...
Final	ـک	ـکـ...	ـگ	ـگـ...
Alone	ک	ک	گ	گ

Before the "verticals" (*alef*, *lâm* and *kâf/gâf*) the vertical of *kâf/gâf* is bent forward toward the following vertical.

کا   کا   کك   ککک   گل   گل   کلم   گم

Group 12

Lâm, a connector, is the only letter under this shape group. It is like *alef* but connects forward. *Lâm* takes a special form *(lâm-alef,* see Additional Signs) when followed by *alef.*

Initial	ل	‌لـ	Final	ل	ـل
Medial	ل	‌لـ	Alone	ل	ل

Group 13

A connecting letter, *mim* is the only representative of this group. See notes to Groups 3 and 6.

Initial	م	‌مـ or ‌مـ	Final	م	ـم
Medial	م	‌مـ	Alone	م	م or م

Kâf/gâf and *lâm* followed by *mim* are written thus:

كم كـ لم لـ گما گا لمس لمـ

Group 14

A non-connector, *vâv* is the only representative of this group.

Initial/alone	و	‌و	Medial/final	‌و	‌وـ

See note to *sin/shin* (Group 6). In a few words *vâv* following *khe* is silent, as in خویش *khish* and خواهش *khâhesh.*

Group 15

A connector, *he-havvaz* is the only letter whose various shapes have no apparent connection one with another. It also has variant shapes in handwriting in all but the alone form.

Initial	ه	‌هـ or ‌هـ	Final	ه	ـه or ـه

Medial   ِ   ...ـحـ."or...ـۀ""   Alone   ه   ة

THE VOWELS

â is written	(1) word-initially with *alef-madde*	آن	*ân*
	(2) elsewhere with *alef*	بابا	*bâbâ*
i is written	(1) word-initially with *alef-ye*	این	*in*
	(2) elsewhere with *ye*	بینی	*bini*
u is written	(1) word-initially with *alef-vâv*	اوت	*ut*
	(2) elsewhere with *vâv*	روپوش	*rupush*
ay is written	(1) word-initially with *alef-ye*	ایوان	*ayvân*
	(2) elsewhere with *ye*	سیل	*sayl*
aw is written	(1) word-initially with *alef-vâv*	اولاد	*awlâd*
	(2) elsewhere with *vâv*	جو	*jaw*

The "short" vowels *(a, e, o)* are indicated initially by *alef*:

اسب *asb*   اسم *esm*   الفت *olfat*

The short vowels are not normally written or indicated non-initially. Where confusion might arise they can be indicated by the following signs, written over or under the letter they follow in pronunciation.

ـَ   *a* (called *fathe* or *zebar*), as in کَل *kal*

ـِ   *e* (called *kasre* or *zir*), as in گِل *gel*

ـُ   *o* (called *zamme* or *pish*), as in گُل *gol*

Final -*e* is written with *he-havvaz*. This purely orthographic convention is called "silent *he*" to distinguish it from the "real *he*," which also occurs word-finally.

خانه *khâne*   مرده *morde*   ده *deh*   ابله *ablah*

When the glides *ay* and *aw* are to be indicated with a vowel-point, they are, contrary to Arabic usage, indicated with *zir* and *pish* respectively.

سیل *sayl*   جُو *jaw*

A consonant followed by no vowel is indicated by a small circle above the consonant. This sign is called *sokun* or *jazm*.

جزم *jazm*   اسم *esm*

Additional letters and signs.

(1) *Lâm-alef* is merely an orthographic convention to avoid the shape ل. Like *alef,* it is a non-connecting letter.

لا *lâl*   سلاسل *salâsel*   وكلا *vokalâ*

(2) *Madde* (always written on *alef*) serves as

(a) all initial *â-,* as in آل *âl* and آمد *âmad.*

(b) internal glottal stop followed by *-â-* (i.e., *-'â*) in most cases (but see 5 below), as in مآثر *ma'âser,* ایدآل *ide'âl* and تآتر *te'âtr.*

(c) *Lâm* followed by *alef-madde* is written with the *lâm-alef* ligature, as in لآلی *la'âli.*

(3) *Te-tammat,* the Arabic *tâ' marbūta,* is word-final only. It occurs in Arabic loan-constructions and is pronounced as *-t* invariably preceded by the vowel *a.* It almost always has the *tanvin* termination (see next entry). This letter is often replaced in typography by *te.*

(4) The Arabic adverbial termination, called *tanvin* and pronounced *-án,* must be "carried" by an *alef,* as in مثلا *masalan* and واقعا *vâqe'an.* When *tanvin* occurs on *te-tammat,* it should not have the *alef* bearer, as

xxix

نسبةً *nesbatan* and دفعةً *daf'atan*. Most writers of modern Persian, how-ever, treat these words as though the *te-tammat* were *te* and write them with *alef,* as نسبتا *nesbatan* and دفعتا *daf'atan.*

(5) The *hamze* is the sign of the glottal stop. It is theoretically pre-sent and carried by *alef* for all initial vowels except *â.*

اسب *asp*   إسم *esm*   الفت *olfat*

Non-initially there are complicated rules for the bearer of the *hamze* in Arabic words; however, since misspellings are frequent in Persian, it is considerably less time-consuming for the student simply to learn the spelling of words with *hamze* as they occur. Bearers of the *hamze* may be

(a) *alef,* as in مساله *mas'ale*

(b) an undotted "tooth," as in مسائل *masâ'el*

(c) *vâv,* as in سؤال *so'âl,* and

(d) nothing, as in شیء *shay'* .

Most modern writers tend to write internal *hamze* on the undotted "tooth" as مسئله *mas'ale,* سئوال *so'âl* and مسئول *mas'ul.*

(6) The *tashdid* (also called *shadde)* indicates gemination, or dou-bling, of a consonant. It is not usual to write the *tashdid,* although it may be provided where confusion might arise.

ماده	*mâde*	بنا	*banâ*	سلام	*salâm*
مادّه	*mâdde*	بنّا	*bannâ*	سلّام	*sallâm*

The doubling that results from compounding is not indicated by the *tashdid* but by writing both consonants, as in پررو *por-ru,* پاك كن *pâk-kon* and تیززبان *tiz-zabân.*

(7) The connecting line between letters can be extended indefinitely without affecting the word, as حــــرف *harf.*

Summary of the Alphabet (non-connectors indicated by asterisk):

NAME OF LETTER	ALONE FORM	FINAL FORM	MEDIAL FORM	INITIAL FORM	TRANS- SCRIPTION
*alef	ا	ا	ا	ا	–
be	ب	ب	ب	ب	b
pe	پ	پ	پ	پ	p
te	ت	ت	ت	ت	t
se	ث	ث	ث	ث	s
jim	ج	ج	ج	ج	j
che	چ	چ	چ	چ	ch
he-hotti	ح	ح	ح	ح	h
khe	خ	خ	خ	خ	kh
*dâl	د	د	د	د	d
*zâl	ذ	ذ	ذ	ذ	z
*re	ر	ر	ر	ر	r
*ze	ز	ز	ز	ز	z
*zhe	ژ	ژ	ژ	ژ	zh
sin	س	س	س	س	s
shin	ش	ش	ش	ش	sh
sâd	ص	ص	ص	ص	s
zâd	ض	ض	ض	ض	z
tâ/tayn	ط	ط	ط	ط	t
zâ	ظ	ظ	ظ	ظ	z
ayn	ع	ع	ع	ع	'
qayn	غ	غ	غ	غ	q
fe	ف	ف	ف	ف	f
qâf	ق	ق	ق	ق	q

kâf	ك	ـك	ـكـ	كـ	k
gâf	گ	ـگ	ـگـ	گـ	g
lâm	ل	ـل	ـلـ	لـ	l
mim	م	ـم	ـمـ	مـ	m
nun	ن	ـن	ـنـ	نـ	n
vâv	و	ـو	ـو	و	v
he-havvaz	ه	ـه	ـهـ	هـ	h
ye	ى	ـى	ـيـ	يـ	y

Additional Combinations and Signs

lâm-alef	لا	ـلا	ـلا	لا	*lâ*
te-tammat	ة	ـة			*-atan*
alef-madde	آ	آ	آ	آ	*â*
alef-tanvin	اً	ـاً	ـاً	اً	*-an*
hamze	ء				'
tashdid	ّ				(doubling)

Numerals

The Persian numerals, written like English from left to right, are as follows:

۱	1	۶	6
۲	2	۷	7
۳	3	۸	8
۴	4	۹	9
۵	5	۱۰	10

Pronunciation Exercise

Practice pronouncing the following words. Remember that stress falls on the final syllable unless an enclitic (indicated by the hyphen) has been added. Pay particular attention to the difficult clusters and to stress and intonation and notice the various homophonous letters.

بر	bar	نرخ	nerkh	گول	gul
بار	bâr	غنچه	qonche	قرض	qarz
باری	bâr-i	قاشق	qâshoq	ارز	arz
باری	bâri	چپق	chopoq	شرح	sharh
باربر	bârbar	قلقلكی	qelqelaki	ارج	arj
باربری	bârbar-i	جامه	jâme	گری	gery
باربری	bârbari	جامع	jâme'	قلب	qalb
سر	serr	تابه	tâbe	كهف	kahf
سری	serr-i	تابع	tâbe'	برق	barq
سری	serri	تابه‌ای	tâbe-i	فسق	fesq
قحط	qaht	تابعی	tâbe'-i	رزق	rezq
قحطی	qahti	ژاله	zhâle	عشق	eshq
بحث	bahs	مژه	mozhzhe	سقف	saqf
بحثی	bahs-i	مبل	mobl	ركن	rokn
صحن	sahn	اصل	asl	طعم	ta'm
صحنها	sahnhâ	اهل	ahl	ذقن	zeqn
نقص	naqs	حسن	hosn	بطن	batn
مكث	maks	خشم	khashm	دفن	dafn
جم	jam	جوانمرد	javânmard	اسبسوار	asbsavâr
جمع	jam'	صحت	sehhat	مفصل	mofassal
جمعی	jam'-i	وجه	vajh	جبر	jabr
جمعی	jam'i	صلح	solh	چتر	chatr
جمعها	jam'hâ	فهم	fahm	بدر	badr
جمعهانی	jam'hâ-i	سرو	sarv	فكر	fekr
لطمه	latme	عضو	ozv	قعر	qa'r
دكمه	dokme	پررو	porru	فقر	faqr
معروف	ma'ruf	پارو	pâru	صفر	sefr
غرق	qarq	گل	gol	طبل	tabl

xxxiii

رطل	ratl	وهم	vahm	دلقپوش	dalqpush
عدل	adl	مهد	mahd	رنجبر	ranjbar
شكل	shekl	سنگسار	sangsâr	مدحسرا	madhsarâ
لعل	la'l	دستبرد	dastbord	رفع	raf
شغل	shoql	درختكار	derakhtkâr	شرع	shar'
قفل	qofl	دردناك	dardnâk		

Reading Exercise

Read the following words, which contain only the "apparent" vowels *â*, *i*, *u* and final *e*.

ویلا	وادی	بامدادان	بانو
طاق	شیروانی	صابون	عام
پول	گام	ثانی	دور
موش	زیر	آی	چیز
گوناگون	پیچید	لولیان	دیوانه
ساز	گیج	خوب	قاضی
واژگونی	کاشیکاری	عاق	ماچ
موم	حاجی	دیر	روئیده
دیو	یاغی	اینجا	حالا
آلوبالو	قیر	آقایان	قال
وول	آفتاب	تیپ	روح
میز	هیچگاه	گوشت	زین
خیس	چاپ	روحانیون	واچیدیم
بیبال	نوری	دادیم	کوچگاه
لال	پور	واگیره	هارون
شاهانی	تور	باطلاق	باغها
وادار	آبدار	چوب	ژاله
واصی	کاخ	کوچی	روباه
گول	گریا	هامان	داغ
بینی	قو	داشتیم	طوپ

Part One   بخش اول

The Grammar of   دستور زبان
Modern Persian   فارسی معاصر

Lesson One

§1 Word Order. Normal word order in Persian is subject–predicate–verb. Finite verbs almost always take their proper place as the last element in a phrase or sentence. However, the copulative verb ("is, are, was, were"), which serves only to express a predicative state and not existence, may be followed by other matter (prepositional phrases, adjective modifiers, etc.) modifying the predicate.

§2 Stress and intonation. All nouns and adjectives in Persian are stressed on the final syllable. Primary sentence-stress (´), characterized by a very high rising pitch, falls on the last stressed syllable before an affirmative verb.

irân dar mashreqzamín-ast
"Iran is in the east."

Whereas the affirmative copula ("is, are") may never receive stress at all, the negative copula, like all negatives, takes primary stress. A secondary stress, characterized by a falling pitch (`), falls on the preceding stressed syllable.

âmrikâ dar mashreqzamìn níst
"America is not in the east."

1

§3 Gender. Persian lacks gender distinction altogether. There is no grammatical distinction of masculine, feminine or neuter.

§4 State of the noun. There is no definite article ("the") or indefinite article ("a") in Persian. The Persian noun exists instead in two states, the absolute and the non-specific.

4.1 The noun in its absolute state, i.e., with no suffix or enclitic, indicates both the specific singular and the generic, which in English in generally rendered by the plural. Thus, *ketâb* means both "the book" (about which we already know something) and "books" (in general).

کتاب خوب است. *ketâb khub-ast.*	The book (specific) is good. / Books (generic) are good.
کوه بزرگ است. *kuh bozorg-ast.*	The mountain is large. Mountains are large.

4.2 The non-specific state of the noun is formed by adding the indefinite enclitic, an unstressed -*i*, to the noun. Because this ending is enclitic, and therefore unstressed, the final syllable of the absolute state retains the stress. The non-specific state indicates "a certain, a particular" thing or "one of a class."

کتابی *ketâb-i (ketâˊbi)*	a book, any book, one book, a certain book, some book or other, some particular book
میزی *miz-i (mízi)*	a table, any table, one table, a certain table, some table or other, some particular table

§5 Orthography of the indefinite enclitic. The indefinite enclitic is spelled as a *ye* added directly to nouns ending in consonants (as above). Note that the *ye* is joined directly to nouns ending in "connecting" letters but not, of course, to nouns ending in any of the seven non-connecting letters.

5.1 When added to words ending in -*â* or -*u*, the indefinite is spelled with *hamze–ye* (ئی) or *ye–ye* (یی) (*hamze–ye* will be preferred in this book).

دانا ‹ دانائی   *dânâ* › *dânâ-i*   a sage

دانشجو ‹ دانشجوئی   *dâneshju* › *dâneshju-i*   a student

5.2 In words ending in the "silent" *he* and *ye*, the indefinite enclitic is generally spelled with *alef–ye* (ای).

خانه ‹ خانه‌ای   *khâne* › *khâne-i*   a house

صندلی ‹ صندلی‌ای   *sandali* › *sandali-i*   a chair

Care must be taken to distinguish the **silent *he***, which is merely an orthographic convention to indicate a final vowel, from the **real *he***, which is a true consonant and thus adds the indefinite enclitic directly.

         خانه ‹ خانه‌ای   *khâne* › *khâne-i*   a house

but   کوه ‹ کوهی   *kuh* › *kuh-i*   a mountain

§6 **Adjectival order.** Attributive adjectives normally follow nouns they modify. When the noun is in the non-specific state, the adjective follows immediately.

کتابی خوب   *ketâb-i khub*   a good book

کشوری قدیمی   *keshvar-i qadimi*   an old country

کوهی بزرگ   *kuh-i bozorg*   a large mountain

§7 **The plural.** The plural marker that may be added to all nouns in Persian is *hâ*, which is suffixed directly to the noun in the absolute state; it takes the stress and renders the specific plural.

کتاب ‹ کتابها   *ketâb* "the book" › *ketâbhâ* "the books"

کشور ‹ کشورها   *keshvar* "the country" › *keshvarhâ* "the countries"

the → ha

3

7.1 When the final consonant of the noun can be connected orthographically, the plural suffix is usually joined directly, although it is sometimes left separate (كتاب ها or كتابها).

7.2 When added to a noun ending in the silent *he,* the plural suffix is **never** joined, although it may be connected to the real *he.*

خانه‌ها > خانه   *khâne > khânehâ* "the houses"

كوه‌ها or كوهها > كوه   *kuh > kuhhâ* "the mountains"

§8 **The non-specific plural.** The non-specific plural is formed by adding the unstressed indefinite enclitic to the plural. The plural suffix retains the stress. The non-specific plural denotes "some" or "several." The orthographic rule given above in §5.2 applies.

كتابهائی	*ketâbhâ-i*	some books, several books
خانه‌هائی	*khânehâ-i*	some houses, several houses

8.1 Adjectives that modify plural nouns do not agree in number but always remain singular. As in the singular (§6), attributive adjectives follow a non-specific noun directly.

كتابهائی خوب	*ketâbhâ-i khub*	some good books
كشورهائی قديمی	*keshvarhâ-i qadimi*	some old countries
كوههائی بزرگ	*kuhhâ-i bozorg*	some large mountains

Vocabulary

بد	*bad* bad		در	*dar* door, gate	
بزرگ	*bozorg* big, large, great		صندلی	*sandali* chair	
پاك‌كن	*pâkkon* eraser		قديمی	*qadimi* old, ancient	
خانه	*khâne* house		قلم	*qalam* pen	
خوب	*khub* good, well		كتاب	*ketâb* book	
			كشور	*keshvar* country	

4

كوچك *kuchek* little, small   ميز *miz* table

كوه *kuh* mountain   نو *naw* new

گچ *gach* (piece of) chalk

Exercise 1

(1) For the following words give (1) the non-specific singular (e.g, *pâkkon-i*), (2) the specific plural (e.g., *pâkkonhâ*), and (3) the non-specific plural (e.g., *pâkkonhâ-i*):

۱ کشور، ۲ کتاب، ۳ خانه، ٤ قلم، ٥ میز، ٦ صندلی، ۷ کوه، ۸ در

(b) Read and translate the following phrases:

۸ کتابی نو	۱ میزی بزرگ
۹ قلمی خوب	۲ صندلیهائی خوب
۱۰ میزهائی نو	۳ کشوری کوچك
۱۱ خانهای نو	٤ کوهی بزرگ
۱۲ گچی کوچك	٥ خانه‌هائی قدیمی
۱۳ کشورهائی بزرگ	٦ قلمهائی بد
۱٤ دری کوچك	۷ پاك‌کنهائی قدیمی

(c) Give the Persian for the following:

1. small mountains
2. old houses
3. an old table
4. a new chair
5. an old country

6. a good pen
7. a good eraser
8. big doors
9. bad books
10. new pieces of chalk

Lesson Two

§9 Demonstrative adjectives and pronouns.

9.1 The demonstrative adjectives *in* ("this, these") and *ân* ("that, those") modify both singular and plural nouns. They invariably precede the nouns they modify.

این کتاب	*in ketâb*	this book
این کتابها	*in ketâbhâ*	these books
آن قلم	*ân qalam*	that pen
آن قلمها	*ân qalamhâ*	those pens

9.2 As demonstrative pronouns *in* ("this") and *ân* ("that") refer to the singular, while the plurals *inhâ* ("these") and *ânhâ* ("those") refer to plurals.

این خوب است	*in khub-ast.*	This is good.
اینها خوبند	*inhâ khub-and.*	These are good.
آن بد نیست	*ân bad nist.*	That isn't bad.
آنها بد نیستند	*ânhâ bad nistand.*	Those (they) aren't bad.

§10 Verbal agreement with the plural. As a general rule, plurals of inanimate nouns take singular verbs.

این کتابها خوب است.	*in ketâbhâ khub-ast.*	These books are good.

6

| آن کشورها قدیمی نیست. | *ân keshvarhâ qadimi nist.* | Those countries are not old. |

In very short sentences with the verb "to be," however, where a plural subject is separated from its verb by no more than a predicate adjective, noun or short prepositional phrase, a plural subject usually takes a plural verb. In longer sentences, especially in complex constructions and with most finite verbs other than "to be," plurals of inanimate nouns (things) take singular verbs, while only animate plurals (people) take plural verbs.

| این کتابها خوبند. | *in ketâbhâ khub-and.* | These books are good. |
| این پسرها زرنگند. | *in pesarhâ zerang-and.* | These boys are clever. |

With the negative verb "not to be," the singular is usually retained for inanimate plurals.

| این کتابها خوب نیست. | *in ketâbhâ khub nist.* | These books aren't good. |
| این پسرها ایرانی نیستند. | *in pesarhâ irâni nistand.* | These boys aren't Iranian. |

§11 Coordination. The coordinating conjunction is read either as *va-*, added to the second element of the coordination, or—and more idiomatically—as *-o*, an unstressed enclitic added to the first element of the coordination.

| کتاب و قلم | *ketâb-o qalam or ketâb va-qalam* | book(s) and pen(s) |
| میز و صندلی | *miz-o sandali or miz va-sandali* | table(s) and chair(s) |

The indefinite enclitic usually appears only once at the end of a series of non-specific nouns.

| کتاب و قلمی | *{ketâb-o qalam}-i* | a book and pen |

گچ و پاك كنی {gach-o pâkkon}-i		a piece of chalk and (an) eraser

§12 Adverbs. Adverbs invariably precede adjectives.

بسيار خوب	besyâr khub	very good
كاملاً نو	kâmelan naw	brand new
قلمی بسيار خوب	qalam-i besyâr khub	a very good pen
كتابهائی كاملاً نو	ketâbhâ-i kâmelan naw	some brand new books

§13 Interrogative sentences.

13.1 An interrogative sentence that contains no interrogative words (who, what, where, why when, which) is signalled by a rising inflection of voice and not by rearrangement of words (as in English). The intonation that accompanies the interrogative sentence in Persian should be learned by imitation of the tape or instructor.

این خوب است.	in khub-ast.	This is good.
این خوب است؟	in khub-ast?	Is this good?

13.2 Interrogative words tend not to come first in a Persian sentence unless absolutely unavoidable. Interrogatives follow the subject and adverbs of time and immediately precede the predicate.

آن چه بود؟	ân che bud?	What was that?
آن جوان كی بود؟	ân javân ki bud?	Who was that young man?
ايران كجاست؟	irân kojâ-st?	Where is Iran?
علی كی آمد؟	ali kay âmad?	When did Ali come?

An exception to the general rule is chérâ ("why?"), which often comes at the beginning of an interrogative sentence.

چرا اينجا نيست؟	chérâ injâ nist?	Why isn't he here?

8

Vocabulary

Nouns and adjectives

آمریکا *âmrikâ* America *Emira*

آمریکائی *âmrikâi* American

آن *ân* that (adj. & pron.)

ایران *irân* Iran

ایرانی *irâni* Iranian

این *in* this (adj. & pron.)

بچه *bachche* child

پنجره *panjare* window

تهران *tehrân* Tehran

جوان *javân* young, young person

شهر *shahr* town, city

خیلی *kháyli* very, much, many, a lot; too much, too many

در *dar* in (prep.)

کاملاً *kâmelan* completely *an*

کجا *kojâ* where?

نخیر *nákhayr* no

ولی *váli* but

Verbs — *not stress*

است *-ast* (he, she, it) is

اند *-and* (they) are

بود *-bud* (he, she, it) was

بودند *-budand* (they) were

نبود *nábud* (he, she, it) was not *stressed*

نبودند *nábudand* (they) were not

نیست *nist* (he, she, it) is not

نیستند *nístand* (they) are not

Adverbs, prepositions, &c.

آنجا *ânjâ* there

اینجا *injâ* here

بسیار *besyâr* very, very much

بله ، بلی *bále* yes

چرا *chérâ* why?

Exercise 2 *an →that, in →this*

(a) Make predicates from the noun–adjective combinations given in parentheses (make appropriate changes for plural, non-specific, &c., e.g. *ânhâ (kuh - kuchek)-and > ânhâ, kuhhâ-i kuchek-and)*:

add ee (S) to the word

١ این ، (جوان - ایرانی) است .

٢ آن ، (کوه - بزرگ) است .

٣ آنها ، (بچه - بد) بودند .
  aadad bad bakne

٤ تهران ، (شهر - بزرگ) است .

٥ این ، (کشور - قدیمی) است .

٦ آنها ، (میز - کوچك) بودند .

9

children are not pl. because it is a unmodified (generic) children

۷ آنها ، (کتاب - کوچک) بودند .   ۹ آنها ، (پنجره - کوچک) اند .

۸ اینها ، (صندلی - نو) بودند .   ۱۰ آمریکا ، (کشور - بزرگ) است .

(b) Determine whether the demonstrative given is a pronoun or adjective, and give the proper form:

۶ (آن) کتابی قدیمی بود .   ۱ (این) جوان ایرانی است .

۷ (این) صندلی‌ای نو بود .   ۲ (آن) شهری بزرگ است .

۸ (آن) پنجره‌هائی کوچک اند .   ۳ (آن) بچه‌هائی خوبند .

۹ (این) کشورهائی بزرگ اند .   ۴ (این) کشور قدیمی است .

۵ (آن) میزها کوچک بودند .

(c) Give both affirmative and negative answers to the following questions:

۶ این میز و صندلی خوبند ؟   ۱ آن جوان ایرانی است ؟

۷ آن شهر در آمریکاست ؟   ۲ آن کشورها بسیار قدیمی اند ؟

۸ آن کوه خیلی کوچک است ؟   ۳ این بچه کوچک است ؟

۹ این کتابها قدیمی اند ؟   ۴ آن میزها خوبند ؟

۱۰ این گچ و پاک‌کن خوبند ؟   ۵ آن صندلی کاملاً نو است ؟

(d) Read and translate the following into English:

۱ آن کوه در آمریکا نیست .

۲ آن کتابها چرا اینجا نیست ؟

۳ آن میزها بزرگ نیست ولی خوب است .

۴ آن شهر چرا بد است ؟

۵ آمریکا کشوری بزرگ است ولی قدیمی نیست .

۶ آن ایرانی‌ها کجا بودند ؟

۷ این میز و صندلی بزرگ و خوبند .

۸ ایران کشوری قدیمی است و تهران شهری بزرگ است در ایران .

۹ آن جوان ایرانی نیست ، آمریکائی است .

۱۰ اینها کتابهائی بسیار خوبند .

(e) Translate into Persian: *turn in english- Persian*

1. Those Iranians are not here.
2. They were there.
3. That table is too[1] small.
4. The books and pens are in the house.
5. These are very good chairs.
6. Where is that city?
7. Tehran is in Iran.
8. Those children are Iranian.

Supplementary Vocabulary: Courtesy Phrases

سلام	*salâm*	Hello.
صبح بخير	*sobh bekhayr*	Good morning.
صبح شما بخير	*sobh-e shomâ bekhayr.*	Good morning to you.
حال شما چطور است؟	*hâl-e shomâ chetawr-ast?*	How are you?
بد نيست. حال شما چطور است؟	*bad nist. hâl-e shomâ chetawr-ast?*	Not bad. How are you?
حال من هم بد نيست، قربان شما.	*hâl-e man-ham bad nist, qorbân-e shomâ.*	Not bad either, thanks.
خدا حافظ.	*khodâ hâfez.*	Goodbye.

---

[1]There is no word in Persian equivalent to the English "too" in this meaning as distinguished from "very"; the sense of "too much" and "too little" is conveyed by context and/or voice intonation.

Lesson Three

§14 The *ezâfe*. The *ezâfe* is a construction that is indicated by an unstressed enclitic vowel *(-e)* and serves to link syntactically related nouns and adjectives together. It is not normally indicated orthographically. There are two types of *ezâfe,* the attributive adjectival and the possessive (to be introduced in §21 below).

14.1 The attributive adjectival *ezâfe* links an attributive adjective to a noun in the absolute state and renders a definite sense (modified nouns cease to function as generics).

كتاب نو	*ketâb-e naw*	the new book
ميز كهنه	*miz-e kohne*	the old table

(a) When added to nouns ending in consonants and in *-i*, the *ezâfe* is not usually indicated orthographically, although it can be written with the *kasre/zir* vowel and may be given by careful editors in highly ambiguous contexts.

(b) When added to words ending in *-â* and most words ending in *-u*, the *ezâfe* is pronounced *-ye* and the letter *ye* is written.

كتابهای خوب	*ketâbhâ-ye khub*	the good books
دانشجوی زرنگ	*dâneshju-ye zerang*	the clever student

(c) When added to words ending in the silent *he,* the *ezâfe* is indicated by a *hamze* written above the *he* and is pronounced *-ye.* This indi-

12

cation, though fairly frequent, is not always given in printed texts, as in the second example below.

| خانهٔ بزرگ | *khâne-ye bozorg* | the big house |
| بچه بد | *bachche-ye bad* | the bad child |

14.2 A series of attributive adjectives not coordinated by the conjunction is linked by the *ezâfe*.

| خانهٔ قدیمی بزرگ قرمز | *khâne-ye qadimi-e* | the big old red house |
| | *bozorg-e qermez* | |

Adjectival order, a crucial feature of English, is not fixed in Persian. Multiple adjectives describing a single noun may come in any order whatsoever, the emphasis falling in descending order away from the noun. Thus,

خانهٔ بزرگ قدیمی قرمز
khâne-ye bozorg-e qadimi-e qermez

خانهٔ قرمز بزرگ قدیمی
khâne-ye qermez-e bozorg-e qadimi

خانهٔ قدیمی قرمز بزرگ

and *khâna-ye qadimi-e qermez-e bozorg*

all mean "the big old red house."

14.3 When the indefinite enclitic falls on the noun, no *ezâfe* intervenes between the noun and its adjective, as described in §6 above.

(a) When a noun in the non-specific state is modified by more than one adjective, the adjectives are linked by the conjunction *-o*.

| خانه‌ای قدیمی و بزرگ و قرمز | *[khâne]-i [qadimi-o* | a big old red house |
| | *bozorg-o qermez]* | |

(b) The indefinite enclitic may also fall at the end of a attributive adjectival series, i.e., after the adjective modifiers. In this case the ad-

13

jectives are all linked by the *ezâfe* and do not require the conjunction. There is no essential difference in meaning whether the indefinite suffix is added to the noun itself or to the end of the adjectival sequence.

خانهٔ قدیمی بزرگی

[khâne-ye qadimi-e bozorg]-i

خانه‌ای قدیمی و بزرگ

[khâne]-i [qadimi-o bozorg]

a big old house

14.4 Adverbial modifiers precede adjectives directly in the *ezâfe* construction.

خانه‌ای بسیار بزرگ

[khâne]-i [besyâr bozorg]

خانهٔ بسیار بزرگی

[khâne-ye besyâr bozorg]-i

a very big house

پزشکی نسبةً مشهور

[pezeshk]-i [nesbatan mashhur]

پزشك نسبةً مشهوری

[pezeshk-e nesbatan mashhur]-i

a relatively famous physician

§15 The noun in the predicate position.

15.1 The unqualified noun, i.e., not modified by an attributive adjective or prepositional phrase, occurs, as a categorical predicate of the copulative verb, in the absolute state and indicates membership in the class. The unqualified noun is **singular** and **absolute** regardless of the number of the subject.

این کتاب است.	*in, ketâb-ast*	This is a book.
اینها کتابند.	*inhâ, ketâb-and.*	These are books.
علی دانشجوست.	*ali, dâneshju-st.*	Ali is a student.
علی و اکبر دانشجو اند.	*ali-o akbar, dâneshju-and.*	Ali and Akbar are students.

14

پدر علی پزشک بود .	*pedar-e ali, pezeshk-bud.*	Ali's father was a physician.
پدرهای آن بچه‌ها پزشک بودند .	*pedarhâ-ye ân bachchehâ, pezeshk-budand.*	Those children's fathers were physicians.

15.2 When the predicate noun is modified by an adjective or by any other type of descriptive phrase (such as a prepositional phrase), it is placed in the non-specific state. As previously noted (§14.3), in such constructions the indefinite enclitic may be attached either to the noun or to the adjective.

علی دانشجوئی زرنگ است .

ali, [dâneshju]-i [zerang]-ast.

علی دانشجوی زرنگیست .

ali, [dâneshju-ye zerang]-i-st.

Ali is a clever student.

آقای جعفری پزشکی مهربان بود .

âqâ-ye ja'fari, [pezeshk]-i [mehrbân]-bud.

آقای جعفری پزشک مهربانی بود .

âqâ-ye ja'fari, [pezeshk-e mehrbân]-i-bud.

Mr. Ja'fari was a kind physician.

In negative sentences, however, the indefinite enclitic falls on the adjective and not on the noun.

علی دانشجوی زرنگی نیست .

ali, dâneshju-ye zerang-i níst.

Ali is not a clever student.

آقای جعفری پزشک مشهوری نبود .

âqâ-ye ja'fari, pezeshk-e mashhur-i nábud.

Mr. Ja'fari was not a famous physician.

15.3 In good literary prose style, in such constructions the affirmative present and past-absolute copulative verb tends to intervene between the noun and its modifiers when the noun carries the indefinite enclitic.

علی دانشجوی زرنگیست.

ali, dâneshju-ye zerang-i-st. (normal)

علی دانشجوئیست زرنگ.

ali, dâneshju-i-st zerang. (literary)

Ali is a clever student.

پزشك مهربانی بود.

pezeshk-e mehrbân-i-bud. (normal)

پزشکی بود مهربان.

pezeshk-i-bud mehrbân. (literary)

He was a kind physician.

معلمی در شیراز است.

mo'allem-i dar shirâz-ast. (normal)

معلمیست در شیراز.

mo'allem-i-st dar shirâz. (literary)

He is a teacher in Shiraz.

15.4 With plural subjects, an unmodified predicate noun is in the **absolute singular,** while a modified predicate noun is in the **indefinite plural.**

<div dir="rtl">اینها کتاب است (اند).</div>	*inhâ, ketâb-ast (-and).*	These are books.
<div dir="rtl">اینها کتابهای مفیدی نیست.</div>	*inhâ, ketâbhâ-ye mofid-i nist.*	These are not useful books.

Vocabulary 3

<div dir="rtl">پسر</div>	*pesar* boy, son	<div dir="rtl">دانشجو</div>	*dâneshju* (university) student
<div dir="rtl">تنبل</div>	*tambal* lazy	<div dir="rtl">دانشگاه</div>	*dâneshgâh* university
<div dir="rtl">خراب</div>	*kharâb* broken, ruined	<div dir="rtl">دربارۀ</div>	*darbâre-ye* about, concerning
<div dir="rtl">خوشحال</div>	*khoshhâl* happy		

زرنگ   *zerang* clever, smart

زن   *zan* woman, wife

کهنه   *kohne* old, worn-out

مرد   *mard* man (not woman)

مشهور   *mashhur* famous, well-known

مفید   *mofid* useful

نسبةً   *nesbatan* relatively, fairly (also spelled نسبتاً, particularly in modern typeset)

Exercise 3

(a) Transform the following noun–adjective phrases into nonspecific *ezâfe* constructions (e.g., *ketâb-i khub > ketâb-e khub-i*):

١ دانشجوئی زرنگ

٢ پسرهائی خوشحال

٣ کشوری مشهور

٤ خانه‌هائی خراب

٥ مردی بزرگ

٦ بچه‌هائی بسیار زرنگ

٧ مردی خیلی تنبل

٨ کتابهائی نسبةً مفید

٩ دانشجوهائی خیلی خوب

١٠ دانشگاهی کاملاً نو

(b) Give both affirmative and negative answers to the following:

١ آنها بچه‌اند؟

٢ این دانشگاه قدیمی است؟

٣ معلمهای خوبی بودند؟

٤ تهران شهر خوبی است؟

٥ اینها ، مردهای تنبلی اند؟

٦ آن بچه‌ها ایرانی اند؟

٧ آن دانشگاه مشهور در ایران است؟

٨ این کتابها دربارهٔ ایران اند؟

٩ آن قلم کهنه مفید بود؟

١٠ آن پسرهای کوچک تنبل زرنگند؟

(c) Read and translate:

١ تهران شهریست بزرگ و نسبةً قدیمی.

٢ آن خانه‌های کهنه خراب بودند.

٣ آنها پسر نیستند ، مردند.

٤ این پسر تنبلی نیست.

٥ آن دانشجوی زرنگ در دانشگاه نیست.

٦ چرا در این شهر کتاب خوبی نیست؟

٧ در آن دانشگاهها دانشجوها تنبل نیستند .

٨ آن کتاب اینجا نیست. کجاست؟

٩ این کتابهای قدیمی دربارهٔ ایران اند؟

١٠ آن مردیست بسیار مشهور در ایران .

(d) Translate into Persian:

1. That old pen is broken.
2. He is not a student.
3. They are good students.
4. He is not in Tehran, but he is happy.
5. Those big old houses are perfectly good.
6. This is a relatively old country.
7. They are clever boys.
8. Where is that man?
9. They weren't in that old city.
10. The children weren't there.

Lesson Four

§16 Pronouns. The personal (subject) pronouns are:

من	*man* I		ما	*mâ* we
تو	*to* you		شما	*shomâ* you
او	*u* he, she		ایشان	*ishân* they ~used as a very respected singular
آن	*ân* he, she, it		آنها	*ânhâ* they

16.1 Although they have other uses, these are basically subject pronouns and for the present may be used only as emphatic verbal subjects.

16.2 The second-person plural pronoun, *shomâ,* is generally used, like the English "you" and the French *vous,* as both the singular and plural second person. The singular second-person pronoun, *to,* like the French and Italian *tu,* is reserved for God, intimate friends and relatives, small children, social inferiors, and for derogatory usage.

16.3 Although *ishân* is properly the third-person plural pronoun, in modern Persian it is used almost exclusively as the "polite" singular to refer deferentially to a singular third person. The demonstrative pronouns are used for all third persons, animate and inanimate, while the true pronouns *u* and *ishân* are reserved for animate beings only.

§17 Present copula. The present copula (the English verb "to be") expresses a predicative state, as in "he is good." In their simplest form the copulas are enclitics joined to the predicate.

م... ‌*-am* I am	یم... *-im* we are
ی... *-i* you are	ید... *-id* you are
است *-ast* he/she/it is	...ند *-and* they are

Since the copulas, as well as all verbal forms in Persian, convey adequate information to the hearer as to person and number, the personal pronouns are not necessarily expressed.

17.1 Orthographically the enclitic forms are joined directly to the preceding word when it ends in a consonant. Although *ast* may be joined in this manner (and the *alef* dropped), it is generally left as a separate word.

cons.→ no alef

خوبم (من) *(man) khub-am*	خوبیم (ما) *(mâ) khub-im*
خوبی (تو) *(to) khub-i*	خوبید (شما) *(shomâ) khub-id*
خوب است (او/آن) *(u/ân) khub-ast*	خوبند (آنها) *(ânhâ) khub-and*

17.2 When joined to words ending in *-e* and *-i,* an *alef* is used:

e & i → alef used

بچه‌ام *bachche-am*	بچه‌ایم *bachche-im*
بچه‌ای *bachche-i*	بچه‌اید *bachche-id*
بچه است *bachche-ast*	بچه‌اند *bachche-and*

ایرانی‌ام *irâni-am*	ایرانی‌ایم *irâni-im*
ایرانی‌ای *irâni-i*	ایرانی‌اید *irâni-id*
ایرانی است *irâni-ast*	ایرانی‌اند *irâni-and*

17.3 Joined to words in *-â* and *-u,* the enclitics are written as follows. Note that the *alef* of *-ast* is dropped.[1]

â & u

کجام (من) *(man) kujâ-am*	کجانیم (ما) *(mâ) kujâ-im*
کجائی (تو) *(to) kujâ-i*	کجائید (شما) *(shomâ) kujâ-id*

---

[1]As a general orthographic rule, the *alef* of *ast* is dropped after *â* and unstressed *-i.* The *a* of *ast* may optionally be dropped after *u* and stressed *i.*

(آنها) کجااند (ânhâ) kujâ-and	(آن) کجاست (ân) kujâ-st
دانشجوئیم dânishju-im	دانشجوام dânishju-am
دانشجوئید dânishju-id	دانشجوئی dânishju-i
دانشجواند dânishju-and	دانشجوست dânishju-st

§18 The negative copula. The negative copula is formed by adding the personal enclitic endings to *nist*, itself the third-person singular negative.

نیستم *nístam*	نیستیم *nístim*
نیستی *nísti*	نیستید *nístid*
نیست *níst*	نیستند *nístand*

§19 *Kist* and *chist*. When immediately followed by *-ast* or *-and*, the interrogatives *che* ("what") and *ki* ("who") combine to form *chist(and)* and *kist(and)*.

آن چیست؟	*ân chist?*	What's that?
آن بچه کیست؟	*ân bachche kist?*	Who is that child?
آن بچهها کیستند؟	*ân bachchehâ kist-and?*	Who are those children?
این کتابها دربارۀ چیست؟	*in ketâbhâ darbâre-ye chist?*	What are these books about?

Vocabulary 4

آقا *âqâ* gentleman, sir, Mr.   خانم *khânom* lady, Miss/Mrs./ Ms.

When *âqâ* and *khânom* precede family names, they take the *ezâfe*, as *âqâ-ye alizâde* "Mr. Alizadeh," *khânom-e alizâde* "Miss/Mrs./Ms. Alizadeh." Before or after given names there is no *ezâfe*, as *âqâ ali, ali âqâ, khânom maryam, maryam khânom*. In normal social situations Iranians address each other by title and family name; in fairly familiar situations the given name and title are used. The given name alone is considered excessively familiar.

پزشك *pezeshk* doctor, physician

جعبه *ja'be* box

چه *che* what? (with -ast, chist)

سبز *sabz* green

سفید *sefid* white

سیاه *siâh* black

قرمز *qermez* red

معلم *mo'allem* teacher

کی *ki* who? (with -ast, kist)

همیشه *hamishe* always

Exercise 4 *for Friday*

(a) Give the appropriate form of the verb "to be" in the present and past:

۱۱ این خانمها مهربان ــ؟   ٦ شما معلم ــ؟   ۱ من همیشه خوشحال ــ.

۱۲ تو بچهٔ خوبی ــ؟   ۷ این آقا کی ــ؟   ۲ آنها تنبل ــ.

۱۳ شما پزشك ــ؟   ۸ آن چه ــ؟   ۳ شما بچه نــ.

۱٤ من ایرانی ــ.   ۹ ما کجا ــ؟   ٤ تو بچه ــ.

۱٥ آن آقا ، کجا ــ؟   ۱۰ آن جعبه بزرگ ــ.   ٥ ما پزشك نــ.

(b) Give the correct form of the words in parentheses as predicates:

٦ این کتابها (نسبةً مفید) بودَ.   ۱ ما (دانشجوی خوب) ایم.

۷ آن مردها (پزشك بزرگ) اند در ایران.   ۲ شما (پزشك مشهور) اید.

۸ من (دانشجو) ام در دانشگاه تهران.   ۳ شما (دانشجو) اید؟

۹ آن ، (بچه) است زرنگ ولی تنبل.   ٤ او (مرد خوشحال) است.

۱۰ این جوانها (دانشجو) بودند.   ٥ آنها (بچه زرنگ) بودند.

(c) Give the Persian for the following:

1. Who is that kind man?
2. What is in that big black box?
3. Why aren't you happy?
4. I'm not a doctor; I'm a teacher in this city.
5. Who is that woman?
6. Isn't she Mrs. Alizadeh?
7. I'm a student in this university.

Supplementary Vocabulary: Courtesy Phrases

خوش آمدید	*khósh-âmadid*	Welcome.
متشکرم	*motashakker-am*	Thank you.
مرسی	*mérsi*	Thank you.[1]
خیلی ممنون	*kháyli mamnun*	Much obliged.[2]
خواهش میکنم	*khâhésh-mikonam*	You're welcome.[3] Please.[4]
بفرمائید	*béfarmâid*	Please.[5]

---

[1]The French *merci* has become as almost universal casual "thank you."
[2]This phrase has a slightly old-fashioned ring to it, but it is still quite common.
[3]As a reply to "thank you."
[4]Used when requesting something.
[5]Used when offering something.

Lesson Five

§20 The vocative. The vocative, or direct address, is formed by shifting the stress of a noun from its normal position to the first syllable. In names with preceding titles, the stress is shifted to the first syllable of the title. There is no orthographic representation of this phenomenon.

بچه	*bachché*	child
بچه	*báchche*	Hey, kid!
خانم علوی	*khânom-e alaví*	Ms. Alavi
خانم علوی	*khâ´nom-e alavi*	O Ms. Alavi!

§21 The possessive *ezâfe*. The *ezâfe* construction is also used to link together two syntactically related nouns or noun and pronoun.

21.1 The nouns linked by the *ezâfe* indicate possession by the latter of the former:

خانۀ علی	*khâne-ye ali*	Ali's house
کتابهای بچه	*ketâbhâ-ye bachche*	the child's books

Since attributive adjectives must follow immediately the nouns they modify, they intervene between the possessor and the thing possessed in the possessive *ezâfe* construction.

کتاب بزرگ بچۀ کوچك	*[ketâb-e bozorg]-e* *[bachche-ye kuchek]*	the small child's big book

24

قلمهای کهنهٔ دانشجوی تنبل	*[qalamhâ-ye kohne]-ye [dâneshju-ye tambal]*	the lazy student's old pens

21.2 The subject pronouns given in §16, as well as the interrogative *ki,* are used as second members of the *ezâfe* construction to indicate possession.

کتاب من	*ketâb-e **man***	my book
مادر مهربان شما	*mâdar-e mehrbân-e **shomâ***	your kind mother
قلمهای نو آنها	*qalamhâ-ye naw-e ânhâ*	their new pens
بچهٔ کیست؟	*bachche-ye kist?*	Whose child is he?

21.3 The *ezâfe* construction, while called possessive, is used extensively in Persian and ranges into meanings far beyond the English possessive. It is used, in fact, to indicate any type of syntactical relationship between two nouns.

راه تبریز	*râh-e tabriz*	the road to Tabriz, Tabriz Road
دانشجوی دانشگاه	*dâneshju-ye dâneshgâh*	university student
کجای ایران؟	*kojâ-ye irân*	whereabouts in Iran?

Several of these idiomatic constructions have already been introduced, such as *âqâ-ye* and *khânom-e,* the *ezâfe* being required by the nouns *âqâ* and *khânom* before family names.

(a) Many prepositions, like *darbâre-ye,* take their complements through the *ezâfe.* These should be learned as items of vocabulary.

(b) All geographical locations require the *ezâfe* between the geographical formation and the proper name.

دریای مدیترانه	*daryâ-ye mediterâne*	the Mediterranean Sea
کوه دماوند	*kuh-e damâvand*	Mount Damavand

(c) All proper names of towns, cities, streets, buildings, etc. are linked to the generic noun by the *ezâfe*.

شهر تهران	*shahr-e tehrân*	the city Tehran
خیابان اصفهان	*khiâbân-e esfahân*	Isfahan Avenue
کشور ایران	*keshvar-e irân*	the country Iran

21.4 The indefinite enclitic does not intervene in a possessive *ezâfe* construction as it does in the adjectival *ezâfe*. When the first noun is indefinite, the phrase *yek-i az* ("one of") and the plural is used with true possessives; with other types of *ezâfe, yek* may precede the construction.

یکی از کتابهای من	*yek-i az ketâbhâ-ye man*	one of my books, a book of mine
یک دانشجوی دانشگاه	*yek dânishju-ye dâneshgâh*	one (a) university student
یکی از دانشجوهای دانشگاه تهران	*yek-i az dâneshjuhâ-ye dâneshgâh-e tehrân*	one of the students of Tehran University

§22 **The long copula.** The long forms of the copulas, which are always written separate and receive stress, are as follows.

هستم	*hástam* I am		هستیم	*hástim* we are
هستی	*hásti* you are		هستید	*hástid* you are
هست	*hást* he/she/it is		هستند	*hástand* they are

22.1 The long forms are used for the existential state ("I am, I exist") and where the predicate is a preceding prepositional phrase, normally rendered in English by "there is" or "there are."

علی هست.	*ali hast.*	Ali is (exists).
در آشپزخانه غذائی هست.	*dar âshpazkhâne qazâ-i hast.*	There is some food in the kitchen.

26

در خانهٔ او کتابهای خوبی هست.	dar khâne-ye u ketâbhâ-ye khub-i hast.	There are some good books in his house.

22.2 Whereas the short enclitic copulas cannot be stressed, the long forms may be stressed and are therefore used for emphasis, as in the following exchange:

علی ایرانی است.	ali irâní-ast.	Ali is Iranian.
نخیر، ایرانی نیست.	nákhayr, irâni níst.	No, he isn't Iranian.
چرا، ایرانی هست!	chérâ, irâní hást!	Oh yes he is Iranian.

22.3 Following words ending in vowels, the long copulas are often used, especially in every-day speech, to avoid the conjunction of two vowels, especially two like vowels. This applies particularly to the second person singular and the first and second persons plural. In this case the long copula does not take stress.

when word ends w/ a vowel → hastam

من ایرانی هستم.	man irâní-hastam.	I'm Iranian. *(use n)*

Hastam is used here to avoid *irâní-am,* a combination that is also fairly tolerated in spoken Persian.

آنها کجا هستند؟	ânhâ kojâ-hastand?	Where are they?

Hastand is used here to avoid *kojâ-and,* a combination that is avoided whenever possible.

شما آمریکائی هستید؟	shomâ âmrikâi-hastid?	Are you American?

Hastid is used here to avoid *âmrikâí-id,* a combination that is avoided whenever possible.

اینها کتابهای خوبی هستند.	inhâ, ketâbhâ-ye khub-i-hastand.	These are good books.

Hastand is used here to avoid *ketâbhâ-ye khúb-i-and,* unstressed *i* following by *a,* a combination that is tolerated but often avoided in spoken Persian.

Vocabulary 5

از *az* from (prep.)

اسم *esm* name

امروز *emruz* today

راه *râh* road, way

على *ali* Ali (masc. given name)

علیزاده *alizâde* Alizadeh (family name)

با *bâ* with, by (prep.)

برای *barâ-ye* for (prep.)

به (بـ...) *be* to (prep.; may be written separate or joined directly to following word)

پدر *pedar* father

دختر *dokhtar* girl, daughter

جا *jâ* place

جدید *jadid* new

دور (از) *dur* distant, far (*az* from)

مادر *mâdar* mother

مریم *maryam* Maryam (fem. given name)

نزدیك *nazdik* near, close (with *ezâfe* or *be*, to)

یك *yek* one, a (adj., precedes word it modifies)

یکی *yek-i* one (pronoun)

Exercise 5

(a) Give both affirmative and negative answers:

۶ اینها کتابهای ما هستند؟

۷ راه تهران از اینجاست؟

۸ تهران شهر بزرگ ایران است؟

۹ او پدر خانم علیزاده است؟

۱۰ آقای علیزاده با شما بود؟

۱ این بچه پسر شماست؟

۲ شما دختر او هستید؟

۳ او مادر علی است؟

٤ من پدر آن بچه‌ام؟

۵ کتابهای شما اینها هستند؟

(b) Give appropriate answers to the following:

۳ کشور شما چیست؟

٤ آن دخترها با شما بودند؟

۱ کتابهای جدید ما کجا هستند؟

۲ خانهٔ شما به اینجا نزدیك است؟

۸ اسم شما چیست؟   ٥ کتاب پسر کوچك او در خانه است؟

۹ امروز کجا بودند؟   ٦ تهران از اینجا دور است؟

۱۰ این برای کیست؟   ۷ خانهٔ من نزدیك خانهٔ شماست؟

(c) Change the following to the "one of" construction (e.g., *ketâb-e man > yek-i az ketâbhâ-ye man*):

٥ پسر مادر من   ۱ کتاب جدید علی

٦ راه دور آن کشور   ۲ خانهٔ آقای علیزاده

۷ دانشجوی دانشگاه   ۳ شهر ایران

۸ خانهٔ این شهر   ٤ بچهٔ آن زن

(d) Read and translate into English:

۱ خانهٔ جدید مادر و پدر شما کجاست؟

۲ امروز آن مرد مهربان ایرانی در آن شهر بود.

۳ شهر تهران از آمریکا خیلی دور است.

٤ خانم علیزاده، شما مادر آن دختر کوچك هستید؟

٥ خانهٔ آنها کجای تهران بود؟

٦ یکی از این کتابهای نو برای علی است.

(e) Translate into Persian:

1. What is that little boy's name?
2. Is this for your wife?
3. No, it's not for her; it's for my little daughter.
4. What is that new book of yours about?
5. We aren't Iranians; we're Americans.
6. Your house is not far from the city.

Review I

(a) Review the vocabulary lists for Lessons 1–5.

(b) Read and translate the following:

١ این آقا معلم است.

٢ آن خانم معلمیست بسیار مهربان.

٣ دختر کوچك شما همیشه خوشحال بود.

٤ آقا، در آن جعبهٔ بزرگ چیست؟

٥ دانشجوهای دانشگاه کجااند؟

٦ این قلم کهنه کاملا خراب است.

٧ ایشان زنهای نسبةً زرنگی اند.

٨ پدر او پزشکی بود در یکی از شهرهای ایران.

٩ معلم آن جوان زرنگ ایرانی شمائید؟

١٠ اینها صندلی‌های خوبی نیست.

(c) Translate the following into Persian:

1. What was his name?
2. Our house is fairly near Tehran.
3. Iran is a large and very old country.
4. Where are my books and pens?
5. The windows in (of) this house are very small.
6. Aren't you a student?
7. What was that book about?
8. Isn't your new pen green?
9. No, it's not green; it's black.
10. There are some very small houses in this city.

1) ra-n the (used when referring to something specific)

Lesson Six

§23 The infinitive. All Persian infinitives end in stressed *-dán* or *-tán*. Following vowels and voiced consonants the ending is *-dan;* following voiceless consonants the ending is *-tan.*

ماندن	*mândan*	to remain
دادن	*dâdan*	to give
گرفتن	*gereftan*	to take

Although in quoting items of vocabulary the Persian infinitive is equated with the English infinitive, in fact their uses hardly ever coincide. The idiomatic uses of the Persian infinitive will be introduced later.

§24 The past stem and the past absolute tense. The past absolute tense of all verbs is formed by (1) dropping the infinitival ending *-an,* giving a past stem in *-d* or *-t,* and (2) adding the following enclitic personal endings:

م...	*-am* (I)	یم...	*-im* (we)
ی...	*-i* (you)	ید...	*-id* (you)
— —	(he, she, it)	ند...	*-and* (they)

With the addition of the above endings, the stress remains constant on the final syllable of the past stem. An example of the past absolute conjugation, from the verb *gereftan* "to take":

گرفتم *geréftam* I took   گرفتیم *geréftim* we took

گرفتی *geréfti* you took   گرفتید *geréftid* you took

گرفت *geréft* he/she/it took   گرفتند *geréftand* they took

24.1 Expressed pronominal subjects are not necessary in Persian since they are implicit in the verb. The pronouns are expressed only under the following conditions:

(a) special emphasis is given to the pronoun:

شما رفتید؟ *shomâ raftid?*   Did *you* go?

من گرفتم. *man gereftam.*   *I* took (it).

(b) enclitic *-ham* ("too, also") is added to the subject pronoun:

من هم رفتم. **man-ham raftam.**   I went too.

آنها هم آمدند. **ânhâ-ham âmadand.**   They came too.

(c) two different subject pronouns are contrasted:

من رفتم و او ماند. **man raftam-o u**   I went and he stayed.
                    mând.

24.2 The negative past absolute of all verbs is formed by prefixing stressed *ná-*, which removes the stress from its position in the affirmative.

(a) The negative prefix is connected orthographically to all verbs beginning with consonants.

نگرفتیم *nágereftim*   we did not take

نرفتند *náraftand*   they did not go

(b) In verbs beginning with vowels other than *i-*,[1] a -*y*- is infixed between the negative prefix and the *alef* of the stem.

افتادم < نیافتادم   *oftâdam > náyoftâdam*

افزودم < نیافزودم   *afzudam > náyafzudam*

آمد < نیآمد   *âmad > náyâmad*

Some writers, preferring a more "phonetic" orthography, drop the *alef* after the infixed -*y*- in stems beginning with *a*- and *o*- (e.g., either نیفزودم or نیفتادم for *náyafzudam* and either نیافتادم or نیفتادم for *náyoftâdam*). The pronunciation remains the same in either case. In verbs beginning with *â*- the *alef* cannot be dropped, but the retention of the *madde* is a matter of personal preference (e.g., either نیآمد or نیامد for *náyâmad*).

24.3 The past absolute tense corresponds generally to the English simple past.

(a) It indicates an action done once and completed in the past.

به تهران رفتم.   *be tehrân raftam.*   I went to Tehran.

به او قلمی دادم.   *be u qalam-i dâdam.*   I gave him a pen.

(b) The past absolute of stative verbs indicates that the state ceased to pertain in the past.

پدر مهدی استاد بود.   *pedar-e mehdi ostâd bud.*   Mehdi's father was a professor (i.e., he is no longer one).

هیچ چیز نماند.   *hich chiz námând.*   Nothing remained, there was nothing left .

---

[1]There is only one verb in Persian that begins with the vowel *i*-, *istâdan* "to stand, stop." With this verb the negative prefix may be written attached directly to the *alef* as نایستادم (*náistâdam*) or separate as نه ایستادم (same pronunciation).

نماندم. *námândam.*	I didn't stay (i.e., I moved on at some point in the past).

(c) It is used for actions "as good as done" and states just perceived to have come about.

خوب ، رفتم. *khob, raftam.*	OK, I'm gone (I've got to go now).
علی آمد. *ali âmad.*	Here's Ali (he is just perceived to have come).
حالا خوردم. *hâlâ khordam.*	I've just eaten.

§25 The specific direct-object marker. Definite or specific direct objects of verbs are marked by the enclitic *-râ,* which may be either attached orthographically or left separate. This enclitic marks direct objects that are specific, grammatically or semantically. Nouns are construed as specific in the following cases:

(a) all proper names.

ایران را دیدید؟ *irân-râ didid?*	Did you see Iran?
علی را کجا دیدید؟ *ali-râ kojâ didid?*	Where did you see Ali?

(b) all personal and demonstrative pronouns. Note that *man* combines with *-râ* to form the irregular مرا *márâ,* and *to + râ* is spelled ترا, *tórâ.*

مرا کجا دیدید؟ *márâ kojâ didid?*	Where did you see me?
ترا ندیدم. *tórâ nádidam.*	I didn't see you.
آن را گرفتند. *ân-râ gereftand.*	They took it.

(c) all nouns described by demonstrative adjectives or by the possessive *ezâfe.*

آن خانه‌ها‌را ندیدم.	*ân khânehâ-râ nádi-dam.*	I didn't see those houses.
خانهٔ اورا خریدید؟	*khâne-ye u-râ khari-did?*	Did you buy his house?
آن کتابهای شما‌را خریدند.	*ân ketâbhâ-ye shomâ-râ khari-dand.*	They bought those books of yours.
خانهٔ علی‌را ندیدم.	*khâne-ye ali-râ nádi-dam.*	I didn't see Ali's house.

(d) Since the complement of the phrase *yek-i az* ("one of") and the negative *hich yek az* ("none of") is always considered specific, the entire phrase is construed as definite and therefore marked with *-râ*.

یکی از آنها‌را خواستم.	*yek-i az ânhâ-râ khâs-tam.*	I wanted one of those.
هیچیک از کتابهای شما‌را نیآوردم.	*hichyek az ketâbhâ-ye shomâ-râ náyâvor-dam.*	I didn't bring any of your books.

(e) The reflexives *yekdigar* and *hamdigar* ("each other") are construed as definite.

همدیگررا دیدیم.	*hamdigar-râ didim.*	We saw each other.
یکدیگررا ندیدند.	*yekdigar-râ nádidand.*	They didn't see each other.

(f) True indefinite or non-specific direct objects are marked by the indefinite enclitic but not by *-râ*.

صدائی نشنیدم.	*sedâ-i náshenidam.*	I didn't hear a sound.
کتاب دیگری خواستم.	*ketâb-e digar-i khâs-tam.*	I wanted another book (any other book).

However, a specific indefinite object ("a certain...") takes both the indefinite enclitic and the object marker *-râ*.

صدائی‌را شنیدم.	*sedâ-i-râ shenidam.*	I heard a (certain) sound.

35

كتاب ديگرى را *ketâb-e digar-i-râ*   I wanted another
خواستم . *khâstam.*   (particular) book.

Vocabulary 6

آوردن *âvordan* to bring

بودن *budan* to be

چرا *chérâ* yes (in response to a negative question), oh yes (contradicts a negative statement)

چيز *chiz* thing (usually tangible)

خواستن *khâstan* to want

دادن *dâdan* to give

دوست *dust* friend

ديدن *didan* to see

ديروز *diruz* yesterday

ديگر *digar* other

روى *ru-ye* on

شنيدن *shenidan* to hear

كتابخانه *ketâbkhâne* library

گرفتن *gereftan* to take

هم *-ham* (enclitic, may not follow a verb) too, also; (with negatives) either; *ham X ham Y* both X and Y

همديگر *hamdigar* each other

يكديگر *yekdigar* each other

Exercises 6

(a) Give the proper ending for the verbs:

۱ ما (ديدن) .

۲ آنها (آوردن) .

۳ ايشان چه (گرفتن) ؟

٤ او (نشنيدن) .

٥ من (آوردن) .

٦ تو اين را (خواستن) .

۷ شما مرا (ديدن) .

۸ ما (گرفتن) .

۹ آن را اينها (خواستن) .

۱۰ من آنجا (بودن) .

۱۱ ايران را ما (نديدن) .

۱۲ اين صندلى را كى (آوردن) ؟

۱۳ من قلم شمارا (گرفتن) .

۱٤ تو آنهارا به او (دادن) .

۱٥ شما (شنيدن) .

۱٦ دوستهاى ايشان اينهارا براى ما (آوردن) .

۱۷ او در آن شهر (نبودن) .

۱۸ دانشجوها كتابهارا (گرفتن) .

(b) Give affirmative answers to the questions. Contradict the negative statements (e.g., *in khub nist > chérâ, khub-ast*)..

١ این جا خوب نیست؟

٢ اینهارا شما نخواستید؟

٣ آن شهر بد نبود.

٤ آنهارا نیاوردید.

٥ مرا ندیدید؟

٦ دیروز علی و اکبر اینجا نبودند.

٧ آن چیزهارا به علی نداد؟

٨ در خانهٔ دوست شما نیستند.

٩ آن شهر از اینجا دور نیست.

١٠ اسم اورا نشنیدید؟

(c) Read and translate:

١ دوستهای مارا ندیدند.

٢ آن قلم دیگررا خواست.

٣ کتاب مرا به او دادی؟

٤ آنهارا شنیدم.

٥ آن چیزهارا چرا نگرفتید؟

٦ کتابهارا آوردیم.

٧ مادر و پدر شمارا در خانهٔ آقای جعفری دیدم.

٨ اینهارا نخواستیم.

٩ آن‌را شنیدید؟

١٠ اینهارا کی آورد؟

(d) Translate into Persian:

1. Didn't you hear that?
2. My friend brought these books to the library.
3. Who wanted these things?
4. They gave the pens to our friends.
5. I didn't see Maryam's mother yesterday.

6. We too saw them on the table.
7. I didn't bring anything. -Chizi naiovardam
8. They gave them to my friend.
9. I saw you in the library yesterday.
10. Didn't you want this book? Yes, I did.[1]

Supplementary Vocabulary: Countries and Languages

COUNTRY		NATIVE		LANGUAGE	
آلمان	âlmân Germany	آلمانی	âlmâni	آلمانی	âlmâni
آمریکا	âmrikâ USA[2]	آمریکائی	âmrikâi	انگلیسی	englisi
آذربایجان	âzarbâyjân Azer-baijan	آذربایجانی	âzarbâyjâni	ترکی	torki
اتریش	otrish Austria	اتریشی	otrishi	آلمانی	âlmâni
ارمنستان	armanestân Armenia	ارمنی	armani	ارمنی	armani
اروپا	orupâ Europe	اروپائی	orupâi		
اسپانیا	espânyâ Spain	اسپانیائی	espânyâi	اسپانیائی	espân-yâi[3]
افغانستان	afqânestân Afghanistan	افغان	afqân	فارسی، پشتو	fârsi, pashtu
انگلستان	englestân England	انگلیس	englis	انگلیسی	englisi
ایتالیا	itâlyâ Italy	ایتالیائی	itâlyâi	ایتالیائی	itâlyâi
ایران	irân Iran	ایرانی	irâni	فارسی	fârsi
بلژیك	belzhik Belgium	بلژیکی	belzhiki		
بلغارستان	bolqârestân	بلغار	bolqâr	بلغاری	bolqâri
پاکستان	pâkestân Pakistan	پاکستانی	pâkestâni	اردو	ordu
پرتقال	portoqâl Portugal	پرتقالی	portoqâli	پرتقالی	portoqâli

---

[1]For the English short answer, Persian gives the full verb.

[2]Also occasionally referred to by the old-fashioned term اتازونی etâzuni from the French *Etats Unis*.

[3]Also, *espânyol*.

N→ shemal
S→ jenub
W→ gharb
E→ shargh

Country		Demonym	Language
تاجیکستان *tâjikestân* Tajikistan	تاجیک *tâjik*		فارسی *fârsi*
ترکیه *torkiye* Turkey	ترك *tork*		ترکی *torki*
چین *chin* China	چینی *chini*		چینی *chini*
دانمارك *dânmârk* Denmark	دانمارکی *dânmârki*		دانمارکی *dân-marki*
روسیه *rusiye* Russia	روس *rus*		روسی *rusi*
ژاپن *zhâpon* Japan	ژاپنی *zhâponi*		ژاپنی *zhâponi*
سوریه *suriye* Syria	سوری *suri*		عربی *arabi*
سویس *suis* Switzerland	سویسی *suisi*		
سوئد *sued* Sweden	سوئدی *suedi*		سوئدی *suedi*
عراق *erâq* Iraq	عراقی *erâqi*		عربی *arabi*
عربستان *arabestân* Arabia	عرب *arab*		عربی *arabi*
فرانسه *farânse* France	فرانسوی *farânsavi*		فرانسه *farânse*
كانادا *kânâdâ* Canada	کانادائی *kânâdâi*		
كردستان *kordestân* Kurdistan	کرد *kord*		کردی *kordi*
گرجستان *gorjestân* Georgia	گرجی *gorji*		گرجی *gorji*
لبنان *lobnân* Lebanon	لبنانی *lobnâni*		عربی *arabi*
لهستان *lehestân* Poland	لهستانی *lehestâni*		لهستانی *lehestâni*
مجارستان *majârestân* Hungary	مجار *majâr*		مجاری *majâri*
مصر *mesr* Egypt	مصری *mesri*		عربی *arabi*
نروژ *norvezh* Norway	نروژی *norvezhi*		نروژی *norvezhi*
هلند *holand* Holland	هلندی *holandi*		هلندی *holandi*
هند(وستان) *hend(ustân)* India	هندی *hendi*		هندی *hendi*
یونان *yunân* Greece	یونانی *yunâni*		یونانی *yunâni*

Lesson Seven

§26 Compound verbs. The compound verb, the type that accounts for the vast majority of verbs in Persian, consists of a non-verbal element and a verbal element. The non-verbal element may be (1) a noun such as *kâr* "work" as in the compound *kâr-kardan* "to work, to do something," (2) an adjective like *paydâ* "found" as in the compound *paydâ-kardan* "to find," or (3) an adverb like *pish* "forward" in *pish-raftan* "to advance, go forward," or *bar* "up, over" as in *bar-dâshtan* "to pick up."

26.1 In compound infinitives stress is on the final syllable.

بزرگ شدن	*bozorg-shodán*	to grow up
برداشتن	*bar-dâshtán*	to pick up

26.2 In finite compound forms stress falls on the final syllable of the non-verbal element, and voice intonation falls rapidly away on the verbal element, which receives no stress whatsoever.

دیروز از مدرسه برگشتند.	*diruz az madrase bár-gashtand.*	They returned from school yesterday.
قلم مرا پیدا کردند.	*qalam-e ma-râ paydâ´-kardand.*	They found my pen.
کتابهارا برداشتم.	*ketâbhâ-râ bár-dâsh-tam.*	I picked up the books.

40

— budan } never take
— dashtan } "mi" in
The past tense.

26.3 In the negative, the negative prefix takes its place before the verbal element and removes the primary stress from the non-verbal element, leaving a secondary stress on the final syllable of the non-verbal element.

کتابهارا برنداشتند.	*ketâbhâ-râ bàr-nádâsh-tand.*	They didn't pick up the book.
قلم مرا پیدا نکردند.	*qalam-e ma-râ paydâ`-nákardand.*	They didn't find my pen.

26.4 Generic objects form compounds with the verb. They are not marked with the direct-object marker.

کتاب خواندم.	*ketâb-khândam*	I read books.
نامه نوشتند.	*nâme-neveshtand.*	They wrote letters.

§27 The continuous prefix. The verbal prefix *mí-* is added in all tenses to all verbs (except *budan* "to be" and simplex *dâshtan* "to have") to convey a progressive, continuous, or habitual aspect to the action or state of the verb.

mi- habitual, continuous

میرفتم	*míraftam*	I was going, I used to go
به شهر میرفتم که...	*be shahr míraftam ke...*	I was going to town when...
هرروز به شهر میرفتم	*har ruz be shahr míraftam.*	I used to go to town every day.

but

جوان بودم.	*javân budam.*	I was young / I used to be young.
آن کتاب را داشتند.	*ân ketâb-râ dâshtand.*	They had / used to have that book.

Orthographically the continuous prefix may be either left separate or joined to the verb; there is no standard practice. When joined to verbs beginning with *alef,* the prefix may be joined directly to the *alef* or, more "phonetically," the *alef* may be dropped as with the negative pre-

41

fix. When joined to verbs beginning with *â-*, the *alef* is retained, whereas the *madde* may be dropped or not at will.

می رفتم - میرفتم *míraftam* (two spellings)

می‌افتادم - میافتادم - میفتادم *míoftâdam* (three spellings)

می‌آمدم - میآمدم - میامدم *miâmadam* (three spellings)

27.2 In the past absolute of compound verbs the continuous prefix is added to the verbal element. Stress, however, remains on the last syllable of the non-verbal element and does not shift to the prefix as it does in simple verbs.

| در میرفتم | *dár-míraftam* | I was running away |
| درآنجا زندگی میکردیم. | *dar ânjâ zendegí-mikardim.* | We used to live there. |

If, however, the continuousness of the action is to be particularly emphasized, an added stress may fall on the continuous prefix, resulting in a dual stress pattern.

| در میرفتم | *dár-míraftam* | I *was* running away. |
| درآنجا زندگی میکردیم. | *dar ânjâ zendegí-míkardim.* | We *used* to live there (but not any longer). |

27.3 The negative past continuous is formed by prefixing the negative particle to the continuous particle. When followed by *mi-* the negative particle changes to *ne-*. In compound verbs the negative prefix takes primary stress, and a secondary stress falls on the final syllable of the non-verbal element.

در نمی‌رفتم	*dàr-némiraftam.*	I wasn't running away.
آن کتابها را برنمی‌داشتم.	*ân ketâbhâ-râ bàr-némidâshtam.*	I wasn't picking up those books.
دیروز کار نمی‌کردیم.	*diruz kâr-némikardim.*	We weren't working yesterday.

§28 The past participle. The past participle, which, like the English past participle, has a passive force with transitive verbs and a past force with intransitive verbs, is formed by adding stressed -é to the past stem.

رفتن > رفت > رفته   *raftan > raft- > rafte*   "gone"

دیدن > دید > دیده   *didan > did- > dide*   "seen"

پیش‌رفتن > پیش‌رفت >   *pishraftan > pishraft-*   "advanced"
پیشرفته   *> pishrafte*

§29 The past narrative tense. The past narrative is formed by adding the present copulas to the past participle; stress remains on the last syllable of the participle. This tense corresponds generally to the English present perfect, with the important exceptions noted below. The past narrative conjugation of *raftan* is as follows:

رفته‌ام *rafté-am* I've gone   رفته‌ایم *rafté-im* we've gone

رفته‌ای *rafté-i* you've gone   رفته‌اید *rafté-id* you've gone

رفته است *rafté-ast* he/she/it's gone   رفته‌اند *rafté-and* they've gone

The negative is formed by prefixing the stressed negative *ná-* to the participle.

نرفته‌ام *nárafte-am*   نرفته‌ایم *nárafte-im*

نرفته‌ای *nárafte-i*   نرفته‌اید *nárafte-id*

نرفته است *nárafte-ast*   نرفته‌اند *nárafte-and*

29.1 The past narrative is used in Persian for any action that was accomplished or state that pertained in the past, the effects of which are still pertinent or felt to be relevant in some way to a present situation. When historical truths are felt to be of special relevance to the present, or to transcend the past, they are couched in this tense. Compare and contrast the following examples.

شاه عباس پادشاه   *shâh abbâs pâdshâh-e*   Shah Abbas was a
بزرگی بود.   *bozorg-i **bud**.*   great king.

(i.e., he is no longer king: the state no longer pertains and is not considered of relevance to the present)

شاه عباس پادشاه   *shâh abbâs pâdshâh-e*   Shah Abbas was a
بزرگی بوده است.   *bozorg-i **bude-ast**.*   great king.

(i.e., it is still true now that he was both a king and great: the historical validity of the statement holds true today)

بیرونی در غزنی مرد.   *biruni dar qazni*   Biruni died in
                        ***mord**.*   Ghazna.

(a simple statement of fact: at one point in time he died; no special significance for the present)

بیرونی در غزنی مرده   *biruni dar qazni*   Biruni died in
است.   ***morde-ast**.*   Ghazna.

(a historical fact that is still pertinent: it may be a source of pride for the city of Ghazna that Biruni is buried there, or one may be viewing the historical significance of where he died, but the relevance is stated in terms of the present)

پدر علی پزشک بود.   *pedar-e ali pezeshk*   Ali's father used to be
                      ***bud**.*   a physician.

(i.e., he is no longer a physician: he may have taken up another profession or he may be dead. In either case, the "pastness" is stressed)

پدر علی پزشک بوده   *pedar-e ali pezeshk*   Ali's father was a
است.   ***bude-ast**.*   physician.

(i.e., it is of some particular relevance to a present situation that Ali's father was a doctor in the past: his "having been a physician" is stressed, not the pastness of the state)

29.2 The past narrative continuous is formed by adding the continuous prefix to the participle. The negative past narrative continuous is regularly formed.

می‌رفته‌ام	*mírafte-am*	I used to go
نمی‌رفته‌ام	*némirafte-am*	I wasn't in the habit of going

The past narrative continuous is used to describe an act or state that was continuous or habitual in the past, the historical validity of which still holds true now.

ابن سینا در اصفهان زندگی میکرده است.	*ebn-e sinâ dar esfahân zendegi-mikarde-ast.*	Avicenna lived in Isfahan.

Vocabulary 7

Nouns and adjectives

درس *dars* lesson

کار *kâr* work, job, thing (one does)

زبان *zabân* language, tongue

فارسی *fârsi* Persian (language)

انگلیسی *englisi* English (language)

روزنامه *ruznâme* newspaper

صدا *sedâ* voice, sound

مدرسه *madrase* school

Verbs

آمدن *âmadan* to come

برداشتن *bar-dâshtan*[1] to pick up

برگشتن *bar-gashtan* to return, come back, go back, turn around

پیدا کردن *paydâ-kardan* to find

پیش رفتن *pish-raftan* to go forward, advance, progress

خواندن *khândan* to read, call, recite

داشتن *dâshtan*[2] to have, hold

---

[1]This compound of *dâshtan* takes the *mí-* prefix.

[2]Simple *dâshtan* never takes the *mí-* prefix.

45

درس خواندن *dars-khândan* to study

رفتن *raftan* to go

زندگی کردن *zendegi-kardan* to live

کار کردن *kâr-kardan* to work, be doing something

مدرسه رفتن *madrase-raftan* to go to school, attend school

نوشتن *neveshtan* to write

Exercise 7

(a) Give the past habitual/progressive of the verbs in parentheses:

۱ دوست من (نامه نوشتن) .

۲ چرا کار ما (پیش نرفتن) ؟

۳ مادر و پدر من در این خانه (زندگی کردن) .

٤ من از شهر به خانه (برگشتن) .

٥ آن کتابهارا ما (خواندن) .

٦ علی و مریم به مدرسه (رفتن) .

۷ آن چیزهارا من (برداشتن) .

۸ شما از مدرسه (آمدن) .

۹ دوستهای من خیلی (درس خواندن) .

۱۰ او کتاب خوبی (داشتن) .

(b) Give the past narrative of the verbs in parentheses:

۱ من هم یک نامه ای (نوشتن) .

۲ قلم مرا کی (برداشتن) ؟

۳ شما هم (مدرسه رفتن) .

٤ او هم کتابی (نوشتن) .

٥ در این خانه کی (زندگی کردن) ؟

٦ کار شما خیلی (پیش رفتن) .

۷ شما چرا اینهارا (آوردن) ؟

۸ ما فارسی (درس خواندن) .

۹ من خیلی (کتاب خواندن) .

۱۰ آنها صدای شمارا (نشنیدن) .

(c) Translate into Persian: *do it in narrative.*

1. Who has come today?
2. I used to study Persian. *man Phasi das mi-khadan*
3. The newspapers were[1] on the table. *ru miz ast*
4. I used to read a lot of books.
5. They haven't returned from school.
6. You haven't worked today. *emruz kar na-cordid*
7. We were writing letters yesterday. *diruz nameh mi-neveshtim*
8. Haven't they given it to you? *anra be shoma nadodan?*
9. The library had a lot of books.
10. She hasn't gone to school; she's too little.
   un naraft ast mardeseh, u chelee chocheek ast nemi-rafte ast

---

[1]Use the narrative tense.

Lesson Eight

§30 Uses of *che* and *kodâm*.

30.1 Adjectival *che*.

(a) Exclamative. *Che* followed by an adjective is equivalent to the English "how ...!"

چه خوب!	*che khub!*	How good!
این خانه چه آرام است!	*in khâne che ârâm-ast!*	How quiet this house is!

Followed by a noun in the absolute state, *che* means "what sort of, what kind of...?"

این چه شهر است؟	*in che shahr-ast?*	What sort of city is this?

(b) When *che* is followed by a noun, or noun + adjective, in the indefinite state, it means "what a ...!"

چه شهری!	*che shahr-i!*	What a city!
چه ساختمانهائی!	*che sâkhtemânhâ-i!*	What buildings!
حسین چه دوست خوبیست!	*hosayn che dust-e khub-i-st!*	What a good friend Hossein is!

(c) The interrogative adjectival *che* ("what?") is normally followed by a noun with the indefinite enclitic in both the singular and the plural.

48

When the unmodified noun following *che* is construed as non-specific, it does not take *-râ* when it is direct object.

چه شهری؟	*che shahr-i?*	What city?
چه شهرهائی؟	*che shahrhâ-i?*	What cities?
چه کتابی خواندید؟	*che ketâb-i khândid?*	What book did you read?
چه کتابهائی خوانده‌اید؟	*che ketâbhâ-i khânde-id?*	What books have you read?

The modified noun in this construction is usually construed as specific and thus requires *-râ* when direct object even though it bears the indefinite enclitic required by *che*.

| چه شهر بزرگی را دیدی؟ | *che shahr-e bozorg-i-râ didi?* | What big city did you see? |
| چه کتابهای مهمی را خوانده‌اید؟ | *che ketâbhâ-ye mo-hemm-i-râ khânde-id?* | What important books have you read? |

Likewise, unmodified nouns take the object marker when construed as specific.

| چه کتابی را خوانده‌اید؟ | *che ketâb-i-râ khânde-id?* | What (particular) book have you read? |

(d) The plural of *che* is *chehâ* ("what all?").

| آنجا چها دیدید؟ | *ânjâ chehâ didid?* | What all did you see there? |
| چها نگفتم؟! | *chehâ nágoftam?* | What all did I not say?! |

Other interrogatives also admit similar plural constructions.

| کجاها بوده‌اید؟ | *kojâhâ bude-id?* | Where all have you been? |
| کیها رفتند؟ | *kihâ raftand?* | Who (all) went? |

30.2 The interrogative adjective *kodâm* ("which?") precedes the noun it modifies. As direct objects, nouns modified by *kodâm* are construed as specific and require *-râ*.

کدام کتابهارا خوانده‌اید؟	*kodâm ketâbhâ-râ khânde-id?*	Which books have you read?
کدام شهر بزرگ را دیدید؟	*kodâm shahr-e bozorg-râ didid?*	Which big city did you see?

§31 Comparison of adjectives. The comparative suffix for all adjectives is *-tar*. This suffix may be joined to an adjective ending in a connective letter or left separate, except with adjectives ending in the silent *he*, to which no suffix is ever joined.

بزرگ > بزرگتر (بزرگ تر)	*bozórg* big > *bozorgtár* bigger	
کوتاه > کوتاهتر (کوتاه تر)	*kutâh* short > *kutâhtár* shorter	
ساده > ساده‌تر	*sâdé* simple > *sâdetár* simpler	
پیشرفته > پیشرفته‌تر	*pishrafté* advanced > *pishraftetár* more advanced	

31.1 The preposition for the second term of comparison, when it is a noun, pronoun or numeral, is *az*. The *az*-phrase normally precedes the comparative adjective, although it may also follow.

از آن ساده‌تر = ساده‌تر ازآن	*az ân sâdetar = sâdetar az ân*	simpler than that
شما از من بلندترید.	*shomâ az man bolandtar-id (bolandtar az man-id).*	You are taller than I am.

"Much" with the comparative is expressed by *besyâr, kháyli* or *bemarâtib*, which may precede the element of comparison when it precedes the comparative adjective.

زهرا از شیرین خیلی خوشگلتر است. or زهرا خیلی از شیرین خوشگلتر است .	*zahrâ az shirin kháyli khoshgeltar-ast* or *zahrâ kháyli az shirin khoshgeltar-ast.*	Zahra is much prettier than Shirin.
کار من از کار شما بسیار مفیدتر است .	*kâr-e man az kâr-e shomâ besyâr mofidtar-ast.*	My job is much more important than yours.
این کشور بمراتب پیشرفته‌تر از آن کشور است .	*in keshvar be-marâteb pishraftetar az ân keshvar-ast.*	This country is much more advanced than that country.

31.2 The comparative adjective with *az hame* is equivalent to the English "the most ... of all."

این میوه از همه خوشمزه‌تر است .	*in mive az hame khoshmazetar-ast.*	This fruit is the most delicious of all.
رضا بلندتر از همه است .	*rezâ bolandtar az hame-ast.*	Reza is the tallest of all.
ساختمان از همه بلندتر ایران کدام است؟	*sâkhtemân-e az-hame-bolandtar-e irân kodâm-ast?*	Which is the tallest building in Iran?

31.3 The superlative suffix is *-tarin*, which, like the comparative suffix, may or may not be attached orthographically to the adjective (with the exception of the silent *he,* to which it may not be attached).

(a) As an attributive adjective the superlative directly **precedes** the noun it modifies. "In" after a superlative is rendered by the *ezâfe*.

خوشگلترین دختر	*khoshgeltarin dokhtar*	the prettiest girl
خوشگلترین پسرها	*khoshgeltarin pesarhâ*	the best-looking boys
مفیدترین کتاب این کتابخانه	*mofidtarin ketâb-e in ketâbkhâne*	the most useful book in this library

51

مفیدترین کتابهای این کتابخانه	*mofidtarin ketâbhâ-ye in ketâbkhâne*	the most useful books in this library
سختترین روز زندگانی من	*sakhttarin ruz-e zendegâni-e man*	the most difficult day of my life
سختترین روزهای زندگانی من	*sakhttarin ruzhâ-ye zendegâni-e man*	the most difficult days of my life

(b) As predicate, the superlative **must** be followed by a noun; it never occurs as a free predicate adjective (instead, the *-tar az hame* construction given above is used).

آن روز از همه سختتر بود .	*ân ruz, az hame sakhttar-bud.*	That day was the most difficult (of all).
آن بود سختترین روز زندگانی من .	*ân-bud sakhttarin ruz-e zendegâni-e man.*	That was the most difficult day of my life.
بلندترین ساختمان تهران اینست .	*bolandtarin sâkhtemân-e tehrân in-ast.*	This is the tallest building in Tehran.

Note particularly the order of the second and third examples above: equational sentences with demonstratives as subjects and specific/definite predicates have either the copulative verb between the subject and predicate, as in the second example *(ân-bud ...)*, or the order of subject and predicate reversed, as in the third example *(... in-ast)*. That is, in either case the equational verb follows the demonstrative immediately.

(c) The superlative adjective followed by the *ezâfe* and a plural noun renders "the most ... of ..."

| سختترین روزهای زندگانی من | *sakhttarin-e ruzhâ-ye zendegâni-e man* | the most difficult (one) of the days of my life |
| مشهورترین دانشگاههای ایران | *mashhurtarin-e dâneshgâhhâ-ye irân* | the most famous of the universities in Iran |

52

| پیشرفته‌ترین کشورهای مشرق‌زمین | *pishraftetarin-e kesh-varhâ-ye mashreqza-min* | the most advanced of the countries of the East |

31.4 Irregular comparatives and superlatives.

(a) Although colloquially *khubtar* and *khubtarin* are occasionally heard, the preferred comparative and superlative forms of *khub* are derived from the now obsolete adjective *beh* ("good") > *behtar* "better," *behtarin* "best."

| این کتاب بهتر از آن کتاب است. | *in ketâb behtar az ân ketâb-ast.* | This book is better than that book. |
| اینست بهترین جای شهر ما. | *in-ast behtarin jâ-ye shahr-e mâ.* | This is the best place in our city. |

(b) The comparative form of *besyâr* and *ziâd* ("much, many") is *bishtar* ("more," also occasionally simply *bish*).

| این از آن بیشتر است. | *in az ân bishtar-ast.* | This is more than than. |

31.5 Both the adverbial "more than ever" and the adjectival "more ... than ever" are rendered by the phrase *bish az pish*.

| کار ما بیش از پیش پیش میرفت. | *kâr-e mâ bish az pish pish-miraft.* | Our work was progressing more than ever. |
| آن تاجر بیش از پیش موفق است. | *ân tâjer bish az pish movaffaq-ast.* | That merchant is more successful than ever. |

31.6 In comparative sentences of the type given above, the preposition for the second term of comparison is *az*. In the following cases, the conjunction of comparison, *tâ,* is used:

(a) when the second term falls after the main verb.

53

| شما بیشتر کار کردید تا من. | shomâ bishtar kâr-kar-did tâ man. | You worked more than I (did). |
| این ساده‌تر است تا آن. | in sâdetar-ast tâ ân. | This is simpler than that. |

(b) when the second term is preceded by a preposition or is a direct object.

| بیشتر برای آنها کار کردم تا برای شما. | bishtar barâ-ye ânhâ kâr-kardam tâ barâ-ye shomâ. | I did more work for them than (I did) for you. |
| آن را بیشتر دوست داشتم تا این را. | ân-râ bishtar dust-dâshtam tâ in-râ. | I liked that better than this. |

(c) when the comparison is not based on any distinct quality.

| این بیشتر آب است تا شراب. | in bishtar âb-ast tâ sharâb. | This is more water than (it is) wine. |
| بیشتر ده است تا شهر. | bishtar deh-ast tâ shahr. | It's more a village than (it is) a city. |

Vocabulary 8

آرام	ârâm quiet, calm	زود	zud early; quick, fast
آسان	âsân easy	زمستان	zemestân winter
بلند	boland tall, high; loud	سخت	sakht hard, difficult
به‌به	bah bah wow!, oh! (exclamation of delight, surprise, approval, etc.)	سرد	sard cold
		کدام	kodâm which? (adj.)
		کوتاه	kutâh short, low
بهتر	behtar better	گرم	garm warm
بیشتر	bishtar more	نامه	nâme letter
تا	tâ than	وای	vây woe!
تابستان	tâbestân summer	همهٔ	hame-ye all (of) [for
روز	ruz day		"all this" and "all

that," *hame* combines with *in* and *ân* as *inhame* and *ân-hame*, often written together as one word, e.g., *inhame kâr* "all this work," but *hame-ye in kâr* "all of this work"]

هر *har* every, each (precedes word it modi-

fies, as *har ruz* "every day")

هرکدام *harkodâm* each one

همه‌چیز *hamechiz* everything

هیچ *hich* (+ interrogative) any, ever; (+ neg.) no, none [*hich* precedes a noun in the nonspecific state, as *hich chiz-i* "nothing"]

Exercise 8

(a) Change the following statements to exclamations using *bah-bah* or *vây* (e.g.: *in khub-ast > bah-bah! in, che khub-ast!*)

۱ آن شهر آرام بود .

۲ دختر خوبیست .

۳ آن درس سخت بود .

۴ زمستان سردی بود .

۵ این تابستان گرم است .

۶ کار سختی بود .

۷ مدرسهٔ قدیمی‌ایست .

۸ امروز روز سردیست .

۹ دیروز گرم بود .

۱۰ اینها کتابهای آسانی اند .

(b) Make questions of the following using *che* or *kodâm*:

۱ در ایران شهرهائی دیدم .

۲ در آمریکا کار می‌کردید .

۳ دیروز کاری کردند .

۴ در خانهٔ علی نامه‌ای خواندیم .

۵ امروز روزنامه خوانده‌ام .

55

۶ از آنجا کتابهائی برداشتند .

۷ آن خانم چیزهائی میخواست .

۸ مریم چیزهائی به شما داده است .

(c) Answer the following questions:

۱ کدام شهرهای ایران را دیده‌اید ؟

۲ دیروز کدام کتاب را خواندند ؟

۳ از روی میز علی کدام نامه را برداشتید ؟

٤ آن مرد کدام چیزرا گرفته است ؟

۵ مریم در کدام دانشگاه درس خوانده است ؟

۶ ما دانشجوهای کدام دانشگاهیم ؟

۷ شما پدر کدام دخترید ؟

۸ به کدام کتابخانه رفتند ؟

(d) Make sentences using the comparative (e.g.: *in—bozorg—ân > in bozorgtar az ân-ast*):

۱ این خانه - آرام - آن خانه‌های دیگر

۲ امروز - گرم - دیروز

۳ این درس - آسان - آن درس

٤ زمستان - سرد - تابستان

۵ این کار - سخت - آن کار

۶ من - درس خواندن - شما

۷ روزنامه‌های تهران - خوب - آن دیگرها

۸ ما - زود آمدن - شما

۹ آنها - زود برگشتن - من

۱۰ او - نامه نوشتن - من

(e) Make superlative constructions two ways (e.g.: *in khâne bozorg-ast > (1) bozorgtarin khâne in-ast, (2) khâne-ye bozorgtar az hame in-ast):*

۱ این کتابها خوبند .

۲ آن مرد بلند است .

۳ این کار سخت است .

٤ دیروز گرم بود.

٥ امروز روز سردی است.

٦ این دانشجوها زرنگند.

٧ علی مرد مشهوریست.

٨ این درس آسان است.

٩ این پسر کوتاه است.

١٠ آن آقا پزشکیست خوب.

Lesson Nine

§32 Other plurals. In addition to the suffix -*hâ,* which can be used to form the plural of any noun in Persian, especially in the more informal spoken idiom, there are several other plural formations in the literary language.

32.1 Substantives denoting animate beings, parts of the body that occur in pairs, and a few other nouns (determined by idiomatic usage) form their plurals by suffixing -*ân.*

(a) This suffix is added directly to all nouns ending in consonants and -*i.*

آن > آنان	*ân > ânân*	those, they
مرد > مردان	*mard > mardân*	men
ایرانی > ایرانیان	*irâni > irâniân*	Iranians
دست > دستان	*dast > dastân*	hands
درخت > درختان	*derakht > derakhtân*	trees

(b) When this suffix is added to nouns ending in silent *he,* the *he* is dropped and a -*g*- is infixed before the plural suffix.

دیده > دیدگان	*dide > didegân*	eyes
بچه > بچگان	*bachche > bachchegân*	children
پرنده > پرندگان	*parande > parandegân*	birds

58

(c) With nouns ending in -*â* and with most nouns ending in -*u*, a -*y*- is infixed before the plural suffix.

Qaru-Pian

| دانشجو > دانشجویان | *dâneshju > dânesh-juyân* | students |
| دانا > دانایان | *dânâ > dânâyân* | learned (people) |

(d) Certain nouns ending in -*u* do not take the -*y*- infix:

| بازو > بازوان | *bâzu > bâzuân* | arms |
| بانو > بانوان | *bânu > bânuân* | ladies |

32.2 The Arabic "feminine" plural suffix -*ât* is used to form the plurals of many Arabic words as well as of a sizeable class of words of Persian (and even Turkish) origin.

انتخاب > انتخابات	*entekhâb > entekhâbât*	elections
طبقه > طبقات	*tabaqe > tabaqât*	classes, strata
ده > دهات	*deh > dehât*	villages
فرمایش > فرمایشات	*farmâyesh > far-mâyeshât*	orders
ایل > ایلات	*il > ilât*	tribes

Persian words ending in silent *he* and in -*i* infix -*j*- before the -*ât* suffix.

silent he → jat

میوه > میوجات	*mive > mivejât*	fruits
کارخانه > کارخانجات	*kârkhâne > kâr-khânejât*	factories
سبزی > سبزیجات	*sabzi > sabzijât*	greens

32.3 The Arabic "masculine" plural suffixes -*in*, except to words that already end in -*i*, in which case the suffix is -*un*.

| معلم > معلمین | *mo'allem > mo'allemin* | teachers |
| مامور > مامورین | *ma'mur > ma'murin* | agents |

| انقلابى > انقلابیون | enqelâbi > enqelâbiun | revolutionaries |
| روحانى > روحانیون | ruhâni > ruhâniun | clerics |

32.4 The Arabic "broken" plural. A vast number of Arabic words form the plural by a rearrangement of internal vowels. Fortunately for the student of modern Persian, few Arabic plurals are now in common use. In classical texts, however, Arabic words normally take their own Arabic plurals; the student's only recourse is the dictionary.

كتاب > كتب	ketâb > kotob	books
فكر > افكار	fekr > afkâr	thoughts, ideas
مدرسه > مدارس	madrase > madâres	schools
حقیقت > حقایق	haqiqat > haqâyeq	truths
فیلسوف > فلاسفه	faylasuf > falâsefe	philosophers

§32 Pronominal possessives. Pronominal possession is expressed either by the noun *mâl* ("property") or by the demonstrative adjective *ân* followed by the possessive *ezâfe* construction.

آن خانه مال آنهاست.	*ân khâne, mâl-e ânhâ-st.*	That house is theirs.
اینها مال کیست؟	*inhâ mâl-e kist?*	Whose are these?
آن مال من است.	*ân, mâl-e man-ast.*	That is mine.
این خانه مال پدر جواد است.	*in khâne mâl-e pedar-e javâd-ast.*	This house is Javad's father's.

Mâl tends to be used in modern Persian, whereas *ân-e* has fallen from every-day use except in more literary styles. Note the ellipsis of the second copula in the examples below. From this a general rule may be drawn: in parallel clauses containing identical verbs, one verb (usually the second) may be omitted.

| خانۀ علی بزرگ است ولی آن جواد بزرگتر. | *khâne-ye ali bozorg-ast, vali ân-e javâd bozorgtar.* | Ali's house is big, but Javad's is bigger. |

صدای من بلند است ولی مال مهدی بلندتر.	sedâ-ye man boland-ast, váli mâl-e mehti bolandtar.	My voice is loud, but Mehti's is louder.
روزنامه‌های اصفهان خوب است ولی آنهای تهران بهتر.	ruznâmehâ-ye esfahân khub-ast, váli ânhâ-ye tehrân behtar.	The newspapers in Isfahan are good, but those in Tehran are better.

Vocabulary 9

انتخاب entekhâb -ât, -hâ election	ده deh -ât village
امسال emsâl this year	زندگانی zendegâni life, life span
امشب emshab tonight	شب shab evening, night
باغ bâq -hâ, -ât garden	میوه mive -hâ, -jât fruit
پارسال pârsâl last year	که -ke that (conj.)
خوشمزه khoshmaze delicious	یا yâ or
دیشب dishab last night	

انتخاب شدن entekhâb-shodan to be/get elected	خریدن kharidan to buy
انتخاب کردن entekhâb-kardan to elect	خوردن khordan to eat, drink
بزرگ شدن bozorg-shodan to grow up, get big	شدن shodan to become
دانستن dânestan to know, realize[1]	گفتن goftan to say

Exercise 9

(a) Answer the following questions:

---

[1]*Dânestan* means "to know (a fact)," like the French *savoir*, when it has the *mi*-prefix (e.g., *mídânestam* "I knew [it]," *némidânestam* "I didn't know"). Without the *mi*- prefix it means "to realize" (e.g., *nádânestam ke...* "I didn't realize that...").

١ آن باغ بزرگ مال شماست؟   ٥ آن قلم مال مریم نیست؟

٢ این جعبهٔ سیاه مال کیست؟   ٦ میدانستید این مال کجاست؟

٣ شما مال این ده نیستید؟   ٧ از آنها کدام یک بیشتر بود؟

٤ این دهات مال کدام شهرند؟   ٨ این مال اوست یا مال آنها؟

(b) Translate the following into English:

١ آن ایرانیان کجا زندگی می‌کردند؟

٢ این دانشجویان بیشتر درس خوانده‌اند تا آنان.

٣ در انتخابات امسال کی انتخاب شده است؟

٤ آنان را هر روز می‌دیده‌ام ولی امروز نیامده‌اند.

٥ پدر علی و مریم به شهر بزرگ رفته و برنگشته است.

٦ چرا آنها را انتخاب کردند؟

٧ نمی‌دانستم که این مال علی است یا مال پدر شما.

٨ دیشب در باغ بزرگی میوهٔ خوشمزه‌ای میخوردیم.

٩ چرا بلندتر نگفتید؟ صدای شما را نشنیدم.

١٠ بچه‌های آن ده همهٔ میوه‌های باغ شما را خورده‌اند.

(c) Translate the following into Persian:

1. Did you grow up in a small town?
2. We used to go to school on (dar) cold winter days.
3. Where did you see Ali and his father yesterday?
4. Which lesson was the easiest of all for you?
5. What good friends we had there!
6. Have you seen the doctor?
7. I have had a very difficult life.
8. We found the best book of all in the university library.

Lesson Ten

§34 The present stem. All simple verbs in Persian have a past stem readily derivable from the infinitive (as seen in §24). The present stem, however, cannot always be derived from the infinitive and must be learned as the second "principal part" of the verb.

34.1 One of the few regularly predictable present stems is that of verbs whose infinitives end in *-idan;* the present stem of almost all such verbs is obtained by removing the *-id-* ending of the past stem.

رسیدن > رسید > رس *residan > resid- > res-* "to arrive"

خریدن > خرید > خر *kharidan > kharid- > khar-* "to buy"

فهمیدن > فهمید > فهم *fahmidan > fahmid- > fahm-* "to understand"

34.2 Verbs whose past stems end in *-nd* generally drop the *-d-* to form the present stem.

ماندن > ماند > مان *mândan > mând- > mân-* "to remain"

خواندن > خواند > خوان *khândan > khând- > khân-* "to read"

34.2 Although there are important exceptions, generally verbs whose past stems end in *-kht-* change the *-kh-* to *-z-* to form the present stem.

دوختن > دوخت > دوز *dukhtan > dukht- > duz-* "to sew"

ریختن > ریخت > ریز *rikhtan > rikht- > riz-* "to pour"

انداختن > انداخت > انداز   *andâkhtan > andâkht- > andâz-* "to throw"

باختن > باخت > باز   *bâkhtan > bâkht- > bâz-* "to lose"

§35 The present indicative. The present indicative tense is formed by prefixing the stressed continuous marker *mí-* to the present stem and adding the following enclitic personal endings:

Mi + stem + ending

م...	*-am* I	یم...	*-im* we
ی...	*-i* you	ید...	*-id* you
د...	*-ad* he/she/it	ند...	*-and* they

Note that these are the same personal endings that are used with the past tense, with the exception of the third-person singular.

The continuous prefix may be joined or left separate, although when there is no orthographic "break" in the stem itself, attachment of the prefix often results in words too long to be read comfortably.

The present indicative conjugation of *gereftan* (present stem *gir-*) is as follows:

میگیرم	*mígiram* I take	میگیریم	*mígirim* we take
میگیری	*mígiri* you take	میگیرید	*mígirid* you take
میگیرد	*mígirad* he/she/it takes	میگیرند	*mígirand* they take

35.1 The negative is formed by adding the negative prefix to the affirmative, which, as in the past, becomes *né-* before *mi-*.

نمیگیرم (نمی‌گیرم)	*némigiram*	I do not take, am not taking
نمیگیری (نمی‌گیری)	*némigiri*	you do not take, are not taking, etc.

35.2 In compound verbs the continuous marker is prefixed to the verbal element, but the non-verbal element retains the stress in the affirmative. In the negative, the negative marker takes primary stress.

64

بر میدارد (بر می‌دارد)	*bár-midârad*	he picks up
بر نمیدارد (بر نمی‌دارد)	*bàr-némidârad*	he does not pick up
بزرگ میشوند (بزرگ می‌شوند)	*bozórg-mishavand*	they grow up
بزرگ نمیشوند (بزرگ نمی‌شوند)	*bozòrg-némishavand*	they do not grow up

35.3 Orthographic and phonetic changes.

(a) When the personal endings are added to stems ending in *-aw-*, the *-w-* ceases to be syllable-final and therefore changes to *-v-* throughout the inflection.

رفتن > رو: میروم ، میروی   *raftan > raw-: míravam, míravi, &c.*

شدن > شو: میشوم ، میشوی   *shodan > shaw-: míshavam, míshavi, &c.*

شنیدن > شنو: میشنوم ، میشنوی   *shenidan > shenaw-: míshenavam, míshenavi, &c.*

(b) With the addition of the personal endings to stems ending in vowels, a *-y-* is infixed before the first- and third-singular and third-plural endings (those that begin with *-a-*) and a *hamze* is infixed before the second singular and the first- and second-person plural endings (those that begin with *-i-*). Examples are *gereftan > gir-* and *âmadan > â-*.

میگویم	*míguyam*	میگوئیم	*míguim*
میگوئی	*mígui*	میگوئید	*míguid*
میگوید	*míguyad*	میگویند	*míguyand*
میآیم	*míâyam*	میآئیم	*míâim*
میآئی	*míâi*	میآئید	*míâid*
میآید	*míâyad*	میآیند	*míâyand*

35.4 The Persian present indicative answers to both the English simple present and the present progressive.

همیشه به آنجا میروم.	*hamishe be ânjâ míravam.*	I always go there.
حالا به آنجا می‌روم.	*hâlâ be ânjâ míravam.*	I'm going there now.

The present indicative also functions as the future in ordinary speech and prose-writing.

فردا به آنجا میروم.	*fardâ be ânjâ míravam.*	I'm going there to-morrow.
پس چه کار میکنید؟	*pas che kâr mikonid?*	So what will you do?

Learn the present stems of these verbs already introduced.

memorize!

آمدن > آ (میآیم، می‌آیم)	*âmadan > â (míâyam)*
آوردن > آور (میآورم، می‌آورم)	*âvordan > âvor (míâvoram)*
بودن > باش (میباشم)	*budan > bâsh (míbâsham*[1]*)*
خریدن > خر (میخرم)	*kharidan > khar (míkharam)*
خوردن > خور (میخورم)	*khordan > khor (míkhoram)*
خواستن > خواه (میخواهم)	*khâstan > khâh (míkhâham)*
خواندن > خوان (میخوانم)	*khândan > khân (míkhânam)*
دادن > ده (میدهم)	*dâdan > deh (mídeham)*
داشتن > دار (دارم)	*dâshtan* (simple) *> dâr (dâram)*[2]
داشتن > دار (میدارم)	*-dâshtan* (compd.) *> -dâr (-mídâram)*[3]
دانستن > دان (میدانم)	*dânestan > dân (mídânam)*

---

[1]The present tense formed from the stem *bâsh-* is an artificial creation used in bureaucratic Persian. The student should use the present copulas for the present tense of *budan*.

[2]Remember that the simple *dâshtan* and a few of its compounds never take the *mi-* prefix in any tense.

[3]As in *bár-midâram*.

دیدن > بین (می‌بینم)   *didan > bin (míbinam)*

رفتن > رو (میروم)   *raftan > raw (míravam)*

شدن > شو (میشوم)   *shodan > shaw (míshavam)*

شنیدن > شنو (میشنوم)   *shenidan > shenaw (míshenavam)*

کردن > کن (میکنم)   *kardan > kon (míkonam)*

گرفتن > گیر (میگیرم)   *gereftan > gir (mígiram)*

گشتن > گرد (میگردم)   *gashtan > gard (mígardam)*

گفتن > گو (میگویم)   *goftan > gu (míguyam)*

نوشتن > نویس (مینویسم)   *neveshtan > nevis (mínevisam)*

Vocabulary 10

بعد از   *ba'd az* after (prep.)   قبل از   *qabl az* before (prep.)

جواب   *javâb -hâ, -ât* answer   سال   *sâl -hâ* year

چطور   *chetawr* how?   سؤال   *so'âl -hâ, -ât* question

حرف   *harf -hâ* word   کی   *kay* when?

فردا   *fardâ* tomorrow   گوش   *gush -hâ* ear

New verbs will be listed henceforth by past and present stems; compounds with familiar verbal elements will be given in the infinitive.

بردن (بر)   *bord-/bar-* to carry, take

جواب‌دادن   *javâb-dâdan* to answer reply (*be* or *-râ* to something)

زدن (زن)   *zad-/zan-* to hit, strike

حرف‌زدن   *harf-zadan* to speak, talk

سؤال‌کردن   *so'âl-kardan* to ask (a question, *az* of someone)

شناختن (شناس)   *shenâkht-/shenâs-* to know[1]

فهمیدن (فهم)   *fahmid-/fahm-* to understand

گذاشتن (گذار)   *gozâsht-/gozâr-* to put, place

---

[1]*Shenâkhtan* is "to know or be acquainted with" a person, like the French *connaître*. In the simple past *shenâkhtan* means "to recognize," e.g., *u-râ míshenâkhtam* "I knew (used to know) him," but *u-râ náshenâkhtam* "I didn't recognize him."

گوش کردن   gush-kardan to listen (be or -râ, to something)

ماندن (مان)   mând-/mân- to stay, remain

Exercise 10

(a) Change the following to the present tense:

۱٦ مارا ندیدید.	۱ بزرگ شدند.
۱۷ آن را شنیدی؟	۲ آن را پیدا کردم.
۱۸ شمارا نشناختند.	۳ آن را نمی‌دانست.
۱۹ آن را گرفته‌ایم.	٤ اینهارا کی خرید؟
۲۰ کی گوش میکرد؟	٥ میوه خورده‌اید؟
۲۱ کجا ماندند؟	٦ ما گفتیم.
۲۲ آنهارا نبردم.	۷ علی نیامد.
۲۳ به این سؤال جواب دادید.	۸ تو چه داشتی؟
۲٤ فارسی حرف میزد.	۹ آنان برنگشتند.
۲٥ آن را روی میز گذاشتم.	۱۰ کجا رفتید؟
۲٦ نفهمیدیم.	۱۱ خیلی درس خواندیم.
۲۷ گوش نمیکردم.	۱۲ این را تو نوشتی؟
۲۸ ایشان چطور بودند؟	۱۳ هیچی نیاوردم.
۲۹ علی را زد.	۱٤ اینهارا نمیخواستید.
۳۰ اینهارا کی برده است؟	۱٥ چه داده‌اند؟

(b) Read and translate the following into English:

۱ قبل از فردا شب همهٔ اینهارا به خانهٔ او می‌بریم.

۲ پدر آن دختران را میشناسم.

۳ صدای مرا خوب می‌شنوید؟ گوش نمی‌کنید؟

٤ این میوهٔ خوشمزه‌را روی میز میگذارم.

٥ نمیگویم که بد بود ولی خوب هم نبود.

٦ به سؤال من جواب نمی‌دهند.

۷ بعد از آن، یک سال ماندیم در آن کشور.

۸ حرفهای شمارا خوب می‌فهمم.

۹ آن را نمی‌خواهم. این را میخواهم.

۱۰ خیلی کار میکنیم. چرا کار ما بیش از پیش سخت میشود؟

(c) Translate the following into Persian:

1. You ask questions, and I'll answer.
2. Don't you know his name?
3. We always speak Persian with her.
4. Which one will you buy?
5. When are they returning from town?
6. We go to school every day, and there we read and write.
7. Ali is taking (carrying) these things to Maryam's house.
8. Do you know my mother and father?
9. I don't understand what he says (his words).
10. Tomorrow we'll put everything near the door, and they'll take [it away].

Review II

(a) Review the vocabulary lists for lessons 6–10.

(b) Read and translate the following:

۱ دیشب من از از همیشه بیشتر درس خواندم.

۲ آرامترین جای این شهر کجاست؟

۳ آنها چه خوب فارسی حرف میزنند!

۴ روز از همه گرمتر این تابستان دیروز بود.

۵ شنیده‌ام که آن شهر یکی از سردترین شهرهای ایران است.

۶ گفتند که بعد از این دانشجویان برنمیگردند.

۷ کدام یکی از اینهارا بیشتر میخواهید؟

۸ چه حرفهای خوبی میزنید!

۹ این نامه‌را در کتابخانهٔ دانشگاه پیدا کرده‌ام.

۱۰ بچه‌ها خوشمزه‌ترین میوه‌هارا از باغ برداشتند و رفتند.

(c) Translate the following into Persian:

1. Last year the work was harder than this year.

69

2. Why didn't they select the best fruits of the garden for us?
3. Does she read both English and Persian?
4. Which school do her sons and daughters go to?
5. All of your answers were good.
6. When will you buy those things for me?
7. I'll carry these, and you carry those.
8. They always put their books on this table.
9. They have understood nothing.
10. Who is the best student in this university?

Lesson Eleven

§36 Pronominal enclitics. The pronominal enclitics, which are used as possessive pronouns, direct objects of verbs and complements of prepositions, are as follows:

-am my, me	*-emân* our, us
-at/-et your, you	*-etân* your, you
-ash/-esh his/her/its, him/her/it	*-eshân* their, them

The second- and third-person singular enclitics are commonly pronounced *-et* and *-esh,* the older pronunciations *(-at, -ash)* being now somewhat bookish except after a final *-e,* where they are always pronounced *-at* and *-ash.*

36.1 The enclitics are attached directly to words ending in consonants and *-i.*

كتابم	*ketâb-am* my book	كتابمان	*ketâb-emân* our book
كتابت	*ketâb-et* your book	كتابتان	*ketâb-etân* your book
كتابش	*ketâb-esh* his/her book	كتابشان	*ketâb-eshân* their book

36.2 In words ending in *-e,* the singular enclitics are spelled with infixed *alef;* the plural enclitics lose their initial *e-.* The pronunciations *-at* and *-ash* are retained for the second- and third-person singular enclitics after words ending in *-e.*

خانهام	*khâne-am* my house	خانهمان	*khâne-mân* our house

71

don't add ا - aleph

خانه‌ات *khâne-at* your house   خانه‌تان *khâne-tân* your house

خانه‌اش *khâne-ash* his/her house   خانه‌شان *khâne-shân* their house

36.3 Following *â* and *u*, a -*y*- is infixed before the pronominal en-clitics.

add a ye

کتابهایم *ketâbhâ-y-am*   کتابهایمان *ketâbhâ-y-emân*

کتابهایت *ketâbhâ-y-et*   کتابهایتان *ketâbhâ-y-etân*

کتابهایش *ketâbhâ-y-esh*   کتابهایشان *ketâbhâ-y-eshân*

رویم *ru-y-am*   رویمان *ru-y-emân*

رویت *ru-y-et*   رویتان *ru-y-etân*

رویش *ru-y-esh*   رویشان *ru-y-eshân*

36.4 Uses of the enclitics.

(a) The enclitics are used as possessive pronouns. As such, there is no appreciable difference between the enclitics and the subject pronouns joined by the *ezâfe,* except that in certain situations the subject pronouns cannot be used (see §37 below), and the enclitic pronouns cannot be stressed. The enclitics are never followed by the *ezâfe* but must fall at the end of an *ezâfe* string.

کشور بزرگمان {*keshvar-e bozorg*}-emân   our great country

دخترهای کوچکش {*dokhtarhâ-ye kuchek*}-esh   his little daughters

Any noun modified by the possessive enclitics in the direct-object posi-tion must be marked by -*râ*.

کشور بزرگمان را ندیدید ؟ *keshvar-e bozorg-emân-râ nádidid?*   Didn't you see our great country?

دخترهای کوچکش را پیدا کرد . *dokhtarhâ-ye kuchek-esh-râ paydâ-kard.*   He found his little daughters.

72

(b) As direct objects, the enclitics may be added to the verb itself or to any other convenient word in the clause. In compound verbs, the enclitics are normally added to the non-verbal element, although they need not necessarily fall in this position. The direct-object enclitics do not take *-râ*.

ندیدمشان.	*nádidam-eshân.*	I didn't see **them**.
می‌بینندش.	*míbinand-esh.*	They'll see **him**.
بازش کردند.	*bâz-esh-kardand.*	They opened **it**.

Although the enclitics are most often used in modern writing as possessives, the usage as direct object is encountered especially in classical quotation and in dialogue representing colloquial speech, where the direct-object enclitics are extensively used.

Note that the addition of the first-person singular enclitic to a third-person singular past verb can result in confusion. In modern Persian, however, the direct-object marker alleviates ambiguity.

	جوادرا زدم.	*javâd-râ zadam.*	I hit Javad.
but	جواد زدم.	*javâd zad-am.*	Javad hit me.

(c) Prepositions that normally take their complements through the *ezâfe* drop it with enclitic complements.

	دربارۀ آن	*darbâre-ye ân*	concerning it
but	دربارهاش	*darbâre-ash.*	concerning it
	برای من	*barâ-ye man*	for me
but	برایم	*barâ-y-am*	for me

In literary Persian the enclitics do not serve as complement of the five "true" prepositions *(be, az, bâ, bar* and *dar).* Other words used as prepositions, all of which take their complements through the *ezâfe,* may take enclitic complements.

§37 Reflexive pronouns. No subject pronoun, expressed or implicit, may be repeated as a possessive or direct object within the clause in which it functions as subject. Only the enclitics serve as possessives referring to the subject. Thus,

| | برادرم را دیدم. | *barâdar-am-râ didam.* | I saw my brother. |
| and | کارتان را کردید. | *kâr-etân-râ kardid.* | You did your work. |

are valid sentences. In these examples, the constructions *barâdar-e man* and *kâr-e shomâ,* though valid elsewhere, could not be used because the pronouns *man* and *shomâ* are subjects, even though implicit, of the verbs *didam* and *kardid.*

37.1 In the third persons singular and plural, the repetition of the subject pronoun implies a change of person. The enclitics are ambiguous as to reference and may refer either to the subject or to another third person.

اکبر برادر اورا دید.	*akbar barâdar-e u-râ did.*	Akbar saw his (i.e., someone else's) brother.
اکبر برادرش را دید.	*akbar barâdar-esh-râ did.*	Akbar saw his (*either* his own *or* someone else's) brother.
برادران ایشان را دوست دارند.	*barâdarân-e ishân-râ dust-dârand.*	They love their (i.e., some other people's) brothers.
برادرانشان را دوست دارند.	*barâdarân-eshân-râ dust-dârand.*	Their love their (*either* their own *or* some other people's) brothers.

37.2 The true reflexive pronoun is خود *khod* (note irregular spelling), which has no person or number inherent in itself but takes its person and number from the subject of the verb of the clause in which it occurs. It can thus signify any person or number and may serve as a possessive as well as a direct object.

| خودرا دیدم. | *khod-râ didam.* | I saw myself. |
| خودرا دید. | *khod-râ did.* | He saw himself. |

خانهٔ خودرا فروختم.	*khâne-ye **khod**-râ forukhtam.*	I sold **my** house.
خانهٔ خودرا فروختید.	*khâne-ye **khod**-râ forukhtid.*	You sold **your** house.
هرکس در خانهٔ خود سلطان است.	*har kas dar khâne-ye khod soltân-ast.*	Everyone is a sultan in his own house ("every man's home is his castle").

Khod is intensified as a reflexive by adding the enclitic pronominals and as such functions as an independent reflexive pronoun. Spoken Persian almost always adds the enclitics to *khod*.

خودم را در آئینه دیدم.	*khod-am-râ dar âine didam.*	I saw myself in the mirror.
خودش را دید.	*khod-esh-râ did.*	He saw himself.

When so intensified as a possessive, *khod* imparts a strong sense of "one's own."

کار خودم را میکنم.	*kâr-e khod-am-râ mikonam.*	I'm doing my own job (and nobody else's).
خانهٔ خودش را فروخت.	*khâne-ye khod-esh-râ forukht.*	He sold his own house (and nobody else's).

Vocabulary 11

آب *âb* water

باز *bâz* open; again, once more, still, even yet (with the comparative and often with -ham, *bâz* means "still, even yet," as in *bâz(-ham) bishtar* "even more, more still")

برادر *barâdar -ân, -hâ* brother

چای *chây* tea

چون *chon* because

چونکه *chon-ke = chon*

حالا *hâlâ* now, at present; *hâlâhâ* these days

خواهر *khâhar -ân, -hâ* sister

75

to class → sar kelas

خود *khod* -self (reflexive pronoun)

ساده *sâde* plain, simple

قهوه *qahve* coffee

کلاس *kelâs* class, classroom

مردم *mardom* people

مهم *mohemm* important

همان *hamân* that very, that same

همین *hamin* this very, this same

همین‌حالا *haminhâlâ* right now, this very instant

هیچوقت *hichvaqt* (with interrog.) ever; (with neg.) never

وقتی‌که *váqtike* when (temporal conj.)

باز آمدن *bâz-âmadan* to come back

باز کردن *bâz-kardan* to open

بستن (بند) *bast-/band-* to shut, close

رسیدن (رس) *resid-/res-* to reach, arrive (*be* at, to)

فروختن (فروش) *forukht-/forush-* to sell

نگاه کردن *negâh-kardan* to look (*be* or *-râ*, at)

Exercise 11

(a) Change the independent pronouns to enclitics:

۱ قلمهای شمارا ندید.

۲ صدای ایشانرا نشنیده‌ایم.

۳ کتاب اورا میخواستی.

٤ کتابهای نو مرا نخوانده‌اند.

٥ خانۀ آنهارا دیده‌ام.

٦ میز کهنۀ مارا علی می‌آوَرَد.

۷ چیزهای اورا از روی میز برمیدارم.

۸ نامۀ مهم شمارا می‌خوانَد.

۹ نامه‌های شمارا روی میز گذاشته‌ام.

۱۰ چای مارا میخورند.

76

(b) Translate into English:

۱ چرا کار خودش را نمیکند؟

۲ این دررا کی باز کرده است؟ من دیروز بستمش.

۳ سؤالش را خوب فهمیدیم ولی او جوابمان را نشنید.

۴ حالا با برادر و خواهرم چای میخورم.

۵ بعد از کار چای میخورید یا قهوه؟

۶ این کارها از آنها خیلی مهم‌تر است.

۷ مردم چرا اورا انتخاب کرده‌اند؟

۸ با اینهمه، هیچوقت به آنجا نمیرسیم.

۹ همیشه با همین قلم قدیمی نامه‌هایتان را می‌نویسید؟

۱۰ برادرانتان را دیدم ولی نشناختمشان.

(c) Translate into Persian:

1. My friends live in a small village near Tehran.

2. They are coming back to their old house because they sold the other house.

3. We saw one of your students yesterday in the library.

4. She is closing one of the windows.

5. Where are you taking (carrying) all that?

6. I won't ever sell my house to them!

7. I'm reading a very important book for class tomorrow.

8. Why are you looking out of (az) the window? What do you see?

9. Do you drink tea or coffee? I drink coffee; I never drink tea.

10. What are you looking at? I'm looking at these Persian books.

1) dustehan dar dehe- kuchek zendegee mikonand.

2)

"e"

mikonam kar keh ast sa'd

میکنم کار کی است ، دو سعی است کی دو

میکردم لو (bud)

mikardam

Lesson Twelve

§38 Cardinal numbers. The cardinal numbers from one to nineteen are as follows. Numerals are written, as in English, from left to right.

(۱) یك	*yek (1)*		(۱۱) یازده	*yâzdah (11)*
(۲) دو	*do (2)*		(۱۲) دوازده	*davâzdah (12)*
(۳) سه	*se (3)*		(۱۳) سیزده	*sizdah (13)*
(٤) چهار	*chahâr (4)*		(۱٤) چهارده	*chahârdah (14)*
(٥) پنج	*panj (5)*		(۱٥) پانزده	*pânzdah (15)*
(٦) شش	*shesh (6)*		(۱٦) شانزده	*shânzdah (16)*
(۷) هفت	*haft (7)*		(۱۷) هفده	*hivdah (17)*
(۸) هشت	*hasht (8)*		(۱۸) هجده	*hizhdah (18)*
(۹) نه	*noh (9)*		(۱۹) نوزده	*nuzdah (19)*
(۱۰) ده	*dah (10)*			

Note the discrepancy between the spelling and pronunciation of 17 and 18.

The tens are as follows (note particularly the spelling of "60").

(۲۰) بیست	*bist (20)*		(٦۰) شصت	*shast (60)*
(۳۰) سی	*si (30)*		(۷۰) هفتاد	*haftâd (70)*
(٤۰) چهل	*chehel (40)*		(۸۰) هشتاد	*hashtâd (80)*
(٥۰) پنجاه	*panjâh (50)*		(۹۰) نود	*navad (90)*

Numbers from 20 on are compounded with the tens and contain the conjunction, which is always read as enclitic *-o,* never as *va-.*

بیست و یك	*bist-o yek*	twenty-one
بیست و دو	*bist-o do*	twenty-two
بیست و سه	*bist-o se*	twenty-three, &c.

The hundreds are similarly compounded with the enclitic conjunction. The only irregularly formed hundreds are 200, 300 and 500. The others are predictably formed from the units. There are no irregularly formed thousands.

(۱۰۰) صد	*sad*		(۱۰۰۰) هزار(یك)	*(yek)hezâr*
(۲۰۰) دویست	*devist*		(۲۰۰۰) دوهزار	*dohezâr*
(۳۰۰) سیصد	*sisad*		(۳۰۰۰) سه‌هزار	*sehezâr*
(٤۰۰) چهارصد	*chahârsad*		(٤۰۰۰) چهارهزار	*chahârhezâr*
(۵۰۰) پانصد	*pânsad*		(۵۰۰۰) پنجهزار	*panjhezâr*
(٦۰۰) ششصد	*sheshsad*		(٦۰۰۰) ششهزار	*sheshhezâr*
(۷۰۰) هفتصد	*haftsad*		(۷۰۰۰) هفتهزار	*hafthezâr*
(۸۰۰) هشتصد	*hashtsad*		(۸۰۰۰) هشتهزار	*hashthezâr*
(۹۰۰) نهصد	*nohsad*		(۹۰۰۰) نه‌هزار	*nohhezâr*

38.1 Numbers are invariably followed by the **singular**. Idiomatically a "counting word," or classifier, intervenes between the numbers and following singular nouns. Although elaborate lists of specific counting words for a variety of items exist (rather like English "flock," "herd," "pride," "covey," etc.), informally they may be replaced by *tâ* ("unit") for practically anything, *dâne* ("grain") for small items, *nafar* ("individual") for people, and *adad* ("item") for commercial items.

سه تا برادر دارم.	*se tâ barâdar dâram.*	I have three brothers.
دو تا کتاب خواندم.	*do tâ ketâb khândam.*	I read two books.
دو دانه پسته خوردم.	*do dâne peste khor-dam.*	I ate two pistachios.

79

| چهار نفر ایرانی دیدم. | chahâr *nafar* irâni didam. | I saw four Iranians. |
| پنج عدد قالیچه | panj *adad* qâliche | five carpets |

Counting words are not used with any words or expressions of time.

دو ساعت ماندم.	do sâ'at mândam.	I stayed two hours.
سه روز آنجا بودیم.	se ruz ânjâ budim.	We were there for three days.
خواهرم شش سال دارد.	khâhar-am shesh sâl dârad.	My sister is six years old.

38.2 All words that indicate weights and measures are themselves construed as counting words.

دو کیلو گوشت	do kilu gusht	two kilos of meat
سه لیتر شیر	se litr shir	three liters of milk
چهار بطری آب	chahâr botri âb	four bottles of water
پنج متر پارچه	panj metr pârche	five meters of cloth
شش فنجان قهوه	shesh fenjân qahve	six cups of coffee
هفت استکان چای	haft estekân chây	seven glasses of tea
هشت جفت جوراب	hasht joft jurâb	eight pairs of socks

38.3 The counters for instances ("once, twice, three times") are *bâr* and *daf'e*. "Per" is expressed by a non-specific noun preceding the number.

سالی دو دفعه	sâl-*i* do *daf'e*	twice a year
هفته‌ای پنج بار	hafte-*i* panj *bâr*	five times a week
ماهی چهار دفعه	mâh-*i* chahâr *daf'e*	four times a month

38.4 Multiples are expressed by *barâbar-e*.

| این هفته قیمت شیر دو برابر (قیمت) هفتهٔ گذشته است. | in hafte qaymat-e shir do barâbar-e (qaymat-e) hafte-ye gozashte-ast. | The price of milk this week is twice what it was last week. |

§39 Ordinal numbers. The ordinal numbers are formed by suffixing *-om* to the cardinal numbers. The ordinals are treated as regular adjectives and follow the nouns they modify with the *ezâfe*. "First" is irregular: *avval*, less commonly *nakhost* ("prime"). In subsequent compound numbers such as 21st, *-o yekom* is used. Of the ordinals, only *dovvom* ("second") and *sevvom* ("third") are irregularly formed. All others are predictable from the cardinals. There is no abbreviation in Persian corresponding to English "1st, 2nd, 3rd, etc."

(روزِ) اول ماه	*(ruz-e) avval-e mâh*	the first (day) of the month
جلسهٔ دوم این کلاس	*jalese-ye dovvom-e in kelâs*	the second session of this class
این دفعهٔ سوم است که میبینمتان.	*in, daf'e-ye sevvom-ast-ke mîbinam-etân.*	This is the third time I've seen you.
خانهٔ پنجم مال ماست.	*khâne-ye panjom mâl-e mâ-st.*	The fifth house on the lane is ours.
بیست و یکم ماه	*bist-o-yekom-e mâh*	the 21st of the month
شمارهٔ صدوسی و یکم این مجله	*shomâre-ye sad-o-si-o-yekom-e in majalle*	the 131st issue of this magazine

39.1 The ordinals may also be formed by adding *-omin* to the cardinals (*avvalin* for "first"). Like the superlatives in *-tarin* (see §31.3), *-omin* ordinals **precede** the nouns they modify and do not occur without a following noun.

اولین روز ماه	*avvalin ruz-e mâh*	the first day of the month
دومین جلسهٔ این کلاس	*dovvomin jalese-ye in kelâs*	the second session of this class
سومین خانهٔ این کوچه	*sevvomin khâne-ye in kuche*	the third house on this lane

Ordinals in *-omin* differ slightly in connotation from ordinals in *-om*. The ordinals in *-omin* indicate order in a series that is liable to change depending on the basis for counting, whereas the ordinals in *-om* indicate a number attached to a noun like a title. For instance,

81

"lesson twelve" in this book is *dars-e davâzdahom,* but if a reader had skipped a lesson it would be the *yâzdahomin dars* ("eleventh lesson") that he had read. The fifth house on a street (counting all houses) is the *khâne-ye panjom-e kuche,* but counting only white houses, it would be, e.g., *sevvomin khâne-ye sefid-e kuche* ("the third white house on the street").

39.2 In addition to the Persian numbers, the following Arabic ordinals should also be learned, especially in the adverbial form, as they are of frequent occurrence.

اول	*avval* first		اولا	*avvalan* firstly
ثانی	*sâni* second		ثانیاً	*sânian* secondly
ثالث	*sâles* third		ثالثاً	*sâlesan* thirdly
رابع	*râbe'* fourth		رابعاً	*râbe'an* fourthly

39.3 With the exception of *nim* "half," the ordinals are also used as fractions.

یك سوم	*yek sevvom*	one third
سه چهارم	*se chahârom*	three fourths
نه دهم کیلومتر	*noh dahom-e kilometr*	nine tenths of a kilo-meter

Also in common use are the Arabic fractions: نصف *nesf* half, ثلث *sols* third, and ربع *rob'* fourth.

Vocabulary

اقلاً	*aqallan* at least (comes @ the beg. of sent.)		تعداد	*te'dâd* number[1]
اول	*avval* first		تقریباً	*taqriban* almost, near-ly
بار	*bâr* time; load		ثانیه	*sânie* second
برابر	*barâbar* together; *barâbar-e* facing, opposite; *dobarâ-bar(-e)* twice as much (as)			

---

[1] As in *te'dâd-e dâneshjuyân-e in kelâs* "the number of students in this class."

82

دفعه	daf' e time (once, twice)	(شمار)	count
دقیقه (دقایق)	daqiqe pl daqâyeq minute	گذشتن (گذر)	gozasht-/gozar- pass (of time); (with az) pass by, go beyond
ربع	rob' quarter[1]	گذشته	gozashte past, last
ساعت	sâ'at -hâ, sâ'ât hour; watch, clock (sâ'at-e divâri wall clock)	ماه	mâh -hâ moon, month
شبانه‌روز	shabâneruz day (24 hours)	نصف	nesf half
شماره	shomâre -hâ number[2]	نفر	nafar person (counter)
شمردن	shomord-/shomâr- to	نیم	nim half
		هفته	hafte week

Exercise 13

(a) Read the following numbers (comma serves as decimal point):

۵۱۱	۱۹۸۳	٦،۲۵	۱۵۷
٤۷۰۲۱	۲٤۲	٦٦	۲،۵
۹۰۱	۱۳٦۱	۷،۷۵	۳۸۹۲

(b) Read and translate into English:

۱ ساعت یک بیست و چهارم شبانه‌روز است.

۲ ثانیه یک شصتم دقیقه است و هر ساعت شصت دقیقه دارد.

۳ این شهر از آن شهر دیگر هفتصد کیلومتر دور است.

۴ دو دقیقه صد وبیست ثانیه دارد و دو شبانه‌روز چهل وهشت ساعت دارد.

۵ امروز و فردا سه تا درس میخوانیم.

۶ این کشور بیشتر از دویست تا روزنامه دارد.

---

[1]With numbers rob' and nim function normally: yek-o rob' "one and a quarter," do-o nim "two and a half." As compounding agents they precede: rob'-sâ'at "quarter hour," nim-sâ'at "half hour."

[2]As in shomâre-ye yek "number one."

۷ ما دوازده سال مدرسه رفته‌ایم.

۸ اقلاً روزی چهار دفعه آنها را می‌بینم.

۹ یک ساعت و نیم در آنجا ماندیم.

۱۰ هر ماه چهار هفته دارد و در هر سال دوازده ماه هست.

(c) Translate into Persian:

1. Are they staying half an hour or three quarters of an hour?
2. This month has thirty-one days.
3. I have two brothers and three sisters.
4. The first lesson was easy, but the second lesson was harder.
5. We worked six hours.
6. I read those five books last week.
7. Do you want those same three green chairs?
8. It's about 3:30 (see Appendix B).
9. Summer and winter have three months each.
10. I've shut that window at least four times today.

Supplementary Vocabulary: Weights and Measures

متر	*metr* meter		گز	*gaz* gaz, ca. 1 yard
کیلومتر	*kilometr* kilometer		فرسخ	*farsakh (farsang)*
سانتیمتر	*sântimetr* centimeter		(فرسنگ)	parasang, ca. 6 km.
گرم	*gram* gram		مثقال	*mesqâl* $1/16$ seer
کیلوگرم	*kilogram* kilogram		سیر	*sir* $1/40$ maund
لیتر	*litr* liter		من	*man* maund, ca. 3 kg.

84

Lesson Thirteen

§40 Relative clauses. As in English, there are two types of relative clause in Persian, the *restrictive* (that which is selective, or determinate) and the *nonrestrictive* (the purely descriptive and nonselective). Both types of clause are introduced by the relative pronoun *-ke,* an enclitic that *must* stand at the head of the relative clause.

40.1 The restrictive relative clause restricts the antecedent and therefore makes it specific. The antecedent of the relative clause is indicated by adding an enclitic *-i* to the noun itself or, if the noun is modified by an adjective, to the end of the adjectival *ezâfe* string, as *mard-i-ke* "the man who...," *khâne-i-ke* "that house that...," *khâne-ye bozorg-i-ke* "the big house that...." The antecedent marker *-i* is omitted (1) when the antecedent is restricted by a possessive pronoun, as *khâne-am-ke* "my house that..." and (2) usually, but not necessarily, when the antecedent already ends in *-i,* as *mard-e irâni-ke* "the Iranian man who..." (also *mard-e irâni-i-ke).*

(a) When the relative pronoun functions as the subject of the subordinate clause, the subordinate verb agrees in number with the antecedent of *ke.*

مردی که آمد...	*mard-i-ke âmad...*	the man who came...
مردانی که آمدند...	*mardân-i-ke âmadand...*	the men who came...

When relative clauses are internal, i.e., followed by the main verb, they are read in an absolute monotone but with a high rising pitch on the

85

final syllable of the clause. Final relative clauses have no special intonation.

مردی که آمد ایرانی است .	*mard-i-ke âmád, irâni-ast.*	The man who came is Iranian.
دخترهائی که دیروز شمارا دیدند به من گفتند .	*dokhtarhâ-i-ke diruz shomâ-râ didánd, be man goftand.*	The girls who saw you yesterday told me.

(b) When the antecedent functions as direct object of the main clause, it is marked by *-râ,* and the order of the enclitics is invariably *-i-râ-ke.*

مردی را که آمد ندیدم .	*mard-i-râ-ke âmad, nádidam.*	I didn't see the man who came.
دخترهائی را که آنجا زندگی میکنند نمی شناسم .	*dokhtarhâ-i-râ-ke ânjâ zendegi-mikonand, némishenâsam.*	I don't know the girls who live there.
نامه‌ای را که روی میز بود فرستادم .	*nâme-i-râ-ke ru-ye miz bud ferestâdam.*	I sent the letter that was on the table.

(c) When the relative is object of the subordinate clause, its function may optionally be marked with a referent pronoun agreeing with the antecedent.

نامه‌ای را که دیروز (آن را) نوشتم فرستادم .	*nâme-i-râ-ke diruz (ân-râ) neveshtam, ferestâdam.*	I sent the letter that I wrote yesterday.
پولی را که به دوستش (آن را) داده است پس میگیرد .	*pul-i-râ-ke be dust-esh (ân-râ) dâde-ast, pas migirad.*	He'll take back the money he gave his friend.

Normally, however, when the antecedent is the direct object of the subordinate clause, the referent pronoun is omitted but the antecedent is marked with *-râ* (by attraction), regardless of its function in the main clause. Note in the following two examples that neither *nâme* nor *film* is the direct object of the verb of the main clause, but they have attracted -râ because they function as direct objects of the relative clauses.

نامه‌ای را که دیروز نوشتم کجاست؟	*nâme-i-râ-ke diruz neveshtam, kojâ-st?*	Where is the letter I wrote yesterday?
فیلمی را که دیشب دیدیم خوب بود.	*film-i-râ-ke dishab didim, khub-bud.*	The movie we saw last night was good.

40.2 "Whose," "of which," etc. In relative constructions that are expressed in English by "whose," "of which," "about which," etc., the referent pronoun **must** be used in Persian. Since the Persian relative -*ke* cannot be moved from the head of the relative clause, the referent pronoun is used to show the syntax of such clauses.

شهری که از آن آمده‌ام از اینجا دور است.	*shahr-i-ke az ân âmade-am, az injâ dur-ast.*	The city from which I have come is far from here.
زنانی که دخترهایشان به تهران رفته‌اند دلواپسند.	*zanân-i-ke dokhtarhâ-yeshân be tehrân raftand, delvâpas-and.*	The women whose daughters went to Tehran are worried.
اطاقی که در آن نشسته‌ایم خیلی کوچک است.	*otâq-i-ke dar ân neshaste-im, kháyli kuchek-ast.*	The room in which we are sitting is very small.
کتابی که درباره‌اش صحبت میکردیم کجاست؟	*ketâb-i-ke darbâre-ash sohbat-mikardim, kojâ-st?*	Where's the book about which we were talking?

40.3 The non-restrictive clause is also introduced by *ke,* and all observations on the syntax of the relative pertain to this type also. The only difference between the restrictive and non-restrictive relative is that the non-restrictive antecedent is **not** marked by -*i*, as *mard ke* "the man, who..." and *khâne ke* "the house, which...." Compare and contrast the following:

احمد که دیروز آمد اینجاست.	ahmad, ke diruz âmad, injâ-st.	Ahmad, who came yesterday, is here.
احمدی که دیروز آمد اینجاست.	ahmad-i-ke diruz âmad, injâ-st.	The Ahmad who came yesterday is here.
آن شهر که ما در آن زندگی میکردیم سرد است.	ân shahr, ke mâ dar ân zendegi-mikardim, sard-ast.	That city, in which we used to live, is cold.
شهری که ما در آن زندگی میکردیم سرد است.	shahr-i-ke mâ dar ân zendegi-mikardim, sard-ast.	The city in which we used to live is cold.

past perfect → I had done something before ... happened

§41 The remote absolute tense. The remote absolute tense, which corresponds generally to the English past perfect, is formed from the past participle followed by the past absolute of *budan.* In the affirmative, stress falls on the last syllable of the participle.

I "had" already

رفته بودم	*rafté-budam*	رفته بودیم	*rafté-budim*
رفته بودی	*rafté-budi*	رفته بودید	*rafté-budid*
رفته بود	*rafté-bud*	رفته بودند	*rafté-budand*

The negative is formed by prefixing *ná-* to the participle.

نرفته بودم	*nárafte-budam*	نرفته بودیم	*nárafte-budim*
نرفته بودی	*nárafte-budi*	نرفته بودید	*nárafte-budid*
نرفته بود	*nárafte-bud*	نرفته بودند	*nárafte-budand*

41.1 Uses of the remote past absolute.

(a) For any remote action or state, although no great amount of time need have elapsed. This usage often renders the sense of the English "already," which has no exact equivalent in Persian.

قبل از آن اورا دیده بودیم.	*qabl az ân u-râ dide-budim.*	We had (already) seen him before that.
پیش از آن وقت برگشته بودند.	*pish az ân vaqt bar-gashte-budand.*	They had (already) returned before that time.

(b) For the anterior of two contrasted verbs in the past.

دیروز شما اورا دیدید ولی ما پریروزهم اورا دیده بودیم.	*diruz shomâ u-râ didid, vâli mâ pariruz-ham u-râ dide-budim.*	You saw her yesterday, but we had already seen her the day before.

When the more remote verb has already been completed before the inception of the second, or less remote, the second verb follows the first and is introduced by *ke* "when."

من رفته بودم که شما آمدید.	*man rafte-budam ke shomâ âmadid.*	I had already gone when you came.
شما به آمریکا برگشته بودید که من به ایران رفتم.	*shomâ be âmrikâ bar-gashte-budid ke man be irân raftam.*	You had already returned to America when I went to Iran.

(c) *Hanuz* "yet, still" and a negative verb in the remote-past clause followed by *ke* renders the idiomatic "scarcely *(hanuz)* had we done something when *(ke)* something happened." hanuz + neg. verb + ke

هنوز وارد اطاق نشده بودیم که آنهارا دیدیم.	*hanuz vâred-e otâq náshode-budim ke ânhâ-râ didim.*	Scarcely had we entered the room when we saw them.
هنوز ننشسته بودم که در باز شد.	*hanuz náneshaste-budam ke dar bâz shod.*	Scarcely had I sat down when the door opened.[1]

hanuz + "just", I had just . . . .

---

[1] I.e., no sooner had I sat down than....

§42 The remote past narrative tense. The remote past narrative is formed from the past participle and the past narrative of *budan*. It is used in cases (a) and (b) of the remote past absolute where the criteria for the past narrative also apply (see §29). This tense will not be encountered frequently.

در آنوقت به سی‌سالگی نرسیده بوده است.   *dar ân vaqt be sisâlegi nâreside-bude-ast.*   At that time he had not yet reached the age of thirty.

Vocabulary 13

اطاق *otâq* room	ساختمان *sâkhtemân* building
اصفهان *esfahân* Isfahan	شیراز *shirâz* Shiraz
پول *pul* money	فاصله *fâsele* distance
ترسیدن *tarsid-/tars-* be afraid (*az* of)	فاصله‌داشتن *fâsele-dâshtan* to be distant (*bâ* from)
تعریف کردن *ta'rif-kardan* define; (with *az*) to tell about, relate[1]	فراموش کردن *farâmush-kardan* to forget
جمعاً *jam'an* in all, in toto	کس *kas -ân* person, one[3]
خوشگل *khoshgel* pretty, handsome	وقت/اوقات *vaqt -hâ/awqât* time
زیاد *ziâd*[2] much, too much	مثل *mesl-e* like (prep.)
	همسایه *hamsâye -hâ/-gân* neighbor
	هنوز *hanuz* still, yet

---

[1]*Az chiz-i ta'rif-kardan barâ-ye kas-i* "to tell somebody about something." Note that the thing about which one tells is the complement of the preposition *az* in Persian, and the person to whom one tells something is the complement of the preposition *barâ-ye.*

[2]In affirmative sentences *ziâd* is usually equivalent to *kháyli* and *besyâr,* although it has a stronger sense of "too much, too many." In negatives *ziâd* generally replaces *kháyli,* e.g., *ân kháyli khub-ast* "that is very good," but *ân ziâd khub nist* "that is not very good."

[3]*Kas* is normally used for "one" in relatives, as *kas-i-ke* "the one who, the person who," and *kasân-i-ke* "those who, persons who." *Hichkas* + negative verb gives "nobody."

Exercise 13

(a) Change the following sentences into restrictive relative phrases (e.g., *ân mard âmad > ân mard-i-ke âmad...*) and then complete the sentence on your own.

۱ درس آسان را خواندیم .

۲ آن ساختمانهای بلند را دیده‌اند .

۳ آن تابستان گرم بود .

٤ پول را داده بودم .

٥ آن زمستان زیاد سرد نبود .

٦ همسایگان رفتند .

۷ آن مردان بسیار پول دارند .

۸ نامه زود رسید .

۹ آن کسان نیامدند .

۱۰ آن دختر خوشگل برگشته است .

(b) Turn the **second** of the two sentences into a restrictive relative clause and embed it into the first sentence (e.g., *(1) ân mard irâni-ast. (2) ân mard âmad. > ân mard-i-ke âmad irâni-ast.)*

۱ آن دانشجو کجاست؟ آن دانشجو دیروز اینجا بوده است .

۲ آن زن را می‌شناسیم . آن زن میوه می‌خرید .

۳ پول زیاد نبود . از ما پول گرفتند .

٤ آن روز ما به شیراز میرویم . آن روز شما میائید .

٥ فاصله زیاد نیست . شیراز با اصفهان فاصله دارد .

٦ اطاق بزرگ نبود . من در آن اطاق زندگی می‌کردم .

۷ همسایه‌مان کی برمیگردد؟ همسایه‌مان به شیراز رفته است .

۸ آن چیزها را فراموش نمیکنم . آن چیزها را روی میز گذاشته‌ام .

۹ آن روز کی بود؟ شما از آن روز تعریف میکردید .

۱۰ آن ایرانیان زرنگند . ما دیروز با آن ایرانیان بودیم .

(c) Translate into Persian:

1. I had scarcely opened the door when I saw him.
2. The house in which we used to live was far from town.
3. I have forgotten the name of the person who was here with you yesterday.
4. Where is the money you took from them?
5. Did you take the clock that was here to some other place?
6. Last month he was in a city that is 200 km. distant from here.
7. I forgot the letter that I put on the table.
8. Is the building your friends live in far from here?
9. It's nearly five kilometers from the school you used to go to.
10. I counted all the things you gave me. There were sixteen in all.

1) nakarden budam

2) mi-kardim

3) ra li

5) beh jaye degan bordid

6) gozashte, fasileh
   (ask Challah bud (ke deust kbnek ba
   — man gozashte dar shari   inja fasee daad)

7) dustaretan

9) ast, miraftid

Lesson Fourteen

§43 The future tense. The future tense is compounded from the present tense of *khâstan* "to want," without the *mí-* prefix, followed by the short infinitive (= past stem). In the affirmative stress falls on the last syllable of the short infinitive.

خواهم گفت	*khâham-góft*	خواهیم گفت	*khâhim-góft*
خواهی گفت	*khâhi-góft*	خواهید گفت	*khâhid-góft*
خواهد گفت	*khâhad-góft*	خواهند گفت	*khâhand-góft*

In compound verbs the auxiliary *khâstan* intervenes between the two parts of the compound. Stress is on the final syllable of the non-verbal element.

برخواهم گشت	*bár-khâham-gasht*	برخواهیم گشت	*bár-khâhim-gasht*
برخواهی گشت	*bár-khâhi-gasht*	برخواهید گشت	*bár-khâhid-gasht*
برخواهد گشت	*bár-khâhad-gasht*	برخواهند گشت	*bár-khâhand-gasht*

The negative future is formed by prefixing *ná-* to the auxiliary.

نخواهم گفت	*nákhâham-goft*	نخواهیم گفت	*nákhâhim-goft*, &c.
برنخواهم گشت	*bàr-nákhâham-gasht*	برنخواهیم گشت	*bàr-nákhâhim-gasht*, &c.

93

Remember that in ordinary usage the present tense is used for the future. The future tense is reserved for fairly emphatic statements about the future.

هیچوقت برنخواهم گشت!	*hichvaqt bar-nákhâham-gasht!*	I shall never return!
همه حتماً خواهند مرد!	*hame hatman khâhand-mord!*	They shall certainly all die!

§44 Other numerical expressions.

44.1 *Chand.*

(a) The interrogative *chand*, invariably followed by the singular (or counting word and the singular[1]), renders "how many?" for countables.

چند (تا) برادر دارید؟	*chand (tâ) barâdar dârid?*	How many brothers do you have?
چند سال در ایران بودید؟	*chand sâl dar irân budid?*	How many years were you in Iran?
چند دفعه به آنجا رفته‌اید؟	*chand daf'e be ânjâ rafte-id?*	How many times have you gone there?

Note especially the expression *chand vaqt* for "how long?"

چند وقت در ایران بودید؟	*chand vaqt dar irân budid?*	How long were you in Iran?

(b) The interrogative ordinal is *chandom*, which functions like ordinals in *-om*, or *chandomin*, which functions like ordinals in *-omin* (i.e., precedes the noun it modifies).

امروز چندم ماه است؟	*emruz chandom-e mâh-ast?*	What day of the month is it today?

---

[1]Time expressions, as with numbers, never take counting words.

| این چندمین دفعه است که میآید؟ | *in chandomin daf'e-ast-ke míâyad?* | How many times has he come?[1] |

For telling time, days of the week, etc., see Appendix B.

(c) Both *chand* and *yek-chand* as declaratives are followed by the singular and mean "several, a few."

(یك) چند تا برادر دارم.	*(yek) chand tâ barâdar dâram.*	I have several brothers.
یکچند سال گذشت.	*yek chand sâl gozasht.*	A few years passed.
امشب آن چند تا کتاب را میخوانم.	*emshab ân chand tâ ketâb-râ míkhânam.*	I'll read those few books tonight.

In this meaning *chand* may also be preceded by the non-specific plural, a more literary usage.

| نمونههائی چند | *nemunehâ-i chand* | several examples |
| سالانی چند | *salân-i chand* | a few years |

44.2 For measurable quantities, the interrogative *cheqadr* "how much, what amount" is used and is followed directly by the noun without *ezâfe*.

| چقدر شکر میخواهید؟ | *cheqadr shekar míkhâhid?* | How much sugar do you want? |
| چقدر آب خوردهاید؟ | *cheqadr âb khorde-id?* | How much water have you drunk? |

44.3 Both *qadr-i* and *kam-i* are used for "a little, a little bit of."

| در نمکدان قدری نمك هست. | *dar namakdân qadr-i namak hast.* | There is a little salt in the saltcellar. |

---

[1]Literally, "this is the 'how-manyeth' time he is coming."

| در چاه کمی آب بود. | dar châh kam-i âb bud. | There was a little water in the well. |
| کمی وقتتان را می گیرم. | kam-i vaqt-etân-râ mígiram. | I'll take a bit of your time. |

44.4 Indefinite numerical expressions such as "two or three," "four or five" are expressed in Persian by the two numbers together.

| دو سه نفر | do-se nafar | two or three people |
| پنج شش سال | panj-shesh sâl | five or six years |

44.5 "More than" is idiomatically expressed by the numerical expression followed by *bishtar*. "Less/fewer than" is expressed by the numerical expression followed by *kamtar*, as in the following examples.

دو تا قلم بیشتر ندارم.	do tâ qalam bishtar nádâram.	I don't have more than two pens.
سه هفته بیشتر نماندیم.	se hafte bishtar námândim.	We didn't stay more than three weeks.[1]
پنج نفر کمتر آنجا بودند.	panj nafar kamtar ânjâ budand.	There were fewer than five people there.[2]

Note the following:

کمتر از صد تومان به من داد.	kamtar az sad tomân be man dâd.	He gave me less than a hundred tomans.
به من صد تومان کمتر داد.	be man sad tomân kamtar dâd.	He gave me a hundred tomans less.
به من صد تومان کم داد.	be man sad tomân kam-dâd.	He gave me a hundred tomans too little.

---

[1]Depending upon context, this sentence also means "we didn't stay three weeks more."

[2]Depending upon context, this sentence also means "there were five people fewer there."

96

44.6 Numerical compounds are generally formed by adding *-e* or occasionally *-i,* as in دوباره *dobâre* "again, once more," دوچرخه *do-charkhe* "bicycle," مرد بیست ساله *mard-e bistsâle* "twenty-year-old man," and اطاق دونفری *otâq-e donafari* "double-occupancy room."

Vocabulary 14

آینده *âyande* coming, next, the future

ارزان *arzân* cheap, inexpensive

آنقدر *ânqadr* so much, that much

اینقدر *inqadr* so much, this much

چرخ *charkh* wheel

چند *chand* (+ sing.) how many?, how much?, several, a few

چقدر *cheqadr* how much?

حتماً *hatman* certainly, surely[1]

قدر *qadr* amount, quantity

قیمت *qaymat (qimat)* price, value

کم *kam* little, little bit, too little, too few

کم دادن *kam-dâdan* to give too little, to shortchange

گذراندن *gozarând-/gozarân-* to spend (time)

گران *gerân* expensive, dear

مردن (میر) *mord-/mir-* to die

نشان دادن *neshân-dâdan* to show

نمونه *nemune* example, sample

---

[1]*Hatman* is often used in the sense of "must," e.g., *hatman raft* "he must have gone" and *hatman injâ-st* "it must be here."

Exercise 14

(a) Give the following in the future tense:

۱ از او میترسد .

۲ در انتخابات کی انتخاب میشود ؟

۳ هیچوقت بزرگ نمیشوی!

٤ برای ایشان تعریف میکنیم .

٥ میدانند .

٦ فراموش میکنید .

٧ آن را به شما نشان نمیدهم.

٨ آن را من میگیرم .

۹ سه هفته در آنجا میگذرانند .

۱۰ آنرا نمیخورم .

۱۱ آنهارا میخریم .

۱۲ او میمیرد .

۱۳ هفتهٔ آینده میروید .

۱٤ گران میخرند .

(b) Answer the following questions:

۱ چند وقت در آن کشور بودید ؟

۲ پارسال چند دفعه به تهران رفتند ؟

۳ چقدر میوه میخواهیم؟

٤ اینرا چند خریدید ؟

٥ امروز چندشنبه است؟

٦ در یک شبانهروز چند ساعت هست؟

٧ ماه گذشته چند روز داشت؟

٨ شما چند سال دارید ؟

۹ این درس چندم این کتاب است؟

۱۰ در خانهتان چند تا اطاق هست؟

(c) Read and translate the following:

۱ قیمتی که برای اینها دادی زیاد نبود.

۲ میدانید کشورهای همسایهٔ ایران چیستند؟

۳ آنها را ارزانتر میخواهم.

٤ حتماً میدانید این کیست.

٥ پولی که از او گرفتهام کم است.

٦ آن ساختمان بزرگی که میبینید دویست تا اطاق بیشتر دارد.

۷ فاصلهای که آن دهات با شهر دارد زیاد نیست.

۸ از کدام همسایهتان تعریف میکردید؟

۹ این نمونهاش است، خودش نیست.

۱۰ هنوز از آنجا بر نگشته بود که خواهرش مرد.

(d) Translate the following into Persian:

1. He's not more than twelve years old [see No. 8 in (b) above].
2. The third house you'll see is ours.
3. We had scarcely reached the garden when their neighbors came.
4. He works so much that I know he won't go.
5. How do you buy those things so cheaply?
6. He'll show you a few examples of his work.
7. Next year we'll spend three weeks in France.
8. Last month we bought two kilograms of very good coffee.
9. Iranians drink tea several times a day, and they almost never drink coffee.
10. Do you know all the students who are in your classes?

Supplementary Vocabulary: Family Relationships

برادر *barâdar* brother

پدر *pedar* father

پدربزرگ *pedarbozorg* grandfather

پدرزن *pedarzan* father-in-law (wife's father)

پدرشوهر *pedarshawhar* father-in-law (husband's father)

پسرخاله *pesarkhâle* cousin (mother's sister's son)

پسردائی *pesardâi* cousin (mother's brother's son)

پسرعمو *pesar' amu* cousin (father's brother's son)

پسرعمه *pesar' amme* cousin (father's sister's son)

خاله *khâle* aunt (mother's sister)

خواهر *khâhar* sister

دائی *dâi* uncle (mother's brother)

دخترخاله *dokhtarkhâle* cousin (mother's sister's daughter)

دختردائی *dokhtardâi* cousin (mother's brother's daughter)

دخترعمو *dokhtar' amu* cousin (father's brother's daughter)

دخترعمه *dokhtar' amme* cousin (father's sister's daughter)

زن *zan* wife

شوهر *shawhar* husband

عمو *amu* uncle (father's brother)

عمه *amme* aunt (father's sister)

مادر *mâdar* mother

مادربزرگ *mâdarbozorg* grand-mother

مادرزن *mâdarzan* mother-in-law (wife's mother)

مادرشوهر *mâdarshawhar* mother-in-law (husband's mother)

ناپدری *nâpedari* stepfather

نامادری *nâmâdari* stepmother

همسر *hamsar* spouse

هوو *havu* second wife (relationship of a second wife to the first)

Lesson Fifteen

§45 The imperative.

45.1 The singular imperative of simple verbs is formed by prefixing *bé-* to the present stem.

بگیر	*bégir!*	Take (it)!
بنشین	*béneshin!*	Sit down!
بزن	*bézan!*	Hit (it)!

(a) When followed in the next syllable by *-o-*, the imperative prefix changes to *bó-*.

بگذار	*bógozâr!*	Put (it) down!

(b) When followed in the next syllable by *-aw-* or *-u-*, the imperative prefix may change, according to regional accent, to *bó-*.

برو	*béraw or bóraw*	Go!
بگو	*bégu or bógu*	Say (something)!

(c) When followed by a verbal stem beginning with a vowel, the imperative prefix becomes *bí-* and is so written.

بیا	*bíâ!*	Come!
بیانداز (بینداز)	*bíandâz!*	Throw (it)!

101

بیافت (بیفت)   *bíoft!*   Fall down!

45.2 The plural imperative is formed by adding the second-person plural ending -*id* to the singular imperative.

بگیرید   *bégirid!*   Take (it)!

بروید   *béravid!*   Go!

بیائید   *bíâid!*   Come!

45.3 The imperative of most compound verbs is formed without the *be-* prefix.[1] *just the present stem, no be*

گم شو!   *gom-shaw!*   Get lost!

دررا باز کنید!   *dar-râ bâz-konid!*   Open the door!

45.4 The negative imperative is formed by prefixing the negative *ná-* to the verbal stem, replacing the *be-* of the affirmative. The negative prefix always receives primary stress, even in compound verbs. Before stems beginning with vowels, a -*y*- is infixed.

نرو!   *náraw!*   Don't go!

گم نشوید!   *gòm-náshavid!*   Don't get lost!

دررا باز نکنید!   *dar-râ bâz-nákonid!*   Don't open the door!

نیائید!   *náyâid!*   Don't come!

نیندازید!   *náyandâzid!*   Don't throw (it).

45.5 When the first syllable of the present stem is an open syllable and contains either -*e*- or -*o*-, that vowel is normally contracted with the addition of the imperative prefixes *bé-*, *bó-* and *ná-*.

---

[1]In classical Persian the imperative of almost all compound verbs is regularly formed without the *be-* prefix. In modern Persian, *true* compounds (i.e., those that are essentially inseparable) like *bardâshtan,* as well as the majority of instances when the compounding verbs are -*kardan* and -*shodan*, also form imperatives without the *be-* prefix. Verbs compounded with -*zadan*, -*keshidan*, &c. tend, particularly in spoken Persian, to take the *be-* prefix, e.g., *hárf bezan* "speak!"

بنشینید	*béneshinid >* *bén'shinid*	Sit down!
بگذارید	*bógozârid > bóg'zârid*	Put (it) down!

The vowel *-a-* is never contracted, as from *bordan, bébarid* "carry (it)!"

45.6 Exceptions. The imperative of two verbs is irregularly formed.

(a) The imperative of *budan* is formed on the stem *bâsh-,* which never takes the *bé-* prefix.

مرد باش! گریه نکن!	*mard bâsh, geryè-nákon!*	Be a man, don't cry!
فعلاً همینجا باشید!	*fe'lan haminjâ bâshid!*	For the time being, stay (be) right here.

(b) The imperative of simple *dâshtan* is formed from the past participle and the imperative of *budan.*

اینرا داشته باش!	*in-râ dâshte-bâsh!*	Hold this!
این نکته‌را در نظر داشته باشید!	*in nokte-râ dar nazar dâshte-bâshid!*	Keep this point in mind!

§46 Resumptive sentence constructions. A common type of sentence in Persian is the resumptive (or topic–comment) sentence, wherein a topic is introduced as subject (topic) of the sentence; the comment then affords some information about that topic. Since the topic-subject is not the subject of the verb of the comment-clause, the topic-subject must be referred to pronominally in its proper position in the comment. Both the independent and the enclitic pronouns are used for this purpose.

آن زنی که در بارەاش صحبت میکردیم، اتفاقاً از در خانهاش رد شدم.	*ân zan-i-ke darbâre-ash sohbat-mikar-dim: ettefâqan az dar-e khâne-ash radd-shodam.*	By chance I passed by the door of the house of the woman we were talking about.

This sentence is equivalent to the sentence *ettefâqan az dar-e khâne-ye zan-i-ke darbâre-ash sohbat-mikardim radd-shodam*. The topicalizer of the example avoids the cumbersome construction.

قالیچهای که دیروز دیدیم، فکر نمیکنید قیمتش کمی گران بود؟	*qâliche-i-ke diruz didim: fekr-némi-konid qaymat-esh kam-i gerân bud?*	Don't you think the price of the carpet we saw yesterday was a bit too much?

Vocabulary 15

اتفاقاً	*ettefâqan* by chance		چنگال	*changâl* fork
اصلاً	*aslan* (+ neg.) not at all		درست	*dorost* right, correct
بشقاب	*boshqâb* plate		درست کردن	*dorost-kardan* to fix, make
بعداً	*ba'dan* afterwards (adv.)		دوست داشتن	*dust-dâshtan*[3] to love
بیرون	*birun* out, outside (*az* of)		صحبت کردن	*sohbat-kardan* to speak, talk
پیر	*pir*[1] old (of people)		ظرف	*zarf* dish
جان	*jân*[2] soul, life		فنجان	*fenjân* cup
			قاشق	*qâshoq* spoon
			قبلاً	*qablan* before (adv.)
			کارد	*kârd* knife

---

[1] *Pir* may follow the noun it modifies as an ordinary adjective (*mard-e pir* "old man," *zan-e pir* "old woman"); it may also precede a noun without *ezâfe* to form a compound, as in *pir-mard* and *pir-zan*.

[2] *Jân* as an enclitic is added to proper names as an endearment, e.g.,

mâdar-jân "mother dear" and *maryam-jân* "dear Maryam."

[3] Like *dâshtan*, *dust-dâshtan* never takes *mí-*. The imperative is also formed like that of *dâshtan*, i.e., *dust-dâshte-bâsh(id)*.

گم شدن *gom-shodan* to get lost

گم کردن *gom-kardan* to lose

لیوان *livân* glass

ماجرا *mâjarâ* adventure

مریض *mariz* sick, ill

نوع/انواع *naw'* pl *anvâ'*[1] kind, sort, type

همانجا *hamânjâ* right there

همینجا *haminjâ* right here

یخ *yakh* ice

آب و مقهب ← *maghab* - before

Exercise 15

(a) Give both the singular and the plural imperatives of the following:

۱۰ زیاد (سؤال نکردن)!

۱۱ این را (گم نکردن)!

۱۲ حرفهایش را (فهمیدن)!

۱۳ آنهارا بمن (نشان دادن)!

۱٤ به سؤالم (جواب دادن)!

۱٥ (رفتن) ، (گم شدن)!

۱٦ با ما (حرف زدن)!

۱۷ اینهارا بیرون (بردن)!

۱۸ برادرت را (نزدن)!

۱ بیرون (رفتن)!

۲ سه روز بیشتر (نماندن)!

۳ این را (داشتن)!

٤ کتابش را همانجا (گذاشتن)!

٥ یکچند روزی همینجا (گذراندن)!

٦ حرفهای مرا (گوش کردن)!

۷ اینهارا ارزان (نفروختن)!

۸ خودرا (شناختن)!

۹ همیشه فارسی (صحبت کردن)!

(b) Read and translate:

۱ آن پیرمردانی که در باره‌شان صحبت میکردیم زنهایشان کجااند؟

۲ اتفاقاً دوستم از همان ماجرا برای ما تعریف میکرد.

۳ حتماً آنهارا قبلاً دیده‌اید.

٤ آقاجان، اینقدر کار نکنید! مریض میشوید!

٥ این نوع سؤال را دوست ندارند.

٦ نفهمیدم چرا جوابی که دادم درست نیست.

---

[1]In the singular *naw'* functions as a counting word, i.e., it is never followed by the *ezâfe;* the plural is normally followed by the *ezâfe*, e.g., *in naw' mardom* "this sort of people" but *anvâ'-e mardom* "sorts of people."

٧ شما همانجا بمانید و این چیزها را برایتان من میآورم.

٨ همین امروز بخرید! هفتهٔ آینده قیمتش کمتر نخواهد بود.

(c) Translate into Persian:

1. Always be (pl) happy!
2. They didn't understand your question correctly.
3. Take (carry) these things out to (for) those old women.
4. When we were going to that village, we got lost three times.
5. I don't like this kind of coffee.
6. Last week I was talking with my friends.
7. Tell me about the adventures you had in Iran.
8. We spent a few days in Shiraz.

Supplementary Vocabulary: Foodstuffs

آب	*âb* water	پیاز	*piâz* onion
آرد	*ârd* flour	تخم مرغ	*tokhm-e morq* egg
آلو	*âlu* plum	تربچه	*torobche* radish
آلوبالو	*âlubâlu* sour cherry	ترشی	*torshi* pickles
اسفناج	*esfenâj* spinach	تره	*tare* chives
انگبین	*angabin* honey	ترهٔ فرنگی	*tare-ye farangi* leek
انگور	*angur* grape	توت	*tut* berry
بادام	*bâdâm* almond	توت فرنگی	*tut-e farangi* straw-
بادنجان	*bâdenjân* eggplant		berry
باقالا	*bâqâlâ* lima bean	جعفری	*ja'fari* parsley
برگ بو	*barg-e bu* bayleaf	چای	*chây* tea
برنج	*berenj* rice	چغندر	*choqondar* beet
	(uncooked)	خردل	*khardel* mustard
بستنی	*bastani* ice cream	خربزه	*kharboze* Persian
به	*beh* quince		melon
پرتقال	*portoqâl* orange	خرما	*khormâ* date
پسته	*peste* pistachio	خیار	*khiâr* cucumber
پنیر	*panir* cheese	دارچین	*dârchin* cinnamon

106

رشته	*reshte* noodle	گردو	*gerdu* walnut
روغن	*rawqan* oil	گشنیز	*geshniz* coriander
ریواس	*rivâs* rhubarb	گل کلم	*golkalam* cauliflower
زردآلو	*zardâlu* apricot	گلابی	*golâbi* pear
زرد چوبه	*zardchube* turmeric	گوجه فرنگی	*gawje-ye farangi*
زعفران	*za'farân* saffron		tomato
زنجبیل	*zanjabil* ginger	گوشت	*gusht* meat
سرشیر	*sarshir* cream	گوشت خوك	*gusht-e khuk* pork
سیب	*sib* apple	گوشت گاو	*gusht-e gâv* beef
سیب زمینی	*sibzamini* potato	گوشت گوسفند	*gusht-e gusfand* lamb
سیر	*sir* garlic	گیلاس	*gilâs* cherry
شبت	*shebet* dill	لوبیا	*lubiâ* string bean
شراب	*sharâb* wine	لیمو	*limu* lemon
شکر	*shekar* sugar (granulated)	لیموسبز	*limu-sabz* lime
شلغم	*shalqam* turnip	ماست	*mâst* yoghurt
شنبلیله	*shambalile* fenugreek	ماهی	*mâhi* fish
شیر	*shir* milk	مرغ	*morq* chicken
طالبی	*tâlebi* melon	موز	*mawz* banana
عدس	*adas* lentil	میخك	*mikhak* clove
فلفل	*felfel* pepper	نان	*nân* bread
قارچ	*qârch* mushroom	نخود چی	*nokhudchi* chickpea
قند	*qand* sugar (lump)	نخود سبز	*nokhud-sabz* green peas
قهوه	*qahve* coffee	نعناع	*na'nâ'* mint
کاهو	*kâhu* lettuce	نمك	*namak* salt
کدو	*kadu* squash	هل	*hell* cardamom
کرفس	*karafs* celery	هلو	*holu* peach
کره	*kare* butter	هندوانه	*hendavâne* watermelon
کشمش	*keshmesh* raisin		
کلم پیچ	*kalam-pich* cabbage	هویج	*havij* carrot

for monday

Review III

(a) Review the vocabulary lists for lessons 11–15.

(b) Read and translate the following:

١ آن غذای خوشمزه‌ای را که دیروز بما دادید ، خودتان درست کرده بودید ؟

٢ آن مرد پیری که همینجا کار میکرد ، اسمش را فراموش کرده‌ام.

٣ در همین اطاق کمی بمانید و درستان را بخوانید.

٤ آن کتاب کهنه را نمیخواهم ، میدانم که مفید نیست.

٥ چون هفتهٔ آینده برادرم از آن شهر دوری که در آنجا کار میکند میاید ، خواهرم هم از جائی که در آن انگلیسی درس میدهد بر میگردد.

٦ بار اولی که آنها را دیدم نمیدانم کی بود.

٧ تعداد دانشجویانی که در این دانشگاه درس میخوانند چند است؟

٨ بعداً فهمیدم که چرا مریض شدم. حتماً از چیزی بود که خورده بودم.

٩ هیچوقت کارهائی را که برای من کرده‌اید فراموش نمیکنم.

١٠ هیچوقت دربارهٔ قیمتی که برای آن چیزها داده است صحبت نخواهد کرد.

(c) Translate the following into Persian:

1. Don't listen to his words.
2. He pays (gives) a lot for the room he lives in.
3. There are nine rooms in their house.
4. Last year we didn't get sick at all.
5. Weren't those people we saw before Iranian?
6. Look here! Don't forget what I told you (my words)!
7. I don't know why you are afraid of them.
8. I had scarcely come when he turned around and left.
9. They had already gone home when you arrived.
10. How many minutes are there in a quarter hour?

Lesson Sixteen

§47 On the nature of compounds. Of the vast number of compound verbs in Persian, we can identify two broad types, close and open compounds. Close compounds are represented in the first place by those whose nonverbal compounding element is a particle or preposition like *bar* in *bar-gashtan* and *bar-dâshtan* or *dar* in *dar-raftan*. Although this type admits into the compound verbal particles such as *mi-* (e.g., *bar-migardam* "I am returning") and pronominal enclitic objects (e.g., *bar-esh-dâshtam* "I picked it up"), noun complements do not intervene in this type.

The second type of close compound consists of verbs like *vâred-shodan* and *kâr-kardan,* which can be "fractured" to admit noun complements, the non-specific enclitic and the plural suffix onto the nonverbal element. Some such compounds may take their complements as "sandwiched" constructions, in which case the complement is linked to the nonverbal element by the *ezâfe*. For instance, an intransitive compound such as *vâred-shodan* "to enter" may take a "sandwiched" complement as in

وارد شهر شدم.   *vâred-e shahr*   I entered the city.
               shodam.

The close compound *kâr-kardan* "to do something" illustrates the fractured compound when the nonverbal element is modified in any way:

آن کاررا کردم.   *ân kâr-râ kardam.*   I did it.

109

کار خوبی کردید. *kâr-e khub-i kardid.*   You did a good job.

کارهای خوبی کرده   *kârhâ-ye khub-i karde-*   He's done some good
است.   *ast.*   things.

As another example, in the construction

جواب ندادید.   *javâb-nádâdid*   You didn't answer,

the close compound of *javâb-dâdan* "to answer" holds, but when a complement is sandwiched, as in

جواب سؤالم را ندادید.   *javâb-e so'âl-am-râ*   You didn't answer my
   nádâdid   question,

the construction can no longer be called a close compound, i.e., it has been split into its component parts and should be thought of as the verb *nádâdid* "you did not give" with a compound object, "the-answer-to-my-question," which takes the direct-object marker *-râ*.

Open compounds represent a loose connection between verb and complement, as in *madrase raftan* "to go to school, attend school" and *dur andâkhtan* "to throw away."

For the time being, all compounds with *-shodan, -kardan, -gashtan* and *-dâshtan* will be considered close compounds unless they are fractured, in which case they become loose (i.e., practically speaking, open) compounds. All compounds with *-keshidan, -oftâdan, -khândan* and *-zadan* will be considered loose compounds.

§48 The present subjunctive. The subjunctive mood in Persian is, with one important exception, used only for complementary constructions, i.e., the subjunctive always depends in some way or follows upon a primary verb in the indicative mood.

Formation of the present subjunctive.

(a) The present subjunctive of simple verbs is formed from the present stem plus the prefix *bé-*, which is identical to the *bé-* prefix of the imperative and follows the same euphonic rules given in §45. Subjunctive verbs of various types are given below:

بگیرم	*bégiram*	بگونیم	*béguim*
بدانی	*bédâni*	بیائید	*bíâid*
بگشاید	*bóg(o)shâyad*	بیفتند	*bíoftand*

(b) The present subjunctive of close compound verbs is character-ized by the lack of any prefix on the verbal element. Stress remains on the final syllable of the non-verbal element.

– no be in closed

دررروم	*dár-ravam*	صحبت‌کنیم	*sohbát-konim*
برداری	*bár-dâri*	برگردید	*bár-gardid*
وارد شود	*vâréd-shavad*	گم شوند	*góm-shavand*

(c) The present subjunctive of open and loose compound verbs is made, like the simple verb, with the prefix *bé-* on the verbal element.

use be in open – if you open separate the words know it's open

حرف بزنم	*hárf bezanam*	دور بیاندازیم	*dúr biandâzim*
کاری بکنی	*kâr-i bokoni*	جوابی بدهید	*javâb-i bedehid*
درس بخواند	*dárs bekhânad*	وارد شهر بشوند	*vâred-e shahr beshavand*

(d) The negative present subjunctive is formed by replacing *be-* with *ná-*. The euphonic rules given in §45 apply. The negative prefix takes primary stress in compound verbs, leaving secondary stress on the nonverbal element.

نگیرم	*nágiram*	نیاندازیم	*náyandâzim*
برنداری	*bàr nádâri*	نیآئید	*náyâid*
وارد نشود	*vârèd náshavad*	گم نشوند	*gòm náshavand*

(e) Exceptions. As in the imperative, *budan* "to be" does not take the *be-* prefix. Its subjunctive inflection is as follows:

باشم	*bâsham*	باشیم	*bâshim*
باشی	*bâshi*	باشید	*bâshid*

111

باشد *bâshad*   باشند *bâshand*

Dâshtan, as in the imperative, forms the subjunctive from the past participle and the subjunctive of *budan*.

داشته‌باشم *dâshte-bâsham*   داشته‌باشیم *dâshte-bâshim*
داشته‌باشی *dâshte-bâshi*   داشته‌باشید *dâshte-bâshid*
داشته‌باشد *dâshte-bâshad*   داشته‌باشند *dâshte-bâshand*

The negative subjunctive is predictably formed from the affirmative: *nábâsham, nádâshte-bâsham,* etc.

§49 Uses of the present subjunctive I. [handwritten: use it when you want to express a:] [handwritten: 1)let him, 2)should I ..., 3)] [handwritten: 1)wish 2)desire 3)possibility]

49.1 The subjunctive mood is used as personal complements of all impersonal verbs and verbal constructions such as *bâyad* "must, should, have to," *nábâyad* "must not, should not, don't have to," *shâyad* "may, might, perhaps" or with negative subjunctive "may not, might not."

باید بروم. *bâyad béravam.*   I must (have to) go.

نباید بمانید. *nábâyad bémânid.*   You don't have to stay.

شاید بگوئیم. *shâyad béguim.*   We may (might) say.

شاید نیایند. *shâyad náyâyand.*   They may (might) not come.

Bâyad and *shâyad* are called "impersonals" because they are "frozen" in the third-person singular, rather like the English "it is necessary." Of *bâyad* there also remains a past third-person singular, *(mi) bâyest,* which reflects the original, now obsolete, infinitive *bâyestan* and which is used synonymously with *bâyad.* A past participle *shâyeste* ("suitable") survives of the original but now obsolete infinitive *shâyestan* that gives *shâyad.* Aside from the fixed third-person singular forms, these verbs have no further inflections in modern Persian.

49.2 The subjunctive is used as a dependent complement of the independent verbs *khâstan* "to want," *tavânestan* "to be able" and *gozâsh-tan* "to allow, let."

112

میخواستم بروم.	*míkhâstam béravam.*	I wanted to go.
میخواهم بروم.	*míkhâham béravam.*	I want to go.
میتوانست بیاید.	*mítavânest bíâyad.*	He was able to come (he could come).
میتواند بیاید.	*mítavânad bíâyad.*	He can come.
بگذارید آنها بیآیند.	*bógzârid ânhâ bíâyand.*	Let them come.
پدرم نگذاشت (که) من بروم.	*pedar-am nágozâsht (ke) man béravam.*	My father didn't let me go.

Direct objects of the dependent subjunctive and prepositional matter generally fall between the independent and dependent verbs. The independent verbs may occur in any tense.

میخواست آنرا به من بدهد.	*míkhâst ân-râ be man bédehad.*	He wanted to give it to me.
میتوانم شمارا ببینم.	*mítavânam shomâ-râ bébinam.*	I can see you.
میخواهند فردا بیایند.	*míkhâhand fardâ bíâyand.*	They want to come tomorrow.
نخواهم توانست بیایم.	*nákhâham-tavânest bíâyam.*	I shall not be able to come.

If there is a change of subject between the independent and dependent verbs, the conjunction *ke* "that" usually appears along with the subject pronoun of the dependent verb.

میخواهم که شما بیائید.	*míkhâham **ke shomâ** bíâid.*	I want you to come.
نمیخواهم که آنها بروند.	*némikhâham **ke ânhâ** béravand.*	I don't want them to go.

49.3 The independent uses of the subjunctive, i.e., where it occurs not as a dependent to a preceding independent verb, are (1) as a jussive ("let, may") in all persons:

برویم!	*béravim!*	Let's go!

113

همانطور که هست باشد.	*hamântawr-ke hast, bâshad.*	Let it be just as it is.
خدا بیامرزدش.	*khodâ bíâmorzad-esh.*	May God have mercy on him.
خدا نکند.	*khodâ nákonad.*	God forbid (lit., "may God not do it")

and (2) as the deliberative interrogative (English "should"):

چه کار کنم؟	*che kâr konam?*	What should I do?
چه بگوید؟	*che béguyad?*	What should he say?
برویم؟	*béravim?*	Should we go?
چرا نرویم؟	*chérâ náravim?*	Why shouldn't we go?

Vocabulary 16

biayad
اینامه دار + ضاب ضعف use it as

امکان	*emkân* possibility		لازم	*lâzem* necessary	
بالاخره	*bel'akhare* finally, at last		لباس	*lebâs* clothes	
چنان	*chonân* such, so, so much[1]		ممکن	*momken* possible	
چنین	*chonin* such, so, so much		غذا	*qazâ* food	
رنگ	*rang* color		همانطورکه	*hamântawr-ke* just as	
			همراه	*hamrâh-e* along with (prep.)[2]	

only occurs in 3 person

امکان داشتن *emkân-dâshtan* to be possible (impersonal + subj.)

انداختن (انداز) *andâkht-/andâz-* to cast, throw, hurl

باید *bâyad* it is necessary, must, should (impersonal + subj.)

---

[1]As adverbs *chonân* and *chonin* are usually followed by *ke* "so much...that." When they modify nouns, the noun must have the nonspecific enclitic *-i*, as *chonân mard-i* "such a man" and *chonin ketâbhâ-i* "such books, books like these."

[2]*Hamrâh* also forms open compounds such as *hamrâh âvordan* "to bring along" and *hamrâh bordan* "to take along."

پوشیدن *pushidan* to cover, clothe, wear, put on (clothes)[1]

تغییر دادن *taqyir-dâdan* to change (transitive)

تغییر کردن *taqyir-kardan* to change (intransitive) ~~goes~~ first in a sentence

توانستن (توان) *tavânest-/tavân-* to be able, can (+ subj.)[2] must have subject

خواستن (خواه) *khâst-/khâh-* to want, be about to (+ subj.)[3]

درآوردن (درآور) *dar-âvord-/dar-âvor- (âvar-)* (close compound) to take off (clothes)

دور انداختن *dur andâkhtan* (open compound) to throw away

شاید *shâyad* may, might, it is fitting (impersonal + subj.); maybe (+ indicative)

فکر کردن *fekr-kardan* to think

گذاشتن (گذار) *gozâsht-/gozâr-* to allow, let (+ subj.)

وارد شدن *vâred-shodan* to enter, come/go in (+ *be* or "sand- wiched" open compound construction)

Exercise 16

(a) Supply the proper subjunctive form of the verbs given in paren- theses, and then translate the following:

۱ امکان دارد که من (نیآمدن).

? naayam

---

[1] The present tense is used only for habitual action *(har ruz sobh lebâs-am-râ mípusham* "I put on my clothes every morning"); the simple past refers exclusively to one act of putting on clothes *(emruz sobh lebâs-am-râ pushidam* "I put on my clothes this morning"); the narrative tense corresponds to the English "be wearing" *(man emruz pirâhan-e sefid-i pushide-am* "I'm wearing a white shirt today").

[2] In the negative past habitual/progressive *tavânestan* implies simple inability; in the simple past negative it implies an attempt that failed, e.g., *némitavânestam bíâyam* "I wasn't able to come," but *nátavânestam bíâyam* "I [tried to or wanted to but] couldn't come." The distinction is not maintained in the present or future tenses.

[3] The past habitual/progressive of *khâstan* implies simple volition, while the past absolute implies "just about to, on the verge of" doing something. Cf. *míkhâs- tam béravam* "I wanted to go" and *khâstam béravam* "I was about to go, I was on the verge of going." There is a way to make a similar distinction in the present, but it involves a construction that will be introduced later. For the time being, ignore this distinction in the present.

۲ شما باید این رنگ را (تغییر دادن) .

۳ میخواهید اینهارا (گم کردن) ؟

٤ همین حالا نمیتوانم (فکر کردن) .

٥ تو هیچوقت نباید در آنجا (نگاه کردن) .

٦ نتوانستند آن را (فروختن) .

۷ نمیخواهید آن در را (بستن) ؟

۸ من شاید اورا (دوست داشتن) .

۹ میتوانند فارسی (حرف زدن) .

۱۰ لازم نیست که او (باز آمدن) .

۱۱ من هم میخواهم کمی (برداشتن) .

۱۲ میتواند خوب (شنیدن) .

۱۳ میتوانی مرا (دیدن) ؟

۱٤ میخواستند اینهارا (دور انداختن) .

۱٥ شاید ما زودتر (رسیدن) .

۱٦ بعداً خواستیم وارد شهر (شدن) .

۱۷ نمیتوانم از آن ماجرا (تعریف کردن) .

۱۸ میخواهید آن قهوه را (خوردن) ؟

۱۹ نمیتوانم این در را (باز کردن) .

۲۰ نمیخواهد آن چیزهارا به من (دادن) .

۲۱ ما باید آنهارا همراه (آوردن) .

۲۲ این شاید درست (بودن) .

۲۳ ممکن نیست من چنین غذائی را (خوردن) .

۲٤ میخواهند که ما بخانه (برگشتن) .

(b) Translate into Persian:

1. I don't want to go there tomorrow.
2. He was just about to throw it away.
3. We want to find the things we lost yesterday.
4. This job is so simple that I don't have to think.
5. I think I got sick from the food I ate in the village last week.
6. Couldn't you give a correct answer to the question?
7. I wanted to answer correctly, but I wasn't able to.

8. Don't let your little brother get lost.
9. Why won't you let me open the door for them?
10. Didn't you want to buy (some) shoes and socks for yourself?

Supplementary Vocabulary: Articles of Clothing

آستین *âstin* sleeve

انگشتر(ی) *angoshtar(i)* ring

بارانی *bârâni* raincoat

بازوبند *bâzuband* bracelet

بلوز *boluz* blouse

بندکفش *band-e kafsh* shoelace

پالتو *pâlto* overcoat

پیراهن *pirâhan* shirt, dress

پیراهنخواب *pirâhankhâb* nightgown

پیژامه *pizhâme* pyjamas

پولور *pulover* sweater

جادکمه *jâdokme* buttonhole

جلیقته *jelitqe* vest

جوراب *jurâb* socks

جوراب نایلن *jurâb-e nâylon* nylons

جیب *jib* pocket

چادر *châdor* veil

چتر *chatr* umbrella

چکمه *chakme* boots

دامن *dâman* skirt

دستکش *dastkesh* gloves

دکمه *dokme* button

دمپائی *dampâi* slippers

روسری *rusari* headscarf

روپوش *rupush* smock

زیپ *zip* zipper

زیرپوش *zirpush* underwear

زیرپیراهن *zirpirâhan* undershirt

ساعت جیبی *sâ'at-e jibi* pocket watch

ساعت مچی *sâ'at-e mochi* wristwatch

سگك *sagak* buckle

سنجاق *sanjâq* pin

سینه بند *sineband* bra

شال گردن *shâl-e gardan* scarf

شرت *short* briefs

شلوار *shalvâr* trousers

عینك *aynak* glasses

عینك دودی *aynak-e dudi* sunglasses

کت *kot* jacket

کراوات *kerâvât* tie

کلاه *kolâh* hat

کفش *kafsh* shoe

کمربند *kamarband* belt

کیف دستی *kif-e dasti* handbag

گالش *gâlosh* galoshes

گردنبند *gardanband* neck-
lace

مایو *mâyo* bathing suit

گوشواره *gushvâre* earring

یقه *yaqe* collar

Supplementary Vocabulary Practice.

1. She's wearing a green skirt. - poosheedas

2. I took my pyjamas off this morning.

3. Aren't you wearing a sweater today?

4. I didn't put on an undershirt this morning.

5. Put on your raincoat!

6. Why are you wearing green socks with those trousers?

7. I wasn't wearing an overcoat at that time.

8. She always wears a white blouse.

9. I want to take my shoes off.

10. I put on my clothes in the morning and take them off at night.

1) اوست

2) daravardan, در آوردم

3) میپوشی چرا سویتر امروز نمیپوشی؟

4) نپوشیدم

7) نپوشیده بودم

Lesson Seventeen

§50 Impersonal constructions.

50.1 *Khosh- âmadan az.* This impersonal construction is equivalent to the English verb "to like"; however, the subject of the English verb is expressed in Persian as a pronominal enclitic after *khosh-,* and the object of the English verb is the complement of the preposition *az.* The verb *âmadan* is invariably impersonal in the third person singular in all tenses.

از آن خوشم آمد.	*az ân khosh-am âmad.*	I liked it.
از آن خوشم میآید.	*az ân khosh-am miâyad.*	I like it.
از کار شما خوشش نمیآید.	*az kâr-e shomâ khosh-esh némiâyad.*	He doesn't like your work.
از چنین کاری خوششان نخواهد آمد.	*az chonin kâr-i khosh-eshân nákhâhad âmad.*	They will not like such a thing.

An infinitive may serve as the complement to the preposition *az* in this construction. Generic objects and compounding complements precede the infinitive; specific and modified objects follow the infinitive with the *ezâfe.*

از صحبت کردن خوششان میآید.	*az **sohbat-kardan** khosh-eshân miâyad.*	They like **to talk.**

از دیدن دوستانمان خوشمان میآید.	*az didan-e dustân-emân khosh-emân miâyad.*	We like **to see** our friends.

Parallel to *khosh- âmadan az* is the construction *bad- âmadan az* "to dislike, to be displeased by."

از این غذا بدم میآید.	*az in qazâ bad-am miâyad.*	I dislike this food.
از فیلمی که دیشب دیدیم بدمان نیآمد.	*az film-i-ke dishab didim bad-emân náyâmad.*	We weren't dis- pleased by the movie we saw last night.

When the "logical" subject of these expressions is other than pronominal, the resumptive construction (§46) is used.

برادر رضا از تهران خوشش نمیآید.	*barâdar-e rezâ: az tehrân khosh-esh némiâyad.*	Reza's brother doesn't like Tehran.
پیرزنهای ده از او بدشان میآمد.	*pirzanhâ-ye deh: az u bad-eshân miâmad.*	The old women of the village disliked her.

50.2 Another common impersonal is *khosh-gozashtan be* ("to have a good time"). The Persian verb is invariably in the third person singular, and the English subject follows the preposition *be*.

بمن خیلی خوش گذشت.	*be man kháyli khosh- gozasht.*	I had a really good time.
آنجا به شما خوش بگذرد.	*ânjâ be shomâ khosh bogozarad.*	May you have a good time there.
به داریوش خوش میگذرد؟	*be dâryush khosh- migozarad?*	Is Darius having a good time?

50.3 In the expressions *khâb- âmadan* "to get sleepy" and *khâb- bordan* "to fall asleep," although *khâb* is actually the subject of both verbs, they are similar to the impersonals in that the English subject is expressed pronominally in Persian.

120

خوابم آمده است.	*khâb-am âmade-ast.*	I've gotten sleepy.
بچه‌ها خوابشان میآید.	*bachchehâ: khâb-eshân miâyad.*	The children are getting sleepy.
خوابم برد.	*khâm-am bord.*	I fell asleep.
بچه‌ها خوابشان برده است.	*bachchehâ: khâb-eshân borde-ast.*	The children have fallen asleep.

§51 Uses of the present subjunctive II. The present subjunctive occurs as a verbal complement of the following expressions. Note that the subordinating conjunction *ke,* like the English "that," may be omitted.

51.1 After all impersonal constructions of possibility, probability and necessity.

امکان دارد (که) نیآیم.	*emkân-dârad (ke) náyâyam.*	It's possible I won't come.
امکان ندارد (که) بیآیم.	*emkân-nádârad (ke) bíyâyam.*	It's not possible for me to come.
لازم بود (که) بروید.	*lâzem bud (ke) béravid.*	It was necessary for you to go.
لازم نبود (که) بروید.	*lâzem nábud (ke) béravid.*	It wasn't necessary for you to go.
احتمال دارد (که) همانجا بمانند.	*ehtemâl-dârad (ke) hamânjâ bémânand.*	It's probable that they will stay there.

51.2 After all personal expressions of desire, will and preference. English equivalents almost all have a complementary infinitive where the persons are the same.

میخواهند برگردند.	*míkhâhand bárgardand.*	They want to return.
میل ندارم به شهر بروم.	*mayl-nádâram be shahr béravam.*	I'm not inclined to go to town.
قصد داشتند آنکاررا بکنند.	*qásd-dâshtand ân kâr-râ bókonand.*	They intended to do it.

121

| ترجیح میدهیم آنطور نباشد. | *tarjíh-midehim ântawr nábâshad.* | We prefer it not to be like that. |

51.3 After expressions of command and prohibition.

| به او گفتم بنشیند. | *be u goftam bén(e)shinad.* | I told him to sit down. |
| فرمودند (که) ما نرویم. | *farmudand (ke) mâ náravim.* | They ordered us not to go. |

51.4 After all expressions of hope.

امیدوارم بازهم شمارا ببینم.	*omidvâr-am bâz-ham shomâ-râ bébinam.*	I hope to see you again.
امیدوارم (که) بتوانم بروم.	*omidvâr-am (ke) bétavânam béravam.*	I hope I can go.
امیدوار بودم که بتوانم بروم.	*omidvâr-budam ke bétavânam béravam.*	I hoped I could go.

Note in the above example that English has a strict sequence of tense in such constructions. There is no sequence of tense in Persian: the complement of a hope is always in the present subjunctive.

| امیدش اینست که همیشه در آنجا بماند. | *omid-esh in-ast ke hamishe dar ânjâ bémânad.* | It is his hope to re-main there always. |

51.5 After expressions of doubt and ignorance.

| شك دارم که بتواند این مطلب را بفهمد. | *shakk-dâram ke bétavânad in matlab-râ béfahmad.* | I doubt he can under-stand this matter. |
| شك داشتند که بیایند یا نه. | *shakk-dâshtand ke bíâyand yâ na.* | They doubted whether they should come or not. |

122

51.6 After expressions of opinion where doubt is implied. Simple statements of opinion where no doubt in implied are in the indicative. Compare the following:

فکر میکنم که آنجاست .	*fekr-mikonam ke ânjâ-st.*	I think he **is** there.
فکر میکنم که آنجا باشد .	*fekr-mikonam ke ânjâ bâshad.*	I think he **may be** there.

51.7 After expressions of emotion when the state or action of the dependent verb is subsequent to or as yet unrealized at the time of the main verb.

میترسم اورا پیدا نکنم .	*mítarsam u-râ paydâ-nákonam.*	I'm afraid I won't find her.
خوشحال میشویم شمارا ببینیم .	*khoshhâl-mishavim shomâ-râ bébinim.*	We'll be happy to see you.

but

خوشحالیم که آمده‌اید .	*khoshhâl-im ke âmade-id.*	We're happy you've come.

Vocabulary 17

آشپزخانه	*âshpazkhâne* kitchen		دراز	*darâz* long
امید	*omid* hope		دیگر	*digar* (+ neg.) no more, no longer
امیدوار	*omidvâr* hopeful		زمین	*zamin* ground, land, earth
بیدار	*bidâr* awake, aware		سرکلاس	*sar-e kelâs* in class, to class
پس	*pas* then, therefore			
پس از	*pas-az* after (prep.)		فرنگی	*farangi* European, non-Iranian
پیشِ	*pish-e* before, in front of		مطلب	*matlab* pl *matâleb*
پیش از	*pish-az* before (prep.)		(مطالب)	matter, topic
تختخواب	*takhtekhâb* bed		معمولاً	*ma'mulan* usually
خواب	*khâb* sleep			

123

احتمال داشتن *ehtemâl-dâshtan* (impersonal + subj.) to be probable

بد- آمد- از *bad- âmad- az* dislike

بیدار شدن *bidâr-shodan* to wake up

خوابیدن (خواب) *khâbid-/khâb-* to sleep, go to sleep, lie down

خوش- آمد- از *khosh- âmad- az* to like

دراز کشیدن *darâz-keshidan* to stretch out

کشیدن (کش) *keshid-/kesh-* to draw, pull, stretch

Some common given names:

جواد	*javâd* Javad (masc.)	شهلا	*shahlâ* Shahla (fem.)
حسن	*hasan* Hassan (masc.)	شیرین	*shirin* Shirin (fem.)
حسین	*hoseyn* Hossein (masc.)	لیلی	*layli* Leili (fem.)
رضا	*rezâ* Reza (masc.)	محمد	*mohammad* Moham-mad (masc.)
زهرا	*zahrâ* Zahra (fem.)	هما	*homâ* Homa (fem.)

Exercise 17

(a) For the following use the *khosh- âmad- az* construction (e.g., *u in âmad > u az in khosh-esh âmad*):

۱ من - آن چیزها - میآید .

۲ شما - این مطلب - نیآمده است .

۳ ما - خوابیدن - میآید .

٤ محمد - کارتان - نیامد .

٥ دانشجویان - زبان فارسی - میآید .

٦ زهرا - درس خواندن - نمیآمد .

٧ من - آن ساعت دیواری - میآید .

٨ آنها - غذای ایرانی - میآید .

٩ شما - چنان کارهائی - نمیآید .

۱۰ تو - آن شهر کوچک - آمده بود .

(b) Give appropriate answers to the following questions:

۱ دیشب ساعت چند خوابیدید؟

۲ دیشب چند ساعت خوابیدید؟

۳ معمولا شبی چند ساعت میخوابید؟

٤ امیدوار است به آنجا برگردد؟

٥ رضا خوابش برده است؟

٦ معمولا ساعت چند خوابتان میآید؟

٧ میتوانند این مطالب را بفهمند؟

٨ کجا میخواهد دراز بکشد؟

٩ دوست ندارید فارسی صحبت کنید؟

۱۰ احتمال دارد که آنها باز بیایند؟

۱۱ میخواهید اینهارا دور بیاندازید؟

۱۲ دیشب به شما خوش گذشت؟

(c) Read and translate the following sentences:

۱ امیدوار بودم امشب لیلی و زهرارا ببینم.

۲ امکان دارد که من امروز پیش پزشك بروم.

۳ معمولا جواد از غذای فرنگی خوشش میآید.

٤ لازم نیست آن چیزهارا به ما نشان بدهند.

٥ باید همهٔ ظرفهارا به آشپزخانه ببریم.

٦ احتمال دارد که من امشب زود بخوابم.

٧ امروز صبح به او گفتم که بهترین لباسهایش را بپوشد.

٨ از زود رسیدن بدش میآید.

٩ ممکن است که رضا دیگر سرکلاس نیآید.

۱۰ از دیدن دوستان ایرانیام و صحبت کردن با آنها خوشم میآید.

(d) Translate into Persian:

1. Last week the things I wanted finally arrived.
2. Is it possible for us to enter that building?
3. I doubt Javad can answer your question.
4. Reza wanted to stretch out on the bed for half an hour.
5. This is at least the third time that we are doing this.

6. No sooner had I picked up the newspaper than I saw it was[1] yesterday's.

7. Who's that Iranian I saw you with last night?

8. I hope they won't come here anymore.

9. Why do you want to live in that old house?

10. I want to take my clothes off and go to sleep.

3) In dafeye sevon ast ke in karra mikonan

7) an Irani ke ba u shoma ra didam kist

---

[1]Use the present tense.

Lesson Eighteen

§52 Totally impersonal constructions.

52.1 The totally impersonal construction is formed of the impersonals *bâyad* ("must") or *shâyad* ("may") with the short infinitive (past stem). The impersonal is equivalent to English expressions with "one" (French *on* and German *man*) or, with transitive verbs, a passive construction.

بايد رفت.	*bâyad raft.*	One must go (*il faut aller*).
شايد گفت.	*shâyad goft.*	One may say, it may be said (*on peut dire*).
نبايد نااميد بود.	*nábâyad nâomid bud.*	One shouldn't be despondent.

52.2 The impersonal construction for "can" with *tavânestan* is made by dropping the third-person singular ending of the present and adding the short infinitive.

ميتوان رفت.	*mítavân raft.*	One can go.
نميتوان گفت.	*némitavân goft.*	One cannot say, it cannot be said.

In the past, the third-person singular form (*mítavânest),* which has no personal ending to begin with, is used with the short infinitive.

میتوانست فهمید.   *mítavânest fahmid.*   One could have understood.

میتوانست گفت.   *mítavânest goft.*   One could say, it could be said.

In modern and spoken Persian *míshod* and *míshavad* are often used as impersonals with the short infinitive in the sense of possibility.

میشود گفت.   *míshavad goft.*   One can say, it's possible to say.

نمیشد باور کرد.   *némishod bâvar-kard.*   One couldn't believe it, it wasn't possible to believe it.

§53 The participial absolute. Sentences in literary Persian are commonly characterized by a high degree of complexity (subordination and co-ordination) and length. In order to relieve the monotony of a number of finite verbs connected by conjunctions, the "participial absolute" is used in sentences that contain more than several parallel verbs. Identical to the past participle (§28), the participial absolute shows neither person nor tense but takes its logical tense from the finite verb at the end of the sentence. When the subject of both the participial absolute and the main verb is the same, that subject is normally expressed before the participial absolute.

حسین وارد اطاق شده نشست.   *hosayn vâred-e otâq shode, neshast.*   Hossein, having come into the room, sat down.

If the subject of the participial absolute is pronominal and different from the subject of the main verb, the pronoun must be expressed.

او وارد اطاق شده همه رفتند.   *u vâred-e otâq shode, hame raftand.*   When he came into the room, everybody left.

The participial absolute may be optionally followed by the co-ordinating conjunction.

بارهای خودمان را بسته (و) براه افتادیم.	*bârhâ-ye khod-emânrâ baste, (va) be râh oftâdim.*	Having tied up our loads, we set out.
فردا به شهر رفته (و) دوستانم را خواهم دید.	*fardâ be shahr rafte, (va) dustân-amrâ khâham did.*	Tomorrow I'll go to town and see my friends.

§54 Reported speech and verbs of sense perception. All speech reported with *goftan* in the past is quoted in the *same tense* in which it was originally stated. In such usage the Persian *ke* that always introduces both direct and indirect speech should be thought of as a type of quotation mark.

گفتم که میآیم.	*goftam ke míâyam.*	I said I **was** coming.
گفت که میآیم.	*goft ke míâyam.*	He said, "I'm coming."
گفت که میآید.	*goft ke míâyad.*	He said he **was** coming.

Similarly, the tense after past verbs of seeing, hearing, knowing, guessing, understanding, etc. (verbs of sense perception) is given in the subordinate clause exactly as it would have been at the moment of perception. This is totally unlike English, where the subordinate verb is sequential according to the tense of the main verb. In Persian, if at the time of perception the verb was present, it remains present; if past, it remains past.

شنیدم که مریضید.	*shenidam ke mariz-id.*	I heard you **were** ill.
وقتی که دیدم که کاظم آنجا نیست حدس زدم که به مدرسه رفته است.	*vâqtike didam ke Kâzem ânjâ nist, hads-zadam ke be madrase rafte-ast.*	When I saw that Kazem **wasn't** there, I guessed he **had gone** on to school.
میدانستم که شما نمیآئید.	*mídânestam ke shomâ némiâid.*	I knew you **weren't** coming.
آنوقت فهمیدم که چرا آنجا نیست.	*ânvaqt fahmidam ke chérâ ânjâ nist.*	Then I understood why he **wasn't** there.

Vocabulary 18

افتادن (افت)   *oftâd-/oft-* to fall, befall

اتفاق افتادن   *ettefâq-oftâdan* for something to happen, occur[1]

باور کردن   *bâvar-kardan* to believe

براه افتادن   *be râh oftâdan* to get under way, start out

بعید   *ba'id* unlikely

پیش آمدن   *pish-âmadan* to come up, happen

حدس زدن   *hads-zadan* to guess

شدن   *shodan* (impersonal) to be possible

نشستن (نشین)   *neshast-/neshin-* to sit, sit down, be seated[2]

واقعه (وقایع)   *vâqe'e* pl *vaqâye'* event, occurrence

Exercise 18

(a) Change the verbs in the following sentences to totally impersonal constructions (e.g., *bâyad béravad > bâyad raft; mítavânad béravad > mitavân raft*):

۱ میتوانم حدس بزنم.

۲ نباید فراموش کنیم.

۳ نمیشود از اینها بترسی.

٤ باید از آن ماجرا تعریف کنند.

٥ ساعت ۱۱ شب باید بخوابیم.

٦ نمیتوانم امیدوار باشم.

۷ نتوانستند آن مطلب را بفهمند.

---

[1]As *diruz ettefâq-i oftâd* "something happened yesterday." In all constructions with this compound verb, *ettefâq* is the subject of *oftâdan*.

[2]The simple past refers only to one instance of sitting down, e.g., *yek sâ'at-e pish injâ neshastam* "I sat down here an hour ago." The narrative tense corresponds to the English "to be sitting, to be seated," e.g., *mâ injâ neshaste-im* "we are sitting here." The present tense is used only of habitual action, e.g., *man hamishe dar haminjâ míneshinam* "I always sit right here."

۸ اینجا نمیشود بنشینید .

۹ نباید حرفهای اورا باور کنید .

۱۰ باید همهٔ اینهارا پیش من ببرند .

(b) Change the underlined verbs to the participial absolute and then translate:

۱ آن اتفاق افتاد و همه برگشتند .

۲ ما براه افتادیم و او در خانه ماند .

۳ واقعهٔ مهمی پیش آمد و نتوانستند بیایند .

٤ آنرا خودم دیدم و باور نمیکنم .

٥ لیلی هنوز نرسیده بود و آنها براه افتادند .

٦ وارد اطاق شدند و نشستند .

۷ به شهر بر میگردیم و همیشه آنجا می‌مانیم .

۸ اورا شناختیم و پیشش رفتیم .

(c) Read and translate into English:

۱ وقتی که فهمیدند که شما نمیخواهید بروید خودشان براه افتادند .

۲ میدانستم که حتماً واقعهٔ خیلی مهمی پیش آمده است .

۳ دیدم که شما در آن ساختمان زندگی میکنید .

٤ حدس زد که چرا هنوز نیامده‌اند .

٥ گفتم که نمی‌شود حرفهایش را باور کرد .

٦ میدانستم که آن اتفاقی که همیشه از آن می‌ترسیدید خواهد افتاد .

۷ شنیدم که همسایگان ممکن است قبل از فردا برگردند .

۸ از کجا میدانستید که زمستان سردی خواهد بود ؟

۹ خیلی بعید است که آن اتفاقی که میگوئید بیفتد .

۱۰ لباسم را درآورده و روی تختخواب دراز کشیده خوابم برد .

(d) Translate into Persian:

1. One can guess that all have gone to sleep.
2. It is not possible to show you those things now.
3. One cannot get lost in that small village.
4. I don't like this color.

5. Should we throw those old things away?
6. Do you believe that such a thing happened?
7. Where do you want to sit?
8. Did Shahla say she was coming to your house tonight?
9. I told Hassan that you wouldn't believe (it).
10. We didn't realize that anything had happened.

Lesson Nineteen

§55 The past subjunctive.

55.1 Formation of the past subjunctive. The past subjunctive is formed from the past participle and the present subjunctive of *budan* (i.e., its formation is similar to that of the past narrative, but the personal endings are subjunctive). Stress remains on the last syllable of the participle in all verbs, simple and compound. The negative past subjunctive is formed by prefixing the negative *ná-* to the participle. Examples of various types are as follows.

رفته باشم	*rafté-bâsham*
برگشته باشی	*bar-gashté-bâshi*
نبوده باشد	*nábude-bâshad*
داشته باشیم	*dâshté-bâshim*
دوست داشته باشید	*dust-dâshté-bâshid*
برنداشته باشند	*bàr-nádâshte-bâshand*

There are no exceptions to this formation. The present and past subjunctives of *dâshtan* are identical.

55.2 Uses of the past subjunctive.

(a) The past subjunctive is used for the doubtful past realization of verbs of necessity ("must have"), possibility ("can have"), desire, wishing, etc., where the complement is anterior to the main verb.

133

باید رفته باشد .	*bâyad rafte-bâshad.*	He must have gone.
باید آن کاررا کرده باشد .	*bâyad ân kâr-râ karde-bâshad.*	He must have done it.
شاید آمده باشند .	*shâyad âmade-bâshand.*	They may have come.
واقعهٔ مهمی باید پیش آمده باشد .	*vâqe'e-ye mohemm-i bâyad pish-âmade-bâshad.*	Some important event must have come up.
نمیتواند آن کاررا کرده باشد .	*némitavânad ân kâr-râ karde-bâshad.*	He can't have done it.
نمیتوانستم آن کاررا کرده باشم .	*némitavânestam ân kâr-râ karde-bâsham.*	I couldn't have done it.
ممکن نیست آن‌را دیده باشید .	*momken nist ân-râ dide-bâshid.*	It isn't possible for you to have seen it.
ممکن نبود آن‌را دیده باشید .	*momken nábud ân-râ dide-bâshid.*	It wasn't possible for you to have seen it.
امیدوارم خیلی به شما خوش گذشته باشد .	*omidvâr-am kháyli be shomâ khosh gozashte-bâshad.*	I hope you have had a really good time.

(b) The past subjunctive is used in past expressions after the conjunctions of condition and concession.

| بشرطی میتوانید بروید که کارتان‌را کرده باشید . | *be shart-i mítavânid béravid ke kâr-etân-râ karde-bâshid.* | You can go provided you have done your work. |
| نمیتوانید یاد گرفته باشید مگر اینکه مدرسه رفته باشید . | *némitavânid yâd-gerefte-bâshid má-gar ínke madrase rafte-bâshid.* | You can't have learned unless you have gone (without having gone) to school. |

| نمیتوانید مسجد گوهر شادرا دیده باشید بجز اینکه مشهد رفته باشید. | *némitavânid masjed-e gawharshâd-râ dide-bâshid **bejoz ínke** mashhad rafte-bâshid.* | You can't have seen the Gawhar-Shad Mosque unless you have gone to Mash-had. |
| حتی اگرهم این کتاب را خودش نوشته باشد افکارش مال او نیست. | ***háttâ agar-ham** in ketâb-râ khod-esh neveshte-bâshad, afkâr-esh mâl-e u nist.* | Even though he may have written this book, the ideas are not his. |

§56 Back-formation of infinitives and denominative verbs. As has been seen, most verbs in Persian have irregular present stems. Many verbs, however, in addition to their original infinitives, have also a "regularized" back-formed infinitive made by adding the regular infinitival ending *-idan* (occasionally *-dan*) to the present stem.

گشتن ‹ گرد ‹ گردیدن   *gashtan > gard- > gardidan* "to turn"[1]

رستن ‹ رو ‹ روئیدن   *rostan > ru- > ruidan* "to grow"

گذاشتن ‹ گذار ‹ گزاردن   *gozâshtan > gozâr- > gozârdan* "to put, place"[2]

This process results in two past stems, usually more or less identical in meaning (although occasionally differing slightly in usage) with one present stem.

The same regular infinitival ending *-idan* is used to form denominative (derived from nouns) verbs.

فهم ‹ فهمیدن   *fahm* "understanding" > *fahmidan* "to understand"

دزد ‹ دزدیدن   *dozd* "thief" > *dozdidan* "to rob"

رقص ‹ رقصیدن   *raqs* "dance" > *raqsidan* "to dance"

---

[1]*Gardidan* is generally used to replace *-shodan* in compounds to avoid excessive repetition. Hence, *vâred-gardidan* could be used to replace *vâred-shodan*.

[2]Note that *gozâshtan* is spelled with zâl, while *gozârdan* is spelled with *ze*.

must come after the noun

§57 Temporal use of *ke*. When the conjunction *ke* is used idiomatically in a temporal sense ("when"), it can never be the first word in the clause; a subject pronoun must be interpolated if necessary. Such temporal clauses generally precede the main clause.

آنها که رفتند ، اکبر آمد .	*ânhâ ke raftand, akbar âmad.*	When they went, Akbar came.
او که مرد تنها ماندند .	*u ke mord, tanhâ mândand.*	When she died they were left alone.
بچه که بودم زندگی ساده‌تر بود .	*bachche ke budam, zendegi sâdetar bud.*	When I was a child life was simpler.
اینطور که حرف میزنی من نمی‌توانم حرفهایت را باورکنم .	*intawr ke harf-mizani, man némitavânam harfhâ-yetrâ bâvar-konam.*	When you talk like this, I can't believe what you say.

The temporal clause follows the main clause only when it introduces a single action that interrupts an on-going, continuous act or when it is preceded by *hanuz* and a negative remote past tense used in the sense of "had scarcely, had barely" (see §41.1c).

کتاب میخواندم که خبرش رسید .	*ketâb mikhândam ke khabar-esh resid.*	I was reading when the news arrived.
رجب صحبت میکرد که مجتبی پا شد و از اطاق خارج شد .	*rajab sohbat mikard ke mojtabâ pâ-shod-o az otâq khârej-shod.*	Rajab was talking when Mojtaba got up and left the room.
به حمام حاج هاشم نزدیک میشدم که قلبم ایستاد .	*be hammâm-e hâjj hâshem nazdik-mishodam ke qalb-am istâd.*	I was approaching the Hajj Hashem Bath when my heart stood still.
من هنوز بیدار نشده بودم که صدای سماوررا شنیدم .	*man hanuz bidâr-náshode-budam ke sedâ-ye samâvar-râ shenidam.*	I had scarcely waked up when I heard the sound of the samovar.

subjunct. + adam

§58 Impersonals with *âdam*. The totally impersonal construction (§52) is used where the impersonal "one" is the subject of the main verb. When the impersonal is other than subject, the impersonal pronoun *âdam* "one" is used. It is always construed as specific.

نمیتوان آدم را باین آسانی گول زد .	*nemitavân âdam-râ be in âsâni gul-zad.*	It's not possible to fool **one** so easily.
نمیگذارند آدم کار خودرا بکند .	*némigozârand âdam kâr-e khod-râ bókonad.*	They won't let **one** do one's work.
چرا آدم را آنقدر اذیت میکنند ؟	*chérâ âdam-râ ânqadr aziyat-mikonand?*	Why do they annoy **one** so?

Vocabulary 19

آنطور	*ântawr*	thus, like that
اگر	*ágar*	if
اینطور	*intawr*	thus, like this
برخاستن (برخیز)	*bar-khâst-/bar-khiz-*	to rise up, stand up (literary)
بشرطی که	*beshart-i-ke*	provided that
پا شدن	*pâ-shodan*	to get up, stand up (colloquial)
پیش / قبل ‑e	*-e pish*	ago
تنها	*tanhâ*[1]	alone, only
(ب)جز	*(be)joz*[2]	(+ neg.) except, only
(ب)جز اینکه	*(be)joz in-ke*	unless
حتی	*háttâ*	even
فکر (افکار)	*fekr* pl *afkâr*	idea, thought

---

[1]As an attributive and predicate adjective, *tanhâ* means "alone, by oneself." When it means "only," it precedes the word it modifies, e.g., *tanhâ chiz-i ke...* "the only thing that...."

[2]*(Be)joz* must have a complementary negative and means "(nothing) except," as in *joz in-râ hich-i némikhâham* "I don't want anything except this," or "I want only this."

فکر کردن *fekr-kardan* to think

قوی *qavi* strong, powerful

کشتن (کش) *kosht-/kosh-* to kill

مگر اینکه *mágar in-ke* unless

مطمئن *motma'enn* sure, certain

نمودن (نما) *nemud-/nemâ-*[1] to appear, seem; represent, show

یاد *yâd*[2] memory

یاد دادن *yâd-dâdan* to teach

یاد گرفتن *yâd-gereftan* to learn

Exercise 19

(a) Give the appropriate past subjunctive form of the verbs in parentheses and then translate:

۱ علی و رضا باید دیروز ——— (رفتن) .

۲ خیلی بعید است چنان واقعه‌ای ——— (پیش آمدن) .

۳ فکر نمیکنم آن اتفاقی که میگفتید ——— (افتادن) .

٤ امکان دارد آنها قبل از ما ——— (براه افتادن) .

٥ امیدوارم که محمد آنهارا به شما ——— (نشان دادن) .

٦ نمی‌توانید این چیزهارا ارزان ——— (خریدن) .

۷ همسایه‌هایتان باید جای دیگری ——— (رفتن) .

۸ آن آقا باحتمال قوی باید دو روز پیش ——— (برگشتن) .

۹ ممکن نیست که من وارد خانهٔ شما ——— (شدن) .

۱۰ او شاید آنهارا ——— (کشتن) .

[handwritten margin notes: "only subjunctive w/ either past or present"; "بعید"; "پیش بیاید"; "for present, add ب"]

---

[1]By itself this verb means "to appear, seem." It is quite often used as a replacement for -*kardan* in compounds to avoid excessive repetition, and in that case it loses its primary meaning. The first vowel of *nemudan* is variable; it is pronounced *nemud-*, *namud-* and *nomud-*.

[2]*Yâd* also occurs in common expressions for which there is no infinitival construction: *yâd-am âmad* "I remembered" and *yâd-am raft* "I forgot." These expressions are used in all tenses and moods. Like the impersonals *khâb-am âmad* and *khâb-am bord*, the verb is always third-person singular with *yâd* as the subject; the subject of the English construction is expressed as a pronominal enclitic after *yâd*.

۱۱ شما نمی‌توانید این را قبلاً ــــــ (دیدن) .

۱۲ امکان ندارد که ما اینهمه را ــــــ (یاد گرفتن) .

۱۳ تنها چیزی که آنها ممکن است ــــــ (ندیدن) این است.

۱٤ شما شاید ــــــ (یاد رفتن) .

۱٥ نمی‌تواند این کار را ــــــ (کردن) بجز اینکه خوب ــــــ (یاد گرفتن) .

یاد بگیراد   بکند   +Future

(b) Read and translate the following:

۱ تنها واقعه‌ای که پیش آمد زیاد مهم نبود.

۲ آنقدر قیمتها گران شده است که مگر اینکه آدم خیلی پولدار باشد
نمی‌تواند کوچکترین چیزی را بخرد .

۳ حدس زدم که خیلی بعید است آنها هم همچنان فکر کنند .

٤ یادتان نرود چند تا تخم مرغ از دکان[1] بیاورید .

٥ ماشین ما پنج دقیقه راه نرفته بود که دهی که در آن ناهار خورده بودیم
ناپدید شد.[2]

٦ فکر می‌کردم که همانجا نشسته‌اید .

۷ بشرطی می‌توانید بنشینید که جا باشد .

۸ پیش از اینکه آن جعبه‌ها را ببندیم مطمئن باشیم که همه چیز درست است.

۹ به او گفتم که همانجا بنشیند و برنخیزد .

۱۰ ساعت شش بعد از ظهر ۲۹ اسفندماه ۱۳۲۹ بود که به اصفهان
رسیدیم .

for Monday

(c) Translate the following into Persian:

1. I must have eaten something bad this morning.
2. He can't have died: I saw him just yesterday.
3. Her life must have been relatively quiet.
4. You can't have seen me last year unless you were in Iran too.
5. Get up (sing.)! Let's go to town.
6. Even the children here seem old: they must have seen a lot of
   evil.

---

[1]*Dokkân* shop, store.

[2]*Nâhâr* lunch; *nâpadid-shodan* to disappear from view.

7. Ali can't have gone to sleep already.
8. It's not possible for them to have thrown all my books away!
9. They should be here at six o'clock, provided nothing bad has happened.
10. The only thing I know is that (in-ast ke) they are sitting in that room.

انشا

Composition. (half a page) Write a short composition either on what you do every morning or on what you did this morning.

اطاق خواب	*otâq-e khâb* bed-room	ریش تراشیدن	*rish-tarâshidan* to shave
بلند شدن	*boland-shodan* to get up	سرکار رفتن	*sar-e kâr raftan* to go to work
بیدار شدن	*bidâr-shodan* to wake up	سرکلاس رفتن	*sar-e kelâs raftan* to go to class
جمع کردن	*jam'-kardan* to gather together	سروصورت شستن	*sarosurat shostan* to wash the face
چای درست کردن	*chây dorost-kardan* to fix tea		
حمام	*hammâm* bath-room	سوار اتوبوس شدن	*savâr-e otobus shodan* to get on a bus
خمیر دندان	*khamir-e dandân* toothpaste	صابون	*sâbun* soap
دستشوئی	*dastshui* wash-basin *(dam-e dastshui* at the washbasin)	صبحانه درست کردن	*sobhâne dorost-kardan* to fix breakfast
دندان پاک کردن	*dandân pâk-kardan* to brush the teeth	غلت زدن	*qalt-zadan* to toss and turn
دندان پاک کن	*dandânpâkkon* toothbrush	قهوه درست کردن	*qahve dorost-kardan* to fix coffee
دوش گرفتن	*dush-gereftan* to take a shower	لباس پوشیدن	*lebâs-pushidan* to get dressed
رختخواب	*rakhtekhâb* bed-clothes, sheets		

کسی که فارسی بلد باشد ⟵

somebody/anybody who knows Persian

↯ anytime it is in subjunctive, makes The sentence indefinite
(use a instead of The)

کسی که فارسی بلد است ⟵

The person who knows Persian.

Lesson Twenty

§59 Uses of the subjunctive III: Adjectival clauses. The subjunctive is used in adjectival clauses of the following types.

59.1 When the antecedent of the relative clause is indefinite. Compare and contrast the indicative with the subjunctive in the following examples:

↯ indefinite
↯ so it is in subj.

دنبال کسی میگردم که فارسی بلد باشد .	*dombâl-e **kas-i** mí-gardam ke fârsi balad **bâshad**.*	I'm looking for someone who knows Persian.[1]
دنبال آن مردی میگردم که فارسی بلد است .	*dombâl-e **ân mard-i** mígardam ke fârsi balad-**ast**.*	I'm looking for the man who knows Persian.
سعی میکنم چیزی را پیدا کنم که بکار ببرم .	*sa'y-mikonam **chiz-i-râ** paydâ-konam ke be kâr **bébaram**.*	I'm trying to find something I can use.
سعی میکنم آن چیزی را پیدا کنم که شما بکار بردید .	*sa'y-mikonam **ân chiz-i-râ** paydâ konam ke shomâ be kâr **bordid**.*	I'm trying to find the thing you used.

This type of indefinite adjectival clause includes all the relative pronouns and conjunctions like *hárche* "whatever," *hárke* "whoever,"

---

[1] In this sentence *kas-i* is indefinite, i.e., anyone who knows Persian will qualify.

141

hárkojâ "wherever," *hárvaqt* "whenever" and *hárchand* "however much." These same relative words are used also as definite, in which case they mean "everything that," "everyone who," "everywhere" and "every time that" and are followed by the indicative. Contrast the following pairs and note especially the present and past subjunctives.

هرکه بیاید باید صبر کند .	*hárke bíâyad, bâyad sabr-konad.*	Whoever comes must wait.
هرکه میاید دلش میخواهد بماند .	*hárke míâyad, del-esh míkhâhad[1] bémânad.*	Everybody who comes wants to stay.
هرکه آمده باشد نمیخواهم اورا ببینم .	*hárke âmade-bâshad, némi-khâham u-râ bébinam.*	Whoever may have come, I don't want to see him.
هرکه رفته است خوشش آمده .	*hárke rafte-ast, khosh-esh âmade.*	Everybody who has gone has liked it.
هرچه بگویم فرقی نمیکند .	*hárche béguyam, farq-i némikonad.*	Whatever I may say, it won't make any difference.
هرچه میگوید درست است .	*hárche míguyad, dorost-ast.*	Everything he says is right.
هرکجا بروم بازهم به همینجا برمیگردم .	*hárkojâ béravam, bâz-ham be haminjâ bar-migardam.*	Wherever I may go, I'll still come back here.
هرکجا میروم چیز جالبی پیدا میکنم .	*hárkojâ míravam, chiz-e jâleb-i paydâ-mikonam.*	Everywhere I go I find something interesting.
هروقت بیاید بگوئید من نیستم .	*hárvaqt bíâyad béguid man nistam.*	Whenever he comes, say I'm not here.

---

[1]The construction *del-esh míkhâhad*, literally "his heart wants," is the normal construction in spoken Persian for "want" in the present tense and provides a contrast with the auxiliary *khâstan* in the present tense, which generally means "about to" (see p. 115, note 3), e.g., *del-am míkhâhad béravam* "I want to go" versus *míkhâham béravam* "I'm about to go, I'm going to go."

| هروقت میاید اقلاً پنج ساعت میماند . | *hárvaqt míâyad aqallan panj sâ'at mímânad.* | Every time he comes he stays at least five hours. |

all negatives & questions have a subjunction

59.2 The subjunctive complements any negative expression.

هیچکس آنجا نبود که فارسی حرف بزند .	*hichkas ânjâ nábud ke fârsi harf-bezanad.*	There was no one there who could speak Persian.
من حمال نیستم که آن صندوقهارا ببرم .	*man hammâl nistam ke ân sanduqhâ-râ bébaram.*	I'm no porter that I should carry those trunks.
اینجا هیچی نیست که بدرد شما بخورد .	*injâ hich-i nist ke be dard-e shomâ bókhorad.*	There's nothing here that could be of any use to you.
هیچ کسیرا ندیدم که آن کتاب را نخوانده باشد .	*hichkas-i-râ nádidam ke ân ketâb-râ ná-khânde-bâshad.*	I never saw anyone who hadn't read that book.
فکر نمیکنم این بدردتان بخورد .	*fekr-némikonam in be dard-etân bókhorad.*	I don't think this will be of any use to you.
این چیزی نیست که آنها ندانند .	*in chiz-i nist ke ânhâ nádânand.*	This is nothing they don't know.

+too

59.3 The subjunctive is used after comparatives with *az ân-ke.* This usage corresponds generally to the English "too...to do something."

| شما باهوشتر از آن هستید که حرفهای اورا باورکنید . | *shomâ bâhushtar az ân hastid ke harfhâ-ye u-râ bâvar-konid.* | You're too intelligent to believe what he says. |
| بزرگتر از آنست که اینطور گریه کند . | *bozorgtar az ân-ast ke intawr gerye-konad.* | He's too big to cry like this. |

59.4 The present subjunctive is used after *kâsh(ki)* "would that, I wish" for wishes in the future. Unfulfilled wishes in the past will be given in §62.

143

| کاش اینطور بماند. | *kâsh intawr bémânad.* | I wish it would stay like this. |
| کاشکی بیایند. | *kâshki bíâyand.* | I wish they would come. |

59.5 The subjunctive is used in descriptive clauses after *mesl-e* "like" and *mesl-e in-ke* "as though."

| مثل گربه‌ای که به بچه‌اش ور برود اصغر با افسر بازی میکرد. | *mesl-e gorbe-i-ke be bachche-ash var-beravad asqar bâ afsar bâzi-mikard.* | Like a cat fooling around with its young, Asghar toyed with Afsar. |
| مثل پلنگی که جفت خودرا گم کرده باشد غرش میکرد. | *mesl-e palang-i-ke joft-e khod-râ gom-karde-bâshad, qorresh-mikard.* | He growled like a panther that had lost its mate. |

§60 Uses of the infinitive.

60.1 The Persian infinitive functions like the English gerund, or verbal noun in "-ing," and is used substantively as the subject of a verb and complement of a preposition.

غم خوردن فایده ندارد.	*qam-khordan fâyede nádârad.*	There's no use in being sad.
از گریه کردن خسته شد.	*az gerye-kardan khaste-shod.*	He grew tired of crying.
قبل از وارد شدن در زدم.	*qabl-az vâred-shodan dar-zadam.*	I knocked before entering.
بچه‌ها شروع به دویدن کردند.	*bachchehâ shoru' be davidan kardand.*	The children started running.

60.2 Adverbial modifiers of the infinitive precede the infinitive and form compounds.

| زود رسیدن فایده ندارد . | *zud-residan fâyede nâdârad.* | There's no use in arriving early. |
| توجه داشته باشید به صحیح نوشتن . | *tavajjoh-dâshte-bâshid be sahih-neveshtan.* | Pay attention to writing correctly. |

60.3 Semantic objects of the infinitive.

(a) Non-determinate and generic infinitival objects precede the infinitive and form compounds.

رخت شستن در چنین خانه‌هائی سخت بود .	*rakht-shostan dar chonin khânahâ-i sakht bud.*	Clothes-washing in such houses was difficult.
تمبر جمع کردن سرگرمی خوبیست .	*tambr-jam'-kardan sargarmi-e khub-i-st.*	Stamp-collecting is a good hobby.
آب گرم کردن مشکل نیست .	*âb-garm-kardan moshkel nist.*	It's not difficult to heat water.

(b) When the subject of the infinitive is not expressed, modified and definite objects are either linked to the infinitive by the *ezâfe* or occur as pronominal enclitics.

شستن رختهای کثیف یك كار همیشگی است .	*shostan-e rakhthâ-ye kasif yek kâr-e hamishegi-ast.*	Washing dirty clothes is a never-ending job.
از دیدنتان خوشحالیم .	*az didan-etân khoshhâl-im.*	We're happy to see you.
بعد از دیدن آنها یادم آمد که آنهارا قبلاً هم دیده بودم .	*ba'd-az didan-e ânhâ, yâd-am âmad ke ânhâ-râ qablan-ham dide-budam.*	After seeing them, I remembered I had seen them before.

(c) Infinitival subjects are linked to the infinitive by the *ezâfe* when there is no object.

145

| قبل از وارد شدن آنها در رفته بودم. | qabl-az vâred-shodan-e ânhâ darrafte-budam. | I had run away before they came in (before their coming in). |
| بعد از سرشناس شدنش دیگر به دوستان قدیمیش سر نمی‌زد. | ba'd-az sarshenâs-shodan-esh digar be dustân-e qadimi-esh sar-némizad. | After becoming well known, he no longer visited his old friends. |

In modern Persian both subject and definite object of an infinitive cannot be expressed together. Such a construction as "my seeing you," classically expressed by *didan-e man shomâ-râ,* must now be circumlocuted as a noun clause ("the fact that I saw you").

(d) When an infinitive serves as complement to an adjective, it is linked by the *ezâfe.*

صبح زود آمادهٔ رفتن بود.	sobh-e zud âmâde-ye raftan bud.	He was ready to go early in the morning.
سرگرم نامه نوشتنیم.	sargarm-e nâme-neveshtan-im.	We're busy writing letters.
مشغول ظرف شستنم.	mashqul-e zarf-shostan-am.	I'm busy washing dishes.
مشغول شستن ظرفهای کثیفم.	mashqul-e shostan-e zarfhâ-ye kasif-am.	I'm busy washing the dirty dishes.

(e) The infinitive after *dar hâl-e* often translates into an English progressive tense (like the French *en train de faire).*

| ما در حال گوش کردن بودیم و او در حال صحبت کردن. | mâ dar hâl-e gush-kardan budim-o u dar hâl-e sohbat-kardan. | We were listening, and he was speaking. |

146

Vocabulary 20

به درد خوردن   *be dard(-e kas-i) khordan*[1] to be of use (to someone)

بلد بودن   *balad-budan*[2] to know (how)

بی آنکه   *bi ân-ke* without[3] ~~followed by subj.~~ *personal*

جالب   *jâleb* nice, interesting

دنبال گشتن   *dombâl-e chiz-i/kas-i gashtan* to look/search for something/somebody

سرگرم   *sargarm*[4] busy *(positive word-pleasurable)*

سعی کردن   *sa'y-kardan* to try (+ present subj.)

سینما   *sinemâ* cinema, movie theater

شروع شدن   *shoru'-shodan* to start, begin (intransitive)

شروع کردن به   *shoru'-kardan* to begin, start (*be* + infinitive, doing something)

شستن (شو)   *shost-/shu-* to wash

غم   *qam* grief

غم خوردن   *qam-khordan* to be sad, grieve

فایده (فواید)   *fâyede* pl *favâyed* benefit, use

فرق   *farq* difference

فرق کردن   *farq-kardan bâ* to make a difference to someone

---

[1]The one for whom something is of use or benefit is expressed as an *ezâfe* complement of *dard*, e.g., *inhâ be dard-e man némikhorand* "these are of no use to me."

[2]What one knows is a noun complement of *balad-budan*, e.g., *fârsi balad-am* "I know Persian." "To know how to do something" is expressed as a following subjunctive, e.g., *balad-am fârsi harf-bezanam* "I know how to speak Persian."

[3]"Without" in English is followed by a gerund; in Persian *bi ân-ke* is followed by a subjunctive, necessarily personal, e.g., *bi ân-ke béravid, némibinid* "without going you won't see it."

[4]Both *sargarm* and *mashqul* are followed by either a complementary noun or an infinitive with the *ezâfe,* or they are preceded by *be* + noun or infinitive, e.g., *man sargarm/mashqul-e in kâr-am* or *man be in kâr sargarm/masqul-am* "I'm busy with this job." *Mashqul* refers to occupation in a rather broad sense, whereas *sargarm* is restricted to pleasurable activities generally.

147

فیلم *film* film, movie

گریه کردن *gerye-kardan* to cry, weep

مثل اینکه *mesl-e in-ke* (+ subj.) as though

مشغول *mashqul* busy, occupied (pos. or neg.)

هرچند *hárchand* however much/many

هرچه *hárche* whatever

هرکجا *hárkojâ* wherever

هرکه *hárke* whoever → regardless of tense indefinite

هروقت *hárvaqt* whenever

می‌آید ← everybody who come

Exercise 20

(a) Complete the following sentences using the verbs given in parentheses and then translate:

۱ دنبال کار جالبی میگردم که ــــ (کردن) .

۲ ما سرگرم ــــ (یاد گرفتن) فارسی هستیم .

۳ فکر میکنید آنها بلدند جواب درستی ــــ (دادن)؟

٤ هرچند زندگانیت سخت ــــ (بودن) ، باید امید ــــ (داشتن) .

٥ بعد از (رسیدن) رضا ، ما همه براه افتادیم .

٦ هرکه چنین سؤالی را ــــ (کردن) حتماً خوب ــــ (یاد نگرفتن) .

٧ شما هرکجا اینها را ــــ (گذاشتن) فرقی نمیکند .

٨ قبل از ــــ (شناختن) اش فکر میکردم کسی دیگر است .

٩ شما هرچه ــــ (گم کردن) باید ــــ (پیدا کردن) .

۱۰ سه ساعت پیش شروع کردم به ــــ (خواندن) این کتاب و هنوز هم ــــ (خواندن) .

۱۱ چرا سعی میکنند جوانتر از آنکه ــــ (بودن) ــــ (نمودن)؟

۱۲ آنطور که او ــــ (گریه کردن) باید اتفاقی خیلی بدی برایش ــــ (افتادن) .

۱۳ آن بچه کوچکتر از آن است که ــــ (مدرسه رفتن) .

(b) Translate into Persian:

1. Whoever said that must not know anything at all.

2. Whatever you do and wherever you go, they will be looking for you.

3. I'm trying to tell you about my friends in Iran.

4. Zahra is too clever to listen to what he has to say.

5. Before coming here, by chance I found something that may be of use to you.

6. I like learning things I didn't know before.

7. He's trying to find something to do tonight.

8. This won't be of any use to you unless you learn it well.

9. I don't think the film has started, and the theater isn't far.

10. He started speaking before he stood up.

Supplementary Vocabulary: Common Materials

The adjectival form is indicated in parentheses. Although almost all materials are theoretically capable of taking the -in ("made of") adjectival, suffix, in practice not all do so.

آجر	*âjor* baked brick, tile	سرب	*sorb(i)* lead
آلومینیوم	*âluminium* aluminium	سفال	*sofâl(in)* clay
آهن	*âhan(in)* iron	سنگ	*sang(i)* stone
ابر	*abr(i)* form rubber	سیمان	*simân* cement
ابریشم	*abrisham(i)* silk	شیشه	*shishe(i)* glass
استخوان	*ostakhân(in)* bone	طلا	*talâ(i)* gold
برنج	*berenj(i)* brass	فلز	*felezz(i)* -ât metal
بلور	*bolur(in)* crystal	قلعی	*qal'i* tin
پارچه	*pârche(i)* cloth	قیر	*qir* tar
پلاستیك	*pelâstik(i)* plastic	کاشی	*kâshi* glazed tile
پشم	*pashm(in)* wool	کاغذ	*kâqaz(i)* paper
پنبه	*pambe(i)* cotton	کاه	*kâh(i)* straw
چرم	*charm(in)* leather	کاهگل	*kâhgel(i)* mudbrick
چوب	*chub(in)* wood	کتان	*kattân(i)* linen
چینی	*chini* china	گچ	*gach(i)* plaster
حلبی	*halabi* tinplate	لاستیك	*lâstik(i)* rubber
خشت	*khesht* brick	مس	*mes(i)* copper

مقوا *moqavvâ(i)* cardboard نقره *noqre(i)* silver

Review IV

(a) Review the vocabulary lists for lessons 16–20.

(b) Read and translate:

۱ هیچ خوشم نمیآید دنبال چنین چیزهائی بگردم .

۲ نمیتوانید حدس بزنید ما کجا بودهایم .

۳ هروقت وارد خانهٔ او میشوند مشغول کار دیگریست .

٤ نه غم خوردنتان نه گریه کردنتان فایده دارد .

٥ معمولاً نمیشود اینهارا تغییر داد .

٦ نمیتوانید ایشانرا قبلاً دیده باشید .

۷ ممکن است آنها بهتر از شما بلد باشند .

۸ باور میکنید که امکان دارد که اوهم چنین کاریرا کرده باشد؟

۹ کار ما زیاد پیش نرفته بود که فهمیدیم لازم است کسی دیگر داشته
باشیم .

۱۰ سعی کن پیش از برگشتن پدرت این چیزهارا دور انداخته باشی

(c) Translate the following into Persian:

1. Don't you want to get under way early tomorrow?
2. It makes no difference to me where you found them. Give
them to me!
3. Before you get up, let me say this.
4. We cannot go forward. What should we do now?
5. Have you forgotten to throw those things away?
6. It's possible for you to have a good time there.
7. He said he was coming, but I don't think he knows the way.
8. What time do they usually go to sleep?
9. He doesn't want to tell about that event.
10. I don't love you anymore.

field رشته (field handwritten)

Additional Vocabulary: Academic Fields and Related Vocabulary

ادبیات *adabiyât* literature

اقتصاد *eqtesâd* economics

الهیات *elâhiyât* divinity

بخش *bakhsh* department

پزشکی/طب *pezeshki/tebb* medicine

تاریخ *târikh* history

تخصص *takhassos* specialization

تطبیقی *tatbiqi* comparative

تمدن *tamaddon* civilization

جامعه‌شناسی *jâme'eshenâsi* sociology

جانورشناسی *jânevarshenâsi* zoology

جغرافیا *joqrâfiâ* geography

جنگلداری *jangaldâri* forestry

حقوق *hoquq* law

خاورشناسی *khâvarshenâsi* oriental studies

دانشکده *dâneshkade* faculty, school

دندانپزشکی *dandânpezeshki* dentistry

رشته *reshte* field

روانشناسی *ravânshenâsi* psychology

روانکاوی *ravânkâvi* psychiatry

ریاضیات *riâziyât* mathematics

زبانشناسی *zabânshenâsi* linguistics

زمینشناسی *zaminshenâsi* geology

زیستشناسی *zistshenâsi* biology

ستاره‌شناسی *setâreshenâsi* astronomy

شیمی *shimi* chemistry

علوم سیاسی *olum-e siâsi* political science

فرهنگ *farhang* culture

فلسفه *falsafe* philosophy

فیزیک *fizik* physics

مردمشناسی *mardomshenâsi* anthropology

معماری *me'mâri* architecture

موسیقی *musiqi* music

مهندسی *mohandesi* engineering

هنرهای زیبا *honarhâ-ye zibâ* fine arts

religion ← مزهب (maz-hab)
religious ← مزهبی
middle-east ← خاور میانه

Lesson Twenty-One

§61 Conditionals. Conditional constructions in Persian are divided into two basic categories, possible and impossible. In the following discussion the two terms protasis (the "if" clause) and apodosis (the result clause) will be used. The word for "if" in Persian is always *ágar*.

61.1 Possible conditionals are further divided into the doubtful and the actual.

(a) In actual conditionals the protasis refers to an action or state that is assumed to be real and actually pertaining. In this type the verb of the protasis is indicative, and "if" really means "since."

اگر میدانید چرا نمیگوئید؟	*agar mídânid, chérâ némiguid?*	If you know, why don't you say so?
اگر میروید میتوانید مارا هم همراه ببرید.	*agar míravid, mí-tavânid mâ-râ-ham hamrâh bébarid.*	If you're going, you can take us along too.

(b) The doubtful conditional *(possible)* is the type in which the condition set forth in the protasis may or may not be fulfilled. In doubtful conditionals referring to present or future time, the verb of the protasis may be either present subjunctive or past absolute; the verb of the apodosis may be present, future or imperative. Although there is very little difference between the present subjunctive and past absolute in the doubtful conditional, the subjunctive implies actual doubt on the part of the speaker as to whether or not the condition can be fulfilled. The past absolute is

152

LESSON TWENTY-ONE

used when the speaker is less concerned with the doubtfulness of the situation than with the eventuality of the condition.

اگر ببینمش (دیدمش) سلام شمارا میرسانم.	*agar bébinam-esh (didam-esh), salâm-e shomâ-râ míresâ-nam.*	If I see him I'll give him your regards.
اگر اورا پیدا کنم (کردم) میکشمش!	*agar u-râ paydâ-konam (-kardam), míkosham-esh!*	If I find him I'll kill him!
اگر بروید (رفتید) اینهارا فراموش نکنید.	*agar béravid (raftid), inhâ-râ farâmush-nákonid.*	If you go, don't forget these.

Doubtful conditionals referring to past time take the past subjunctive in the protasis.

اگر اورا دیده باشید پس میدانید من چه میگویم.	*agar u-râ dide-bâshid, pas mídânid man che míguyam.*	If you've seen him, then you know what I'm talking about.
اگر گناه کرده باشد باید اعتراف کند.	*agar gonâh-karde-bâshad, bâyad e' terâf-konad.*	If he has done something wrong, he should admit it.
اگر چنین کاری را کرده باشد خیلی زحمت کشیده است.	*agar chonin kâr-i-râ karde-bâshad, kháyli zahmat-keshide-ast.*	If he has done such a thing, he has gone to a lot of trouble.

61.2 The impossible conditional, also called contrafactual and irrealis, that is, the conditional that either cannot be fulfilled in the future or cannot have been fulfilled in the past, uses the *past continuous tense* in both protasis and apodosis as the irrealis mood. Inasmuch as Persian does not normally distinguish between past irrealis ("if I had been") and future irrealis ("if I were to be"), the correct tense for translation into English must be gained from context.

اگر می‌آمدید شمارا می‌دیدم.	agar *míâmadid*, shomâ-râ *mídidam*.	If you had come, I would have seen you.[1]
اگر می‌گفتند مجبور میشدیم برویم.	agar *mígoftand*, majbur-*mishodim* béravim.	If they had said so, we would have been obliged to go.[2]
اگر بحرفهای من گوش می‌کردید اینطور نمی‌شد.	agar be harfhâ-ye man gush-*mikardid*, intawr *némishod*.	If you had listened to me, it wouldn't have turned out like this.

Remember that *dâshtan* (and *dust-dâshtan*) and *budan* do not normally take the continuous *mí-* prefix, even in the irrealis.

اگر جای شما بودم آن کاررا نمی‌کردم.	agar jâ-ye shomâ *budam*, ân kâr-râ *némikardam*.	If I had been (were) in your place, I wouldn't have done (wouldn't do) it.
اگر من چنین چیزی‌را داشتم نمیفروختم.	agar man chonin chiz-irâ *dâshtam*, némi-forukhtam.	If I had such a thing, I wouldn't have sold (wouldn't sell) it.

In less formal and colloquial Persian the past irrealis may be expressed in either or both parts of the conditional by the remote past.

اگر اورا دیده بوده بودم به او گفته بودم.	agar u-râ *dide-bu-dam*, be u *gofte-budam*.[3]	If I had seen him, I would have told him.
اگر اینجا مانده بود نمرده بود.	agar injâ *mânde-bud*, námorde-bud.[4]	If he had stayed here he wouldn't have died.

61.3 In conditionals of all types *agar* is often omitted, particularly in less formal Persian. When it is omitted in possible conditionals, the

---

[1] Or, if you were to come, I would see you.

[2] Or, if they were to say so, we would be obliged to go.

[3] Or, *agar u-râ mídidam, be u mígoftam.*

[4] Or, *agar injâ mímând, némimord.*

154

subjunctive is used in the protasis. In contrafactual conditionals both verbs are in the irrealis (past continuous).

بخواهید موفق شوید باید زحمت بکشید.	*békhâhid movaffaq-shavid, bâyad zah-mat-bekeshid.*	If you want to succeed, you must work hard.
کارم تمام بشود همراهتان میآیم.	*kâr-am tamâm béshavad, hamrâh-etân míâyam.*	If my work is finished I'll come along with you.
ترمزم نمیگرفت چکار میکردیم؟	*tormoz-am némi-gereft, chekâr-mikardim?*	If my brakes hadn't held, what would we have done?
نمیگرفت ، فوقش میمردیم و راحت میشدیم.	*némigereft, fawq-esh mímordim-o râhat-mishodim.*	If they hadn't held, at most we would've died and been at peace.

§62 Other irrealis constructions. The irrealis mood (past continuous) is not limited to conditionals but is used for unfulfilled obligation ("should have," cf. "must have" in 55.2a) with *bâyad* and its synonyms *(mí)bâyest(i)*.

باید میرفتم.	*bâyad míraftam.*	I should have gone.
بایست میآمدند.	*bâyest míâmadand.*	They should've come.
بایستی میدانستید که ما نمیآئیم.	*bâyésti mídânestid ke mâ némiâim.*	You should've known we weren't coming.
میبایستی کاری میکردیم.	*míbâyesti kâr-i míkardim.*	We should've done something.

All constructions that normally require the subjunctive are put into the irrealis mood when they are contrafactual.

بهتر بود که دیروز زودتر میرفتیم.	*behtar bud (ke) diruz zudtar míraftim.*	It would have been better for us to have gone earlier yesterday.

| بهتر بود نمی‌آمدید. | *behtar bud némi-âmadid.* | It would have been better if you hadn't come. |

The irrealis mood occurs after *kâsh(ki)* ("would that, I wish") for unfulfilled wishes in the past (cf. §59.4).

کاشکی می‌آمد.	*kâshki miâmad.*	Would that he had come.
کاش من بدنیا نمی‌آمدم.	*kâsh man be donyâ némiâmadam.*	I wish I had never been born.
کاشکی اینجا بودید.	*kâshki injâ budid.*	I wish you were here.

§63 Expressions of temporal duration. In present expressions of temporal duration, where English uses the present perfect, the length of time is given in Persian with *-ast* followed by *ke* (optional) and (1) the present tense of "to be":

| سه سال است (که) اینجا هستم. | *se sâl-ast (ke) injâ hastam.* | I've been here three years. |
| خیلی وقت است (که) اینطور است. | *kháyli vaqt-ast (ke) intawr-ast.* | He's been like this for a long time. |

(2) the past narrative of states, where English uses the present perfect (this category includes most negatives):

شش سال است که اورا ندیده‌ام.	*shesh sâl-ast (ke) u-râ nádideam.*	I haven't seen him for six years.
دو هفته است که از خانه بیرون نرفته است.	*do hafte-ast (ke) az khâne birun nárafteast.*	He hasn't gone out of the house for two weeks.
پنج سال است که شوهرش مرده است.	*panj sâl-ast (ke) shawhar-esh morde-ast.*	Her husband has been dead for five years.
دو ساعت است که همانجا نشسته‌اید.	*do sâ'at-ast (ke) hamânjâ neshaste-id.*	You've been sitting there for two hours.

است + budeham
present + narrative
past + remote absolute (something follows after, normally
bud + mordebud   w/ ke

156

(3) the present continuous of actions, where English uses the progressive present perfect:

دو ساعت است که کار میکنم.	*do sâ'at-ast (ke) kâr-mikonam.*	I've been working for two hours.
سه روز است که باران میبارد.	*se ruz-ast (ke) bârân míbârad.*	It's been raining for three days.

In past expressions of temporal duration, the length of time is given with *-bud* followed by (1) the past absolute of *budan*:

سه سال بود که آنجا بودم که...	*se sâl-bud (ke) ânjâ budam ke...*	I had been there for three years when...

(2) the remote past of states:

شش سال بود که اورا ندیده بودم.	*shesh sâl bud (ke) u-râ nádide-budam.*	I hadn't seen him for six years.
پنج سال بود که شوهرش مرده بود.	*panj sâl bud (ke) shawhar-esh morde-bud.*	Her husband had been dead for five years.

(3) the past continuous of on-going actions:

سه روز بود که باران می‌بارید.	*se ruz bud (ke) bârân míbârid.*	It had been raining for three days.

"Since" followed by the present perfect in English is rendered in Persian by *az váqtike* (or equivalent) followed by the present.

از وقتیکه من اینجا هستم اورا ندیده‌ام.	*az váqtike man injâ hastam, u-râ ná-dideam.*	Since I've been here I haven't seen him.
از وقتی که با امثال آنها سر و کار دارد اورا ندیده‌ایم.	*az váqtike bâ amsâl-e ânhâ sar-o kâr dârad, u-râ ná-dideim.*	Ever since he's been dealing with the likes of them, we haven't seen him.

از روزی که اورا *az ruz-ike u-râ*   He's been like this
میشناسم همینطور است. *míshenâsam,*   ever since the first
hamintawr-ast.   day I came to know
him.

Vocabulary 21

باران	*bârân* rain
باران باریدن	*bârân-bâridan* or *-âmadan* to rain
بایست ، بایستی	*(mi)bâyest(i) = bâyad*
بر	*bar* (prep.) over, upon, at, against (highly idiomatic)
برف	*barf* snow
برف باریدن	*barf-bâridan* or *-âmadan* to snow
پرسیدن	*porsidan* to ask (*az* someone)
تمام	*tamâm-e* all of, the whole...
تمام شدن	*tamâm-shodan* to be finished, over
تمام کردن	*tamâm-kardan* to finish (trs.)
جستن (جو)	*jost-/ju-* to seek[1]
جستجو کردن	*jostoju-kardan* to search for, seek
چراغ	*cherâq* light, lamp
حال (احوال)	*hâl* pl *ahvâl* condition, state
خاموش	*khâmush* silent; off, out (light, machinery)
خاموش کردن	*khâmush-kardan* to turn out, turn off, silence
روشن	*rawshan* lit, light, bright
روشن کردن	*rawshan-kardan* to turn on, light
روغن	*rawqan* oil
عوض کردن	*avaz-kardan* to change (trs.)
ماشین	*mâshin* automobile, car
هوا	*havâ* weather, air

5 preposition

از ، در ، به ، بر ، با ، تا

---

[1]A common enough verb in classical Persian, simple *jostan* has become quite rare in the modern language, its place being taken by *jostoju-kardan*. It is still used in a number of compounds, however.

yâft-/yâb- to find[1] يافتن (ياب)

[handwritten annotations: "baab is used in" ... "compounds"]

Exercise 21

(a) Complete the following with the proper mood and tense:

۱ اگر فردا باران ـــــ (باریدن) ، ما ـــــ (نتوانستن) ـــــ (رفتن) بیرون .

۲ اگر دیروز ـــــ (رفتن) ، من هم همراهتان ـــــ (آمدن) .

۳ اگر فردا ـــــ (رفتن) ، من هم همراهتان ـــــ (آمدن) .

٤ اگر خودت بلد ـــــ (بودن) ، چرا از من پرسیدی؟

٥ اگر از من ـــــ (پرسیدن) ، به او می‌گویم چکار ـــــ (کردن) .

٦ اگر شما چراغها را ـــــ (روشن کردن) ، بهتر می‌بینیم .

۷ اگر فردا هوا خوب ـــــ (بودن) ، من اینها را ـــــ (شستن) .

۸ اگر ما خانهٔ بزرگتری ـــــ (داشتن) ، بهتر ـــــ (بودن) .

۹ اگر همینجا روی تختخواب کمی ـــــ (دراز کشیدن) ،
حالم بهتر ـــــ (شدن) .

۱۰ اگر تو خاموش ـــــ (نشدن) ، من ترا ـــــ (کشتن)!

(b) Complete the following using irrealis constructions:

۱ مریم و شیرین باید خیلی زودتر ـــــ (رسیدن) .

۲ بهتر بود مشغول کار خودتان ـــــ (شدن) .

۳ ما باید آنها را ارزان‌تر ـــــ (خریدن) .

٤ محمد باید قبلاً ـــــ (برگشتن) .

٥ شما بایستی آنها را ـــــ (دیدن) .

٦ رضا میبایست بیشتر ـــــ (درس خواندن) .

۷ آقا ، میبایستی خیلی بیشتر از این ـــــ (کار کردن) .

۸ تو نمی‌بایست آن چراغ را ـــــ (خاموش کردن) .

۹ این نباید با شما ـــــ (فرق کردن) .

---

[1] *Yâftan* is seldom used in modern Persian, and never in colloquial Persian, in its simple state. It was very common in classical Persian and is still used in compounds like *kâr-yâftan* "to find work, get employed."

It would have been better if I started earlier

۱۰ بهتر بود من زودتر ــــ (شروع کردن). میکردم

(c) Give appropriate answers to the following:

۱ چند وقت است حالش اینطور است؟

۲ چند وقت است فارسی درس میخوانید؟

۳ این چراغ چند وقت است روشن شده است؟

۴ چند روز بود باران میآمد؟ *میآمد*

۵ چند وقت است دنبال چنین کاری میگردید؟

۶ چند وقت است روغن ماشینتان عوض نشده است؟

۷ چند وقت است برادران و خواهرانتان را ندیدهاید؟

۸ چند وقت است میخواهند فارسی یاد بگیرند؟

۹ چند سال است که مدرسه میروید؟

۱۰ چند ماه است که در این شهر هستیم؟

(d) Translate into Persian

1. How long has it been raining?
2. We turned on the lights two hours ago, so they've been on for two hours.
3. If he had started earlier, he would have finished his work.
4. If the weather is good tomorrow, we can go to town and buy some things. *present subj* باشد
5. How long ago did you throw that food away?
6. I wish you hadn't said those things to me.
7. No matter how many times (= however much) you ask me, I won't tell you the answer. *naxohad dad (?)*
8. It must have rained last night.
9. You should have put all the lights out when you finished your work. *Yadid, why not mikardid.*
10. If I had known the answer, I wouldn't have asked you.

Additional Vocabulary: Mishaps

بهم خوردن *beham-khordan* to collide

بیمارستان *bimârestân* hospital

بیهوش *bihush* uncon-
scious

پلکان *pellekân* stair,
staircase

تصادف کردن *tasâdof-kardan* to
have an accident

خوردن به *khordan be* to run
into, hit

خیس *khis* wet

دویدن *davidan* to run

راندن (ران) *rând-/rân-* to drive

راننده *rânande* driver

زمین خوردن *zamin-khordan* to
fall down

زیر گرفتن *zir-gereftan* to run
over

سر خوردن *sor-khordan* to slip

شکستن (شکن) *shekast-/shekan-* to
break

غش کردن *qash-kardan* to
faint

کبود شدن *kabud-shodan* to
get bruised

گلگیر *gelgir* fender

له شدن *leh-shodan* to get
mashed

لیز *liz* slippery

لیز خوردن *liz-khordan* to slip,
slide

Write a short composition using as much of the vocabulary given above as you can.

161

Lesson Twenty-Two

§64 Uses of the subjunctive IV: Adverbial clauses. The subjunctive is used in adverbial clauses introduced by certain conjunctions.

64.1 Temporal conjunctions. Note that temporal clauses in Persian tend to precede the main clause, whereas in English the opposite is true.

before (قبل از) → prsnt subj.

(a) All conjunctions meaning "before" *(qabl az in-ke, pish az in-ke)* are invariably followed by the **present** subjunctive, regardless of the tense of the main clause.

قبل از اینکه من بیایم آنها رفته بودند.	*qabl az in-ke man bíâ-yam, ânhâ rafte-budand.*	They had gone before I came.
پیش ازینکه بروید با شما کار دارم.	*pish az in-ke béra-vid, bâ shomâ kâr dâram.*	I want to see you before you go.

ta → prsnt subj.

(b) *Tâ* followed by the negative present subjunctive means "until" (literally, "so long as…not") with reference to future time.

تا شما نروید من هم نمیروم.	*tâ shomâ náravid, man-ham némi-ravam.*	I won't go until you do.
تا کارتان را نکنید نمیتوانید بروید.	*tâ kâr-etânrâ nákonid, némitavânid béravid.*	You can't go until you've done your work.

(c) *Tâ* meaning "by the time that" is followed by the present subjunctive. The verb of the result clause is in the past narrative.

تا برسیم هواپیما رفته است.	*tâ béresim, havâ-paymâ rafte-ast.*	By the time we get there the plane will have gone.
تا شما بیائید دیر شده است.	*tâ shomâ bíâid, dir shode-ast.*	By the time you come it will be too late.

64.2 The conjunctions of purpose (*tâ, tâ ke, tâ in-ke* and *ke* "in order that") introduce a purpose clause. These conjunctions are invariably followed by the present subjunctive, regardless of the tense of the main clause. Whereas temporal clauses precede the main clause, purpose clauses always follow the main clause.

میایم تا شمارا ببینم.	*míâyam tâ shomâ-râ bébinam.*	I'm coming to see you.
آمدم که شمارا ببینم.	*âmadam ke shomâ-râ bébinam.*	I came to see you.
آمده است تا اینکه ماشین را تعمیر کند.	*âmade-ast tâ in-ke mâshin-râ ta'mir-konad.*	He has come to fix the car.

64.3 All conjunctions of concession, provision and exception are followed by the subjunctive, present or past depending upon the temporal relationship to the main clause.

اگرهم بمیرم بازهم میروم.	*ágarham bémiram, bâz-ham míravam.*	Even though I may die, I'm still going.
اگرهم شما دیده باشید بازهم باور نمیکنم.	*ágarham shomâ dide-bâshid, bâz-ham bâvar-némikonam.*	Even though you may have seen it, I still don't believe it.
بشرطی که شما بیائید من هم میایم.	*beshártike shomâ bíâid, man-ham míâyam.*	Provided you come, I'll come too.
بی آنکه با چشم خودم ببینم باور نمیکنم.	*bi ân-ke bâ cheshm-e khod-am bébinam, bâvar-némikonam.*	I won't believe it without seeing it with my own eyes.

163

هرچند کار کنم بجائی *hárchand kâr-konam,*   No matter how much
نمیرسم. *be jâ-i némiresam.*   work I do, I don't
                                          get anywhere.

§65 Participial forms. There are three distinct types of active participle in Persian, (1) the participial of agency, (2) the verbal adjectival participle, and (3) the participle of manner.

65.1 The agent participle, which may be used both adjectivally and substantively as a noun, has two formations, one for simple verbs and another for compounds.

(a) Simple verbs form the agent participle by adding *-(y)ande* to the present stem.

نوشتن > نویس > نویسنده   *neveshtan > nevis- > nevisande* writer

فروختن > فروش > فروشنده   *forukhtan > forush- > forushande* sales-
                                        person

خواندن > خوان > خواننده   *khândan > khân- > khânande* reader,
                                        singer

گفتن > گو >گوینده   *goftan > gu- > guyande* speaker, an-
                                        nouncer

آمدن > آ > آینده   *âmadan > â- > âyande* coming, future

جوینده یابنده است.   *juyande yâbande-ast.*   He who seeks finds.

(b) Compound verbs form the agent participle from the nonverbal element and the simple present stem of the verb.

پاک کردن > پاک کن   *pâk-kardan* to erase > *pâkkon* eraser

دانش جستن > دانشجو   *dânesh-jostan* to seek knowledge >
                               dâneshju student

صبح خاستن > صبح خیز   *sobh-khâstan* to get up early > *sobhkhiz*
                               early riser

بلند گفتن > بلندگو   *boland-goftan* to speak loudly >
                               bolandgu loudspeaker

فارسی‌گو ‹ فارسی‌گفتن *fârsi-goftan* to speak Persian > *fârsigu* Persian-speaking

روزنامه‌نویس ‹ روزنامه‌نوشتن *ruznâme-neveshtan* to write newspapers > *ruznâmenevis* journalist

آبگرمکن ‹ آب‌گرم‌کردن *âb-garm-kardan* to heat water > *âbgarmkon* waterheater

Contrary to this principle of formation, a few modern terms, especially of a commercial nature and loan-translations, form compound agent participles on the pattern of the simple verb.

تحویلگیرنده ‹ تحویل‌گرفتن *tahvil-gereftan* to accept consignment > *tahvilgirande* consignee

امضاکننده ‹ امضا کردن *emzâ-kardan* to sign > *emzâkonande* signatory

65.2 The verbal adjective is formed by suffixing -*(y)â* to the present stem. This form, which means possessed of a quality inherent in the verb, occurs only with and is limited to a very small number of simple verbs, practically limited to the following:

توانا ‹ توان ‹ توانستن *tavânestan* > *tavân-* > *tavânâ* capable

خوانا ‹ خوان ‹ خواندن *khândan* > *khân-* > *khânâ* legible

دارا ‹ دار ‹ داشتن *dâshtan* > *dâr-* > *dârâ* possessing (as in *dârâ-ye sharâyet* qualified)

دانا ‹ دان ‹ دانستن *dânestan* > *dân-* > *dânâ* knowing, wise

بینا ‹ بین ‹ دیدن *didan* > *bin-* > *binâ* sighted, capable of seeing

رسا ‹ رس ‹ رسیدن *residan* > *res-* > *resâ* mature (fruit)

شنوا ‹ شنو ‹ شنیدن *shenidan* > *shenaw-* > *shenavâ* capable of hearing

گویا ‹ گو ‹ گفتن *goftan* > *gu-* > *guyâ* capable of speech

گیرا ‹ گیر ‹ گرفتن *gereftan* > *gir-* > *girâ* attractive

65.3 The participle of manner is formed by adding -*(y)ân* to the present stem. This participle is used adverbially to describe a state or man-

165

ner in which something is done. Verbs that form verbal adjectives in -(y)â do not form participles of manner in their simple states. All compound verbs potentially take this form, although in practice there are not that many in use.

خندان رفت.	*khandân raft.*	She left laughing.
افتان و خیزان از شرابخانه آمدند.	*oftân o khizân az sharâbkhâne âmadand.*	Stumbling and reeling, they came from the tavern.
یارب گویان با مرگ روبرو شدند.	*yârabbguyân bâ marg ruberu-shodand.*	Saying "O Lord," they faced death.
نعره‌زنان حمله کردند.	*na'rezanân hamle-kardand.*	Shouting, they attacked.

65.4 A few other productive agent constructions are as follows.

(1) The suffix -gar, as in کارگر *kârgar* worker (< *kâr* work), آرایشگر *ârâyeshgar* hair dresser (< *ârâyesh* adornment) and مسگر *mesgar* coppersmith (< *mes* copper).

(2) The Turkish agent suffix -chi is particularly productive: پستچی *postchi* mailman (< *post* post), درشکه‌چی *doroshkechi* carriage driver (< *doroshke* carriage), شکارچی *shekârchi* hunter (< *shekâr* hunt).

(3) Arabic agents usually assume the shape $C_1aC_2C_2âC_3$, i.e., a doubled second consonant followed by -â-, as in حراف *harrâf* loquacious (< *harf*), حمال *hammâl* porter, خیاط *khayyât* tailor, and نجار *najjâr* (carpenter).

Vocabulary 22

آماده	*âmâde*	ready
اگرهم	*ágar...ham*	although
بازهم	*bâz-ham*	still, nonetheless, *yet again*

بردن (بر)   *bord-/bar-* to win (game, bet)

بس   *bas* enough; *az bas-ke* so much...that[1]

بعد از آنکه   *ba'd az ân-ke* after (conj.)

بکار بردن   *be kâr bordan* to use, employ

پس از اینکه   *pas az in-ke* after (conj.)

پیش از اینکه   *pish az in-ke* before (+ subj.)[2] *(followed by pr. subj.)*

پیاده   *piâde* on foot, by foot, pedestrian

پیاده رفتن   *piâde raftan* to go on foot

پیاده شدن   *piâde-shodan* to get out, off (of vehicles)

تا   *tâ* until, by the time, in order that (see also Appendix A)

تماشا کردن   *tamâshâ-kardan* to watch

حرکت (حرکات)   *harakat* pl *harakât* motion, movement

حرکت کردن   *harakat-kardan* to take off, start moving

درد   *dard* pain

درد کردن   *dard-kardan* to hurt, ache

دیر شدن   *dir-shodan* to get late (of time)

دیر کردن   *dir-kardan* to be late (of people), to come late

راه افتادن   *(be)râh-oftâdan* to get under way, "hit the road," be on one's way

ساختن (ساز)   *sâkht-/sâz-* to make, build

شام   *shâm* dinner

صبحانه   *sobhâne* breakfast

فرستادن (فرست)   *ferestâd-/ferest-* to send

فرودگاه   *forudgâh* airport

قبل از اینکه   *qabl az in-ke* before (+ subj.)

---

[1]A clause introduced by *az bas-ke* is the main clause in English, and the main clause in Persian is the subordinate clause of English, e.g., *az bas-ke kâr-kardeim, khaste-shodeim* "we've worked so much that we've gotten tired."

[2]Note that *pish/qabl* and *pas/ba'd* are synonymous; *in* and *ân* are also interchangeable in these and other such conjunctions.

کلید *kelid* key, switch

ناهار *nâhâr* lunch

نگهداشتن *negah-dâshtan*[1] to stop (trs.), hold, keep

هواپیما *havâpaymâ* airplane

Exercise 22

(a) Give the agent participles for the following verbs:

۷ کشتن		۱ درس خواندن	
۸ نمودن		۲ بردن	
۹ یاد گرفتن		۳ بار بردن	
۱۰ بطری باز کردن		٤ غم خوردن	
۱۱ کتاب فروختن		٥ شستن	
۱۲ عینك ساختن		٦ لباس شستن	

(b) Change the underlined verbs to participles of manner (make any other necessary adjustments and/or omissions):

۱ از اطاق به اطاق میرفت و چراغ روشن میکرد .

۲ بالاخره رسیدیم ولی پرسیدیم و پرسیدیم .

۳ در حالی که روی تختخواب میفتاد شروع به گریه کرد .

٤ در حالی که بر میخاستند شروع کردند به صحبت کردن .

٥ دراز می‌کشیدم که خوابم برد .

٦ بچه‌ها گریه میکردند و پیش مادرشان آمدند .

۷ همانطور در حالی که حرف میزد برخاست و رفت .

(c) Read and translate into English:

۱ فردا صبح زود آمادهٔ رفتن تهران باشید!

۲ هنوز ناهارمان‌را نخورده بودیم که صدای ماشین محمدرا شنیدیم که میآمد .

---

[1]Like *bar-dâshtan*, *negah-dâshtan* takes the *mi-* prefix and forms a regular subjunctive (*negah-dâram*).

۲ اگر پیاده نمی‌آمدند و با ماشین می‌آمدند، دیر نمی‌کردند.

٤ بهتر است با هواپیما برویم یا میشود با ماشین هم رفت؟

٥ قبل از اینکه باران بیاید ماشین را نزدیك ده كوچكی نگهداشته بودیم.

٦ طوریکه کار ما پیش میرود تا تمام شود ما همه پیر شده‌ایم.

۷ زود باش! نمیخواهم دیر کنم.

۸ از بسکه دیر کرده‌ایم تا به فرودگاه برسیم هواپیما رفته است.

۹ یکی از مشهورترین آوازخوان‌های ایران شَجَریان است.

۱۰ سعی کردم چراغ را روشن کنم ولی نتوانستم کلیدش را پیدا کنم.

(d) Translate into Persian:

1. Stop the car right here. I want to get out.
2. Before you eat dinner, don't forget to wash your hands.
3. I guessed they wouldn't throw those things away.
4. Before eating lunch I like to stretch out and sleep for a few minutes.
5. The announcer is saying something interesting. Let's listen.
6. I usually ask before taking anything from (az ru-ye) his desk.
7. By the time they get here everything will be finished.
8. We can't have dinner until your brother and sister arrive.
9. If you go on foot, you won't arrive until 6 o'clock.
10. I doubt you can get to the airport before the plane takes off.

Additional Vocabulary: Travel

اثاثیه	asâsiye luggage	پرداخت کردن	pardâkht-kardan to pay
اسباب	asbâb belongings, things	پول نقد	pul-e naqd cash
اعلان کردن	e'lân-kardan to announce	تاکسی	tâksi taxi
ایستگاه	istgâh station	ترن	tren train
باربر	bârbar porter	توالت	tuâlet toilet
بازرس	bâzres conductor	درجۀ یك	daraje-ye yek first class
باطل	bâtel invalid	درجۀ دو	daraje-ye do second class
بلیط	belit ticket		

دوسره	*dosare* round-trip	قطار	*qatâr* train
رزرو کردن	*rezerv-kardan* to make a reservation	کارت اعتبار	*kârt-e e'tebâr* credit card
رستوران	*restorân* restaurant	مسافرت کردن	*mosâferat-kardan* to travel
سریع السیر	*sari'ossayr* express		
سکو	*saku* platform	یکسره	*yeksare* one-way
عادی	*âdi* ordinary		

Write a short composition about a trip you have taken.

(رومی) Rumi

"نیک کرد ((ولی نیک برنما "

"He did a good deed, but a good deed that appeared evil."

Lesson Twenty-Three

§66 Abstraction of substantives. All substantives (adjectives and nouns) are abstracted by suffixing *-í*. For substantives ending in *-e*, the abstraction is *-gí*.

پیر > پیری   *pir* old > *pirí* old age

سیاه > سیاهی   *siâh* black > *siâhí* blackness

بچه > بچگی   *bachche* child > *bachchegí* childhood

آماده > آمادگی   *âmâde* ready > *âmâdegí* readiness

دیوانه > دیوانگی   *divâne* mad > *divânegí* madness

پزشك > پزشکی   *pezeshk* physician > *pezeshkí* (the study of) medicine

دندانپزشك > دندانپزشکی   *dandânpezeshk* dentist > *dandânpezeshkí* dentistry

نماینده > نمایندگی   *nemâyande* representative > *nemâyandegí* representation

The abstracted adjective is used in the expression *be in* (or *ân*) ...*í*, equivalent to the English "so" or "such a."

باین زودی نرویم.   *be in* zudí náravim.   Let's not go so early.

خانهای بآن بزرگی ندیده بودم.   *khâne-i be ân bozorgí nádide budam.*   I had never seen a house so big (such a big house).

171

The abstracted adjective is also used in the idiom *be ...í-e ân*, equivalent to the English "as...as (that)."

این به خوبی آن است.	*in be khubí-e ân-ast.*	This is as good as that.
این به سختی آن نیست.	*in be sakhtí-e ân nist.*	This is not so hard as that.
خانه‌ای به بزرگی آن را ندیده بودم.	*khâne-i be bozorgí-e ân-râ nádide budam.*	I had never seen a house as big as that one.

66.1 The abstractions of substantives relating to offices and ranks are often used by extension not only for the office or rank itself but also for the place where the office is conducted.

آتش نشان *âteshneshân* fire extinguisher > آتش نشانی *âteshneshâni* fire department

کتابفروش *ketâbforush* bookseller > کتابفروشی *ketâbforushi* book store

شهربان *shahrbân* chief of police > شهربانی *shahrbâni* police headquarters

شهردار *shahrdâr* mayor > شهرداری *shahrdâri* mayor's office

66.2 The abstractions are also used to define the purpose for which things are employed.

سوپ خوردن *sup-khordan* to eat soup > سوپخور *supkhor* soup eater > قاشق سوپخوری *qâshoq-e supkhori* soupspoon

رخت شستن *rakht-shostan* to wash clothes > رختشو *rakhtshu* washer > طشت رختشوئی *tasht-e rakhtshui* washtub

ظرف شستن *zarf-shostan* to wash dishes > ظرفشو *zarfshu* dishwasher > مایع ظرفشوئی *mâye'-e zarfshui* dishwashing liquid

§67 Double-substantive compounds.

Compounds composed of two substantives (noun-noun or adjective-noun) render substantives. Stress, as in all substantives, is on the final syllable. Generally the first element of a double-substantive compound indicates a quality or modification of the second element, as in *shekaste* ("broken") and *del* ("heart"), which form *shekastedél* ("broken-hearted"), and as in *meh-mân* ("guest") and *dust* ("friend"), which form *mehmândúst* ("hos-pitable"). It is often helpful when first encountering a double-substan-tive compound to put the two elements together and add "-ed."

ماهرو *mâhru* "moon-faced" > beautiful

سنگدل *sangdel* "stone-hearted" > hardhearted

درازدست *darâzdast* "long-armed" > aggressive

پریشان خاطر *parishânkhâter* "disturbed-minded" > distressed

کوتاه قد *kutâhqad* "short-statured" > short in stature

Unfortunately not all compounds are quite so transparent in mean-ing, and some have rather extended metaphorical applications.

خرگوش *khargush* "donkey-eared" > rabbit

تردامن *tardâman* "wet-skirted" > disgraced, scandalous

67.1 Particularly productive first elements for this type of com-pound are *khosh-* ("well, good"), *bad-* ("bad, ill") and *bi-* ("without").

خوشلباس *khoshlebâs* well-dressed

بدلباس *badlebâs* ill-dressed

خوشبخت *khoshbakht* lucky, fortunate

بدبخت *badbakht* unlucky, unfortunate

بیکار *bikâr* unemployed, idle

بیحوصله *bihawsele* impatient

A productive second element is *-kâr*.

فراموشکار *farâmushkâr* forgetful

کثافت کار *kesâfatkâr* messy, sloppy

67.2 All double-substantive compounds are abstracted by suffixing *-(g)í*.

شکسته دلی *shekastedelí* brokenheartedness

173

مهماندوستی *mehmândustí* hospitality

درازدستی *darâzdastí* aggressiveness

بدبختی *badbakhtí* misfortune

بیحوصلگی *bihawselegí* impatience

§68 Adjectives/adverbs in *-âne*. The suffix -*(g)âne* is used to make adverbs from words that are primarily adjectival and also to make adjectives of substantives whose primary connotations have become purely nominal.

Although as a general rule most adjectives can be used as adverbs (*ketâb-e khub-i* "a good book" and *khub khâbidam* "I slept well"), there are some words, like *mo'addab* "polite" and *khoshbakht* "lucky," that are by convention exclusively adjectival. Such words add the -*(g)âne* suffix when used adverbially.

مؤدب > مؤدبانه   *mo'addab* polite > *mo'addabâne* politely

خوشبخت > خوشبختانه   *khoshbakht* lucky > *khoshbakhtâne* luckily

Similarly, although most nouns can be used indiscriminately as adjectives, by convention some, like *barâdar* "brother" and *shâ'er* "poet," are used exclusively as nouns. To make them adjectival the -*(g)âne* suffix is added.

برادر > برادرانه   *barâdar* brother > *barâdarâne* brotherly

بچه > بچگانه   *bachche* child > *bachchegâne* childish

شاعر > شاعرانه   *shâ'er* poet > *shâ'erâne* poetic(al), romantic

§69 Magar. The particle *màgar* is used interrogatively with a negative verb when an affirmative answer is expected. The affirmative answer to a negative question is introduced by *chérâ* (like the French *si*), not by *bále*. The particle also occurs as *màgar ná* after an affirmative statement to induce agreement (French *n'est-ce pas?*).

مگر نرفتید؟ چرا رفتم.   *màgar náraftid?*   Didn't you go? Yes, I
                          chérâ, raftam.   did.

مگر خودتان نبودید؟	*màgar khod-etân*	Weren't you there?
چرا بودم ولی ندیدم.	*nábudid? chérâ,*	Yes, I was, but I
	budam váli nádidam.	didn't see it.
فهمیدید ، مگر نه؟	*fahmidid, màgar ná?*	You understand,
		don't you?

Màgar is also used with an affirmative verb when a negative answer is expected. Note especially the English equivalent.

چه میدانند؟ مگر آنجا	*che mídânand? màgar*	What do they know?
بودند؟	*ânjâ budand?*	They weren't there,
		were they?
میآیند مگر؟	*míâyand màgar?*	They aren't coming,
		are they?

Vocabulary 23

آنچه	*ân-che[1]* that which, what
ادامه دادن به	*edâme-dâdan be* to continue
استفاده کردن از	*estefâde-kardan az* to make use of
اشکال	*eshkâl* difficulty, problem
اشکال داشتن	*eshkâl-dâshtan* have a problem, for something to be wrong; *eshkâl-i nádârad* it's all right, "no problem"
اگرنه	*agarná* otherwise
بالا	*bâlâ* up (adv.), upstairs
بالای	*bâlâ-ye* over, above (prep.)
بخشیدن	*bakhshidan* to excuse, forgive *(be)* someone (a mistake, direct object)
پائین	*pâin* down (adv.), downstairs
پیشنهاد کردن	*pishnehâd-kardan* to suggest

---

[1]*Ân-che* is a relative pronoun; when it takes *-râ*, the relative *ke* is added, e.g., *ân-che gozasht* "that which passed," but *ân-che-râ-ke goftid násheidam* "I didn't hear what you said." For persons *ân-ke* is used and is short for *ân kas-i-ke*. *Ân-ke* is not used with *-râ*, the full *ân kas-i-râ-ke* is used instead.

175

تمیز *tamiz* clean

خداحافظی‌کردن با *khodâhâfezi-kardan bâ* to say goodbye to

دوباره *dobâre* again, a second time

دیوانه *divâne* mad, crazy

زیر *zir-e* under, beneath (prep.)

سردرد *sardard* headache[1]

سلام *salâm* hello, greetings

سلام کردن به *salâm-kardan be* to say hello to

شکستن (شکن) *shekast-/shekan-* to break (transitive and intransitive)

کثافت *kesâfat* dirt, dirtiness

کثیف *kasif* dirty

مگر *mágar* see §69

Exercise 23

(a) Read the following words and tell what they mean:

۱ آقائی	۱۱ فراموشکاری	۲۱ پیاده‌روی
۲ بزرگی	۱۲ سختی	۲۲ خوانائی
۳ کوتاهی	۱۳ دوری	۲۳ برادرانگی
٤ کوتاه‌قدی	۱٤ نزدیکی	۲٤ معلمی
٥ سادگی	۱٥ بدخواهی	۲٥ مردمشناسی
٦ زودی	۱٦ زودگذری	۲٦ همسایگی
۷ جوانی	۱۷ پولداری	۲۷ بچگانگی
۸ خوشحالی	۱۸ سفیدی	۲۸ آسانی
۹ باریری	۱۹ کهنگی	۲۹ دوستی
۱۰ دانائی	۲۰ بخشندگی	۳۰ روزنامه‌نویسی

---

[1]Most aches and pains are compounded similarly with *-dard*, as *gushdard* "earache," *kamardard* "backache" (see Supplementary Vocabulary for parts of the body). When *dard* precedes with the *ezâfe*, a metaphorical pain is implied, e.g., *sardard* and *deldard* are "headache" and "stomach ache" in the physical sense, but *dard-e sar* and *dard-e del* are used metaphorically for "pain in the neck" and "heartache."

(b) Answer the following questions:

١ مگر آن نامه‌ها را نفرستادید؟   ٦ فارسی بلدید ، مگر نه؟

٢ به خانهٔ ما نمی‌آیند مگر؟   ٧ مگر آماده نیستید؟

٣ مگر آنها را دیده‌اید؟   ٨ با ماشین میرویم ، مگر نه؟

٤ مگر نمیدانید این چیست؟   ٩ مگر ناهار خوردید؟

٥ مگر آنقدر پول دارید؟   ١٠ مگر نمیدانید آن آقا کیست؟

(c) Read and translate into English:

١ یکی دو تا اشکال داشتیم و اگرنه زودتر میرسیدیم .

٢ در ایران هر وقت آدمی مؤدّب وارد اطاق میشود باید به همه سلام کند .

٣ آنچه آن دیوانه میگوید درد سر میآورد .

٤ دلم را شکستید ولی باز هم غم نمی‌خورم .

٥ به درس خواندنتان حتماً ادامه دهید .

٦ برای این کار از چه میخواهید استفاده کنید؟

٧ خانم ، ببخشید ، وقت است که ما با همدیگر خداحافظی کنیم .

٨ کسی که چنین حرفهائی را باور کند باید خیلی زودباور باشد .

٩ من میخواستم پزشکی بخوانم ولی پدرم پیشنهاد کرد که دندانپزشکی بخوانم .

١٠ شبی بآن سیاهی را هیچوقت ندیده بودم . خوشبختانه چراغ همراه داشتیم .

(d) Translate into Persian:

1. Try to keep this room clean.
2. This is more childishness than madness.
3. Didn't they try to stop the car?
4. Can one get to (reach) those distant cities by airplane?
5. It's unlikely such a thing would happen again.
6. We knew they would be late.
7. Is there any place in this vicinity (*nazdikihâ*) we can sleep tonight?
8. You don't want to forgive someone who has done such a thing, do you?

9. Didn't you say hello to the ladies and gentlemen who came late?

10. You'd better *(behtar-ast ke)* continue with your work, otherwise you'll never finish.

subjunctive because it is hypothetical

Supplementary Vocabulary: Parts of the Body

آرنج	*âranj* elbow	دندان	*dandân* tooth
ابرو	*abru* eyebrow	دهان	*dahân* mouth
استخوان	*ostakhân* bone	رخ	*rokh(sâre)* cheek
اعصاب	*a'sâb* nerves	رگ	*rag* vein
انگشت	*angosht* finger, toe	ریش	*rish* beard
بازو	*bâzu* upper arm	ریه	*rie* lung
بینی	*bini* nose	زانو	*zânu* knee
پا	*pâ* foot	زبان	*zabân* tongue
پستان	*pestân* breast	ساق	*sâq* leg
پشت	*posht* back(side)[1]	ساعد	*sâed* forearm
پلك	*pelk* eyelid	سبیل	*sebil* mustache
پهلو	*pahlu* side	سر	*sar* head
پیشانی	*pishâni* forehead	سینه	*sine* chest
جگر	*jegar* liver	شانه	*shâne* shoulder
چانه	*châne* chin	شکم	*shekam* stomach, belly
چشم	*cheshm* eye	عضله	*azale -ât* muscle
حلق	*halq* throat	عورات	*awrât* private parts
دست	*dast* hand	قلب	*qalb* heart
دل	*del* stomach, heart[2]	کپل	*kapal* buttocks
		کمر	*kamar* waist, back
		گردن	*gardan* neck
		گلو	*golu* throat

---

[1]*Posht* normally refers to the backside; *kamar* is used euphemistically for "back."

[2]When *del* refers to a physical organ (or pain), it means "stomach." Metaphorically it is the "heart" in all applications. *Qalb* is the physical heart only, and *me' de* is the physical organ stomach.

178

گوش *gush* ear

گونه *gune* cheek

لب *lab* lip

مچ *moch* wrist, ankle

مژه *mozhe* eyelash

معده *me'de* stomach

ناخن *nâkhon* fingernail

مو *mu* hair

179

Lesson Twenty-Four

§70 "As...as possible." The English "as...as possible" is rendered in Persian by *hárche* and the comparative adjective.

باید هرچه زودتر برسیم .	*bâyad hárche zudtar béresim.*	We must arrive as soon as possible.
با صدای هرچه بلندتری گفتم .	*bâ sedâ-ye hárche bolandtar-i goftam.*	I spoke in as loud a voice as possible.
هرچه بیشتر سعی کردند .	*hárche bishtar sa'y-kardand.*	They tried as hard as they could.

Adverbial constructions formed from *bâ* ("with") or from abstracted compound substantives are modified by the phrase *-e harche tamâmtar* in order to circumlocute an impossibly long *harche...tar* construction.

با احترام هرچه تمامتر تعظیم کرد .	*bâ ehterâm-e harche tamâmtar ta'zim-kard.*	He bowed as respectfully as possible.
با شکسته‌نفسی هرچه تمامتر دنبال حرفهایش را گرفت .	*bâ shekastenafsi-e harche tamâmtar dombâl-e harfhâ-yeshrâ gereft.*	He began to speak again as self-deprecatingly as possible.

§71 "The more...the more." The idiom "the more...the more" is rendered in Persian by *harche ...tar, ...tar*.

180

| هرچه بیشتر بهتر. | *harche bishtar,* *behtar.* | The more, the better. |

Clauses introduced by *harche* with reference to future time and situations that may not take place take a subjunctive verb.

هرچه بلندتر بگوئید بهتر می‌شنوند.	*harche bolandtar béguid, behtar míshenavand.*	The louder you speak, the better they will hear.
هرچه زودتر راه بیفتیم زودتر میرسیم.	*harche zudtar râh bíoftim, zudtar míresim.*	The earlier we hit the road, the earlier we'll arrive.
هرچه اورا بیشتر ببینید کمتر دوستش خواهید داشت.	*harche u-ra bishtar bébinid, kamtar dust-est khâhid-dâsht.*	The more you see of him, the less you'll like him.

With reference to past or present continuous tenses, the indicative mood is used.

| هرچه اورا بیشتر می‌بینم بیشتر دوستش دارم. | *harche u-râ bishtar míbinam, bishtar dust-esh dâram.* | The more I see him, the more I like him. |

§72 Factitive verbs. The factitive verbal formation ("to make or cause to do or be") is achieved by suffixing the regular infinitival ending -*ân(i)dan* to the present stem of the simple verb.

رسیدن > رس > رساند(ی)دن

residan to arrive > *res-* > *resân(i)dan* "to make something arrive, deliver"

خوابیدن > خواب > خواباند(ی)دن

khâbidan to sleep > *khâb-* > *khâbân(i)dan* to put to sleep, to lay (something) down

برگشتن > برگرد > برگرداند(ی)دن

bar-gashtan to return > *bar-gard-* > *bar-gardân(i)dan* to return (something), bring/take back

181

گذشتن > گذر > گذراندن(ی)دن

gozashtan to pass (int.) > *gozar-* > *gozarân(i)dan* to make
pass, spend (time)

این نامه‌را کی می‌رساند؟	*in nâme-râ ki míresâ-nad?*	Who will deliver this letter?
باید بچه‌هارا به مدرسه برسانیم.	*bâyad bachchehâ-râ be madrase béresânim.*	We have to take the children to school.
بچه‌هارا خواباندید؟	*bachchehâ-râ khâbân-did?*	Did you put the children to bed?
اورا روی زمین خواباندند.	*u-râ ru-ye zamin khâbândand.*	They laid him down on the ground.
بعد بر می‌گردانمت.	*ba'd bar-migardânam-et.*	I'll bring you back later.
خواهش میکنم این کتابهارا به کتابخانه برگردانید.	*khâhesh-mikonam, in ketâbhâ-râ be ketâb-khâne bar-gardânid.*	Please return these books to the library.
روزی‌را دور از محیط شلوغ شهر در بیابان میگذراندند.	*ruz-i-râ dur az mohit-e sholuq-e shahr dar biâbân mígozarân-dand.*	They were spending a day in the country, far from the crowded milieu of the city.

The only exception in factitive formation is *neshastan* "to sit," the
factitive of which is *neshândan* "to sit (someone) down, quell (rebel-
lion), quench (fire)."

بفاصلة سیصد چهارصد قدم دورتر از جمع زیر درختی مرا نشاندند.	*be fâsele-ye sisad–chahârsad qadam durtar az jam', zir-e derakht-i, márâ neshândand.*	They sat me down under a tree at a distance of three or four hundred paces from the group.

Factitive compounds and participles are regularly formed.

نامه‌رساندن > نامه‌رسان	*nâme-resândan* to deliver letters > *nâmeresân* messenger

آتش نشاندن > آتش نشانی *âtesh-neshândan* to extinguish fire > *âtesh-neshâni* fire department

§73 Verbal nouns.
Verbal nouns are formed from many verbs by suffixing *-(y)ésh* to the present stem.

دانستن > دان > دانش *dânestan* to know > *dân-* > *dânesh* knowledge

فرمودن > فرما > فرمایش *farmudan* to order > *farmâ-* > *farmâyesh* order, command

رفتن > رو > روش *raftan* to go > *raw-* > *ravesh* method, manner

آموختن > آموز > آموزش *âmukhtan* to learn > *âmuz-* > *âmuzesh* instruction

گشتن > گرد > گردش *gashtan* to turn > *gard-* > *gardesh* stroll

پروردن > پرور > پرورش *parvardan* to train > *parvar-* > *parvaresh* education

کوشیدن > کوش > کوشش *kushidan* to strive > *kush-* > *kushesh* attempt

Many of these verbal nouns then combine with simple verbs to form compounds, like *dânesh-jostan* "to seek knowledge" (whence *dâneshju* "student"), *parvaresh-dâdan* "to nourish," *gardesh-kardan* "to take a stroll," and *kushesh-kardan* "to try, attempt."

§74 Infinitival adjectives.
Infinitives form a type of adjective by suffixing *-í*. Depending on the meaning of the verb, this adjectival form means "that which ought to be…," "can or should be…" or "about to be…, on the verge of…." This form often renders the English adjective in "-able." The negative is formed by prefixing *na-* or *nâ-*.

در آن موقع قیافه‌اش دیدنی بود .	*dar ân mawqe' qiâfe-ash **didani** bud.*	At that moment his face was a sight to see.
در آنجا چیز دیدنی نیست .	*dar ânjâ chiz-e **didani** nist.*	There is nothing worth seeing there.

183

قیافهٔ دوست داشتنی داشت.	*qiâfe-ye dust-dâshtani dâsht.*	He had a likeable face.
آنچه گفته است باور نکردنی است.	*ânche gofte-ast bâvarnakardani-ast.*	What he said is unbelievable.
مرتکب گناه نابخشودنی است.	*mortakeb-e gonâh-e nâbakhshudani-ast.*	He has committed an unforgivable sin.

Vocabulary 24

آتش	*âtesh*	fire
آتش گرفتن	*âtesh-gereftan*	to catch fire
آموختن (آموز)	*âmukht-/âmuz-*	to learn
استراحت کردن	*esterâhat-kardan*	to rest
ایستادن (ایست)	*istâd-/ist-*	to stop, stand still
بریدن	*boridan*	to cut
بقدری که	*be qadr-i...ke*	to such an extent that, so much ... that
به نظر آمدن	*be nazar âmadan*	to seem, appear
پر	*por*[1]	full
تشنه	*teshne*	thirsty
تقدیم کردن	*taqdim-kardan*	to offer
خالی	*khâli*	empty, void
خسته	*khaste*	tired
خلوت	*khalvat*	empty, not crowded
دعوت کردن	*da'vat-kardan*	to invite
شلوغ	*sholuq*	crowded

---

[1]*Por* is normally followed by (1) a generic noun with which it forms a compound, as *por-âb* "full of water" or (2) *az* and a generic (absolute) singular or modified plural, as *ketâbkhâne-i por az ketâb* "a library full of books" and *ketâbkhâne-i por az ketâbhâ-ye fârsi* "a library full of Persian books."

فقط *faqat[1]* only

قبول کردن *qabul-kardan* to accept

گرسنه *gorosne* hungry

مدت *moddat* period (of time)

نزدیك بودن/شدن *nazdik-budan* or *-shodan* (impersonal + subj.)
nearly, almost[2]

نشاندن (نشان) *neshând-/neshân-* make sit down; quench, extinguish; quell

Exercise 24

(a) Read and translate the following sentences:

١ بقدری خسته‌ام که فقط میخواهم استراحت کنم .

٢ بازار بقدری شلوغ بود که جای خالی پیدا نمی‌شد .

٣ هرچه تشنه‌تر باشی ، آب خوشمزه‌تر است .

٤ بهتر است با ماشین برویم . اگرنه من نمی‌آیم .

٥ نزدیك بود از گرسنگی و تشنگی بمیریم .

٦ وقتی که دیدم خانهٔ همسایه آتش گرفته است به آتشنشانی تلفن کردم .

٧ هنوز ده کیلومتری از شهر نرفته بودیم که ماشینی روبروی ما ایستاد و مردی پیاده شد .

٨ شما به نظر خسته میآئید . چرا کمی استراحت نمی‌کنید ؟

(b) Translate into Persian:

1. We told her that the earlier we get under way tomorrow morning, the better.

2. I tried as hard as I could to put the fire out, but it was no use.

3. The sooner you send that letter you've written, the sooner it will arrive.

---

[1]*Faqat* either (1) precedes what it modifies, as in *faqat do daf'e raftam* "I only went twice," *man faqat in-râ míguyam* "I'll say only this," or (2) comes at the end of the sentence.

[2]As in *nazdik bud bíoftam* "I nearly fell."

4. Let's take a stroll in the garden before the rain comes.

5. They must have had some difficulty; otherwise they would have been here by now.

6. I've never seen such a dirty room! You don't think I'm going to clean it up, do you?

7. He must be mad if he thinks I'm going to do this again.

8. She came in and very politely offered everyone tea.

9. Shiraz seemed crowded when I arrived, but it is not so crowded as Tehran.

10. Pour some of that dishwashing liquid into the water so that the dishes will come out clean.

Reading Selection

آن مرد آمد و پسر بچه‌هائی‌را که خانه نداشتند دعوت کرد تا با او به

جای بهتری بروند . چون بچه‌ها از او محبت دیده بودند با او رفتند . آن

مرد خوب بچه‌هارا بخانهٔ خودش برد . در خانهٔ آن مرد دو مرد خوب

دیگرهم بودند . آنها به بچه‌ها پول دادند ، شام دادند ، رختخواب گرم هم

دادند و فردا صبح بآنها گفتند اگر میخواهید همیشه دارای یک چنین

زندگی باشید ، باید مطیع و فرمانبردار باشید . بچه‌ها چون محبت دیده

بودند قبول کردند و یک هفته بعد هرکدام در یک نقطهٔ شهر مشغول جیب

بری شدند . و آنچه از استاد آموخته بودند در موقع عمل بکار می‌بردند و

آخر شب‌ها با جیب پر به خانه بر میگشتند و هرچه کار کرده بودند بآن سه

مرد خوب تقدیم میکردند و روزگارشان بخوبی و خوشی میگذشت .

یک روز یکیشان گیر افتاد و در کلانتری بقیه‌را هم لو داد . آنهارا

محاکمه کردند و به دارالتادیب فرستادند . سه ماه در دارالتادیب بودند و

در این مدت از دیگران خیلی چیزها یاد گرفتند .

از توبه ، اثر خسرو شاهانی

2 *mahabbat* affection 4 *rakhtekhâb* bedding (sheets, etc.) 6 *moti'*, *farmânbardâr* (synonyms) obedient 7 *noqte* spot; *jib-boridan* to pick pockets 8 *ostâd* master; *dar mawqe'-e amal* while on the job 10 *ruzegâr* time, days 11 *gir-oftâdan* to get caught, nabbed; *kalântari* police station; *baqiye* the rest, the others; *law-dâdan* to inform on 12 *mohâkeme-kardan* to sentence; *dârotta'dib* reformatory 14 *tawbe* repentance; *asar-e* by

Lesson Twenty-Five

§75 The passive. The passive, which can be made from transitive verbs only, is formed by conjugating, in all tenses and moods, the auxiliary verb *shodan* with the past participle of the verb, as *goftan* to say > *gofte-shodan* "to be said." The passive in Persian is used only when the agent is not expressed. There is no passive construction to render "it was said by me"; such sentences must be expressed in the active ("I said it"). Inanimate instruments are expressed in passive constructions with the preposition *bâ* (see examples below).

چنین چیزهائی دیده نمیشود .	*chonin chizhâ-i dide-némishavad.*	Such things are not (to be) seen.
هیچ سروصدائی از داخل خانه شنیده نمیشد .	*hich sar-o-sedâ-i az dâkhel-e khâne shenide-némi-shod.*	No noise could be heard from inside the house.
این نامه باید هرچه زودتر با پست فرستاده شود .	*in nâme bâyad harche zudtar bâ post ferestâde-shavad.*	This letter must be sent by post as soon as possible.
به نظر میآید که با هفت تیر کشته شده است .	*be nazar míâyad ke bâ hafttir koshte-shodeast.*	It appears that he was killed with a pistol.

187

Compound verbs with transitive verbal elements do not normally form passives. Instead, an intransitive compound with a passive sense is formed by changing the transitive verbal element into a corresponding intransitive one, such as *-kardan > -shodan*.

نام اورا فراموش کردند.	*nâm-e u-râ farâmush-kardand.*	They forgot his name.
نام او فراموش شد.	*nâm-e u farâmush-shod.*	His name was forgotten.
نام برنده‌ را اعلام میکنند.	*nâm-e barande-râ e'lâm-míkonand.*	They will announce the name of the winner.
نام برنده اعلام میشود.	*nâm-e barande e'lâm-mishavad.*	The name of the winner will be announced.
رضارا کتك زدند.	*rezâ-râ kotak-zadand.*	They beat Reza up.
رضا کتك خورد.	*rezâ kotak-khord.*	Reza got beaten up.

§76 Uses of the past participle. The past participle, especially of compound verbs, is often used as an attributive adjective.

آب این قنات زمینها و مزارع کشت‌شدۀ دهکده را آبیاری میکرد.	*âb-e in qanât zaminhâ-o mazâre'-e kesht-shode-ye dehkade-râ âbyâri-mikard.*	The water from this canal irrigated the cultivated lands and fields of the village.
زنها لباسهای نشسته شان‌را در بقچه پیچیدند.	*zanhâ lebâshâ-ye nashoste-shânrâ dar boqche pichi-dand.*	The women wrapped their **unwashed** clothes in bundles.
کف اطاق با گلیمهای پاخورده و زیلوهای نخنما فرش شده بود.	*kaff-e otâq bâ gelim-hâ-ye pâkhorde-o ziluhâ-ye nakhnomâ farsh-shode-bud.*	The floor of the room was spread with **worn** gelims and threadbare rugs.

The past participle is also used as an adjectival complement to the direct object of a verb, in which case it comes as close to the verb as possible.

| یك وقت بود كه من خودرا ميان اين خرابه‌ها ، كوهها و بيابانها گمشده گمان ميكردم. | *yek vaqt bud ke man khod-râ miân-e in kharâbehâ, kuhhâ-o biâbânhâ gom-shode gomân-mikardam.* | There was a time when I thought myself **lost** among these ruins, mountains and deserts. |
| كارهای خودرا كرده و نكرده گذاشت. | *kârhâ-ye khod-râ karde-o nakarde gozâsht.* | She left her chores half **done**. |

The past participle of certain transitive verbs is used as a passive substantive and normally occurs in the plural. This usage often takes the place of relative-clause constructions.

| از گفته‌هايش زياد سر درنياوردم. | *az goftehâ-yesh ziâd sar dar-náyâvordam.* | I didn't get much out of what he said. |
| نوشته‌های اين نويسنده | *neveshtehâ-ye in nevisande* | the writings of this writer |

The past participle of intransitive verbs used substantively gives the force of a perfect participle, as *rafte* "one who has gone," and *raftegân* "those who have gone."

| به ياد درگذشتگان | *be yâd-e dar-gozashtegân* | in memory of those who have passed away |
| فراموش شده‌های عصر گذشته | *farâmushshodehâ-ye asr-e gozashte* | the forgotten things of a by-gone era |

§77 **Diminutives.** The diminutive suffix *-ak* is used for true diminution, denigration and contempt as well as for endearment. It is used for both animates and inanimates.

مرغ ‹ مرغك   *morq* chicken > *morqak* chick

پسر > پسرك   *pesar* boy > *pesarak* kid, dear boy

مرد > مردك   *mard* man > *mardak* fellow

طفل > طفلك   *tefl* child > *teflak* brat, darling child

Many such diminutives are used metaphorically with extended connotations.

عروس > عروسك   *arus* bride > *arusak* doll

صورت > صورتك   *surat* face > *suratak* mask

برف > برفك   *barf* snow > *barfak* frost

The diminutive suffix *-che* is used only for diminution of inanimate objects.

باغ > باغچه   *bâq* garden > *bâqche* garden plot

كتاب > كتابچه   *ketâb* book > *ketâbche* pamphlet

دريا > درياچه   *daryâ* sea > *daryâche* lake

Vocabulary 25

آشنا با   *âshnâ bâ* acquainted with

بدون   *bedun-e* without

پشت   *posht-e* behind

تا   *tâ* up to

تقسيم كردن   *taqsim-kardan* to divide

جلو   *jelaw-e* in front of

جهان   *jahân* world

راست   *râst* right, true

زمان   *zamân* time, era

طرف   *taraf* direction, side; *taraf-e* toward

مجبور   *majbur* obliged (+ subj.)

معروف به   *ma'ruf be* known for

موقع (مواقع)   *mawqe'* pl *mavâqe'* time, opportunity; *dar mawqe'-e* at the time of

نسبت به *nesbat be* in relation to

Exercise 25

(a) Turn the underlined verbs in the following sentences into passives. Delete the agent where necessary.

۱ رضا کتابم را گم کرد .

۲ نمیتوان اینها را شست .

۳ ایشان را روی زمین نشانده‌اند .

٤ آنچه کرده بود بخشیدند .

٥ این را بکار نمی‌بریم .

٦ آن خانه را تازه ساختند .

۷ دلم را شکستید .

۸ آنها مجبورم میکنند که همراهشان بروم .

۹ ماشین را نگهداشته بودند .

۱۰ آنها را در این شهر پیدا نمیکنید .

Reading Selection

مُسلم در بیرون شهر مرو در روستای ماخان زمینی خرید و خانه‌ای

2   ساخت و خاندان خود را در آنجا نشاند . در سال ۱۰۹ هجری که عبد

الرحمن به جهان آمد ، روستای ماخان در سه فرسنگی شهر مرو (که این

4   کودک در آنجا چشم باز کرده بود) با چند روستای دیگر از آن پدرش

بود . مسلم ، پدر عبد الرحمن ، در میان جوانمردان مرو به مقام بسیار

6   بلندی رسیده بود و ایشان بطوع و رغبت وی را براهنمائی و پیشوائی خود

اختیار کرده بودند . (عبد الرحمن در این محیط جوانمردی و بزرگواری ،

8   در میان دلاوران معروف مرو ، رشد کرده و کم کم جوان برومندی شده

بود . مردم مرو و جوانمردان آن دیار پس از مسلم امیدشان به پسر رشید

10   او بود که ، چون وارد زندگی شد ، کنیهٔ ابو مسلم را اختیار کرد و اینک

دیگر "ابو مسلم عبد الرحمن خراسانی" در همهٔ خراسان به جوانمردی و

12   فتوت و بخشندگی و ایران‌پرستی معروف شد .

در آن زمان جوانمردان مرو پسران خود را از خردسالی و از همان

14   روزهای اول که به دبیرستان می‌رفتند و خط می‌آموختند به مسلك و مرام

خود آشنا می‌کردند . و از همان آغاز زندگی ، به آیین ایران قدیم ، سواری

و تیراندازی و مشت‌زنی و شمشیرزنی و کمانداندازی و نیزه اندازی و

زوبین‌بازی را یاد می‌دادند . عبد الرحمن جوان در این فنون از همسالان

خود برتری یافته بود .

16

18

1 *Moslem* masc. proper name; *Marv* Merv, modern Mary, city on the Oxus in Turkmenistan; *rustâ* village 2 *khânedân* family; *abdorrahmân* masc. proper name 3 *farsang* league, *dar se farsangi-e* within 3 leagues of 4 *kudak* child 5 *dar miân-e* among; *javânmard* chivalrous, noble; *maqâm* station 6 *be taw'-o raqbat* willingly; *vay = u; râh-nemudan* to guide; *pishvâ* leader 7 *ekhtiâr-kardan* to select; *mohit* environment; *bozorgvâr* great 8 *delâvar* warrior, brave; *roshd-kardan* to mature; *borumand* worthy, prosperous 9 *diâr* region; *rashid* eldest 10 *konye* nickname; *inak digar* here then 12 *fotovvat* manliness; *parastidan* to worship, serve 13 *khordsâl* young 14 *dabirestân* school (modern high school); *khatt* handwriting; *maslak-o marâm* career and goal 15 *âqâz* beginning; *âyin* custom; *savâr* horseman 16 *tir* arrow; *mosht-zadan* to box; *shamshir* sword; *kamand* lasso; *nize* spear 17 *zubin* javelin; *bâzi-kardan* to play; *fann* pl *fonun* skill, art; *hamsâl* of the same age 18 *bartari-yâftan az* to be superior to

Review V

(a) Read and translate the following into English (unfamiliar words can be found in the Persian-English Vocabulary):

۱ برادرم در وزارتخانهٔ آموزش و پرورش کار میکند و پسردائی‌ام در وزارتخانهٔ خارجه ، ولی تنها کاری که میکنند دفترنشینی و کاغذبازی است .

۲ غرق شوندگان کشتی شکسته امید زندگی را از دست داده هیچ کوششی نمیکردند که خودشان را به جای امن و امانی برسانند .

۳ تا وارد قطار شدیم یک آقای خیلی مهربانی به ما کمک کرد که چمدانهایمان را بالای صندلیها بخوابانیم .

۴ هرچه بیشتر سعی کنید ، احتمال موفق شدن بیشتر میشود .

۵ از چه ابزاری استفاده کرده‌اید که کارتان را باین خوبی انجام دادید؟

۶ رفتارش و حرفهایش بقدری بچگانه است که اگر می‌دیدید و می‌شنیدید باور نمیکردید .

۷ دیروز شما را دیدم که طرف شهربانی میرفتید . مگر در آنجا کار داشتید؟

۸ تا دیر نشده میخواهند یک کاری انجام دهند .

۹ یك ساعت است در همینجا نشسته‌ام منتظر شما .

۱۰ شعار وزارت آموزش و پرورش ایران اینست «توانا بُوَد[1] هرکه دانا بُوَد»
که از حماسهٔ ملی ایران ، یعنی شاهنامهٔ فردوسی ، گرفته شده .

(b) Translate the following into Persian:

1. If I had thought you were coming yesterday, I would have
been here.

2. Before they turned the loudspeaker on, we couldn't hear a
thing.

3. If you've finished all the work you had to do, you can go.

4. If we can find a salesperson in this department store[2] to take
our money, we can buy the things we've selected and get home early.

5. I'm thinking about[3] studying dentistry, but my mother says
that surgeons have a larger (more) income.

6. The books you brought from the library this morning may
have been heavy, but they weren't so heavy as the ones I took back
yesterday.

7. The earlier you get under way, the sooner you'll arrive.

8. You don't know how difficult my life has been. However unlucky you may have been, you haven't been so unlucky as I have.

9. The amount of money they have spent on the house they are
building is unbelievable.

10. The boys who were caught, sentenced and sent to the reformatory learned lots of things from the others with whom they became
friends there.

---

[1]*Bovad*, an archaic present tense from *budan*, = *ast* (see p. 203 §88).

[2]فروشگاه

[3]*(Dar) fekr-e in hastam ke* (+ subj.).

بخش دوم Part Two

دستور زبان Classical and

متون قدیمی Archaic Usages

§78 The *majhul* vowels. Early New Persian had two additional vowels in the vocalic inventory, namely *ê* and *ô,* called the *majhul* vowels.[1] *Ê* was pronounced like the modern *ay,* and *ay* was probably a true diphthong (like the "y" in "why"); *ô* was pronounced like the modern *aw,* which was probably pronounced like the "ow" in "cow." At some point prior to the sixteenth century, and generally within the area that is encompassed by modern Iran, *ê* merged with *i* as *i,* and *ô* merged with *u* as *u.* Thus the older contrast between *shir* "milk" and *shêr* "lion," *sir* "garlic" and *sêr* "satiated" was lost.

In this section the *majhul* vowels will be indicated, but in modern Iran classical Persian is read as though it were modern Persian, so *ê* is always read as *i* and *ô* is read as *u.*

§79 Euphonic -*d*-. When the preposition *be* is followed by a pronoun or a demonstrative beginning with a vowel, it becomes *bed-,* as in *be in > bedin, be ân > bedân, be u > bedu, be ishân > bedishân.*

This classical usage is maintained in modern literary style, especially in certain phrases like بدین وسیله *bedin vasile* "by these means" and بدانسان *bedânsân* "in that manner."

§80 The optative and the negative imperative. The third-person singular optative is formed by replacing the regular third-person singular ending -*ad* with -*âd.* The negative optative prefix is *má-* instead of *ná-.*

که رستم منم کم ماناد نام   نشیناد بر ماتمم پور سام

ke rostam man-am, k' am mámânâd nâm / neshinâd bar ma' tam-am pur-e sâm. For I am Rustam—may my name not endure! May the son of Sâm sit at my funeral. —Firdawsi

The optative of *budan* is irregularly formed as *bâd,* negative *mábâd.*

---

[1]*Majhul* means "unknown," and they are so called because the vowels *ê* and *ô* are unknown to Arabic and cannot be represented by the vowel points in Arabic script.

چنیـن داد پاسخ کـه این نیست داد   بـدیـن روز خـورشیـد روشـن مبـاد

chonin dâd pâsokh ke in nist dâd / bedin rôz khorshêd rawshan mábâd! Thus he answered, "This is not just. On this day may the sun not shine! —Firdawsi

This formation is no longer operative in the modern language. In classical usage the negative prefix *má-* was normally used to form the negative imperative, as *máraw* for modern *náraw* ("don't go") and *gomân mábar ke...* ("don't think that...").

§81 The vocative enclitic. In classical usage, maintained to the present in a few expressions, *-(y)â* is added as a vocative enclitic, as خدایا *khodâyâ* "O God!," شاهنشاها *shâhanshâhâ* "O king of kings!" and حافظا *Hâfezâ* "O Hafiz!" The same enclitic is added to interjections and certain verbals forms, as دردا *dardâ* "oh, woe," دریغا *dariqâ* "oh, alas," and مبادا *mâbâdâ* "oh, may it not be."

When *goft* is used as "he said in response," the enclitic *-â* is often appended.

گفتم ملکا تـرا کجـا جویم من   وز خلعت تو وصف کجا گویم من
گفتا که مرا مجو بعرش و بهشت   نزد دل خود که نزد دل پویم من

goftam malekâ to-râ kojâ juyam man? / vaz khel'at-e to vasf kojâ guyam man? / goftâ ke ma-râ máju be arsh-o be behesht / nazd-e del-e khod, ke nazd-e del puyam man. I said, "O king, where should I search for thee? And how should I describe thy robe of honor?" He said (in reply), "Seek me not on the throne or in heaven but in thine own heart, for I dwell within hearts." —Attar

§82 Dative usages. The enclitic *-râ,* now used as the specific direct-object marker, originally functioned as a dative marker. It indicated both indirect and dative-possessive constructions.

پادشاهی را شنیدم که بکشتن
اسیری اشارت کرد .

pâdishâh-i-râ shenidam ke be koshtan-e asir-i eshârat-kard. I heard **of** a king who indicated that a prisoner should be killed. —Sa'di.

این مژده مرا نیست. *in mozhde ma-râ nist.* This good news is not **for** me. —Sa'di

حـــوران بهشتی‌را دوزخ بـود اعـراف
از دوزخیان پرس که اعراف بهشتست

hurân-e beheshti-râ dôzakh bovad a'râf / az dôzakhiân pors ke a'râf behesht-ast. **For** the houris of paradise purgatory would be hell: ask the inhabitants of hell, for whom purgatory would be paradise. —Sa'di

شتـران بـود مـــرا جملـه نجیـب   در هنر نادر و در شکل عجیب

shotorân bud ma-râ, jomle najib / dar honar nâder-o dar shakl ajib. I had ("there were **to** me") camels, noble all, in craft rare and in form amazing. —Jami

گرچه منزل بس خطرناکست و مقصد ناپدید
هیچ راهی نیست کورا نیست پایان غم مخور

garche manzel bas khatarnâk-ast-o maqsad nâpadêd / hich râh-i nist k' u-râ nist pâyân: qam-mákhor. 'Though the stages are dangerous and the goal not in sight, there is no road **to which** there is not an end: grieve not! —Hafiz

The pronominal enclitics, in addition to the use preserved in modern Persian as possessives and direct objects, also functioned as pronouns in the dative and dative-possessive. It is especially important to note the "floating" quality of these pronominal enclitics, i.e., they do not always have a direct syntactical relationship with the words to which they are affixed but often indicate indirect objects or possession of some other word altogether in the sentence.

چه گویمت؟ *che guyam-at?* What should I say **to you**?

واعظ عذاب دوزخ و میخوارگان مگـو
جـز ایـن فسانـه نیستت افسانۀ دگـر

vâ'ez, azâb-e dôzakh-o maykhâregân mágu! / joz in fasâne nist-at afsâne-i degar? Preacher, don't talk of the torment of hell and wine-drinkers! Don't **you have** any fables besides these? —Fani

198

ز بیقوتیش خاست از جان نفیر   وطن ساخت گرد یکی آبگیر

پس از مدتی کرد آنجا درنگ   درافتاد غوکیش ناگ بچنگ

ze bêquti-ash khâst az jân nafir / vatan sâkht gerd-e yek-i âbgir //
pas az moddat-i kard ânjâ derang / dar-oftâd quk-i-sh nâgah be chang.
Because [the old bird] had nothing to eat there arose a cry from **its**
soul, so it settled by a pond. After dwelling there for a time, suddenly a
frog fell into **its** clutches. —Jami

§83 Prefixing postpositions. Instead of the simple preposition
followed by its complement as in modern Persian *(bar sar-esh* "on his
head"), in Early New Persian what is now the preposition *bar* was
commonly a postposition (i.e., after the noun) and the noun was preceded by *be,* as *be sar-ash bar* "on his head."

که لختی ز زورش ستاند همی   که رفتن بره بر تواند همی

ke lakht-i ze zôr-ash setânad hami / ke raftan be rah bar tavânad
hami. [He prayed] that [God] would take away a bit of his strength so
that he could walk on the road.

بس نامور بزیر زمین دفن کرده اند

کز هستیش بروی زمین بر نشان نماند

bas nâmvar be zêr-e zamin dafn-kardeand / k'az hasti-ash be ru-ye
zamin bar neshân namând. Many a famous one have they buried beneath the earth, of whose existence on the face of the earth no trace
remains. —Sa'di

§84 The perfective aspect; the *be-* prefix. In older Persian
the verbal prefix *bé-* (identical to, and indeed the origin of, the modern
subjunctive and imperative prefix) indicates the perfective aspect of the
verb, that is, the action or state of the verb done once, suddenly or finally (the Greek aorist and French *passé simple*). This usage was
maintained in poetry long after it ceased to function in normal prose-
writing. Since English has no formal way of expressing the perfective
aspect, circumlocutions must be sought for proper translation.

این بگفت و برفت.   *in bégoft-o béraft.* He said this (all at
once) and got up and left.

199

دلم بسوخت. *del-am bésôkht.* My heart went up in flames.

پدر بخندید و ارکان دولت بپسندیدند و برادران بجان برنجیدند. *pedar békhandid-o arkân-e dawlat bépasandidand-o barâdarân be jân béranjidand.* The father broke into laughter, the ministers of state expressed approval, and the brothers smarted with mortal pain. —Sa'di, *Gulistan*

بیزدان بنالید کی کردگار بدینکار این بنده را پاس دار

be yazdân bénâlid k' ay kerdegâr / bedin kâr in bande-râ pâs-dâr. All at once he cried out to God, "O Maker, protect this slave in this endeavor." —Firdawsi

آن پیر لاشه را که سپردند زیر خاک
خاکش چنان بخورد کزو استخوان نماند

ân pir-e lâshe-râ-ke sepordand zêr-e khâk / khâk-ash chonân békhord k' azu ostakhân nâmând. That old corpse they entrusted to the earth, the earth so gobbled it up that not even the bones remain. —Sa'di

§85 Cho(n). In modern Persian *chon* usually occurs as *chon-ke* and means "because." In classical Persian, however, *chon* (and its shortened form *cho)* poses special problems because it can be a causal conjunction ("because, since, as"), a temporal/conditional conjunction ("when, if"), a preposition ("like") and an interrogative ("how?"). When followed directly by a verb, it is usually a conjunction, but otherwise only context determines how it is used.

چو قاصد شد پیام او برد شد شیشهٔ مهر در میان خرد

cho qâsed shod, payâm-e u bord / shod shishe-ye mehr dar miân khord. **When** the messenger went, he took his message: thus was the vial of love between them shattered. —Nizami

شخصی همه شب بر سر بیمار گریست
چون روز شد او بمرد و بیمار بزیست

200

shakhs-i hame shab bar sar-e bêmâr gerist / chon rôz shod, u bémord o bêmâr bézist. A person wept all night over a sick man. **When** day came, he died and the sick man lived. —Sa'di

چو پیش یوسف آمد ابن یامین   نشاندش همنفس بر تخت زرین

cho pêsh-e yusof âmad ebn-e yâmin / neshând-ash hamnafas bar takht-e zarrin. **When** Benjamin came before Joseph, he sat him next to himself on the golden throne. —Attar

اگر صد سال گبر آتش فروزد   چو یکدم اندر آن افتد بسوزد

agar sad sâl gabr âtesh forôzad / cho yekdam andar ân oftad, bésôzad. Although a Zoroastrian kindles the flame for a hundred years, **when (if)** he falls into it for an instant, he is consumed. —Sa'di

چه باشد ار شود از بند غم دلش آزاد
چو هست حافظ مسکین غلام وچاکر دوست

che bâshad ar shavad az band-e qam del-ash âzâd / cho hast hâfez-e meskin qolâm-o châkar-e dôst? What would happen were his heart released from the bonds of grief, **since** poor Hafiz is a slave and servant to the beloved? —Hafiz

تنها نه منم ستم رسیده   کو دیده که صد چو من ندیده

tanhâ na man-am setam-reside / ku dide ke sad cho man nádide? It is not I alone who have suffered oppression. Where is the eye that has not seen a hundred **like** me? —Nizami

دوران بقا چو باد صحرا بگذشت
تلخی وخوشی وزشت وزیبا بگذشت

dawrân-e baqâ cho bâd-e sahrâ bóg'zasht / talkhi-o khoshi-o zesht-o zêbâ bóg'zasht. The era of existence passes **like** a desert wind: bitterness and sweetness, ugly and beautiful pass away. —Sa'di

پادشاه خویش را دانسته ام   چون روم تنها چو نتوانسته ام

pâdishâh-e khêsh-râ dâneste-am / chon ravam tanhâ, cho nat'vâ-neste-am? I know my king, [but] **how** can I go alone, unable **as** I am? —Attar

201

§86 The continuous-progressive marker *hami*. The older continuous marker is *hami*. Like its modern reflex *mi-*, it may be prefixed to the verb, although it often follows the verb, especially in poetry.

همی بود بوس و کنار و نبید

hami bud bôs-o kenâr-o nabêd. There was continual kissing, embracing and wine. —Firdawsi

چشمانش همچنان در چشمخانه همی گردید

cheshmân-ash hamchonân dar chashmkhâne hami gardid. His eyes kept on turning in their sockets. —Sa'di

بوی جوی مولیان آید همی   یاد یار مهربان آید همی

bu-ye juy-e Muliân âyad hami / yâd-e yâr-e mehrbân âyad hami. The scent of the Mulian river is coming; the memory of the beloved friend is coming. —Rudaki

§87 The past habitual and conditional. Whereas the *hami* marker gives the continuous-progressive sense ("to keep on doing, to do over and over"), the past habitual ("used to") was formed in older Persian by the addition of an enclitic *-i* to the past verb. This form is defective and occurs only in the first and third persons. Like the modern past habitual it was also used for the irrealis mood.

رفتمی *raftami*		رفتیمی *raftimi*	
—	—	—	—
رفتی *rafti*		رفتندی *raftandi*	

صیادان آنجا بسیار آمدندی	*sayyâdân ânjâ besyâr âmadandi-o*
و بدان نواحی دام نهادندی.	*bedân navâhi dâm-nehâdandi.* Hunters used to come there often and used to set snares. —Kashifi

خواجهٔ بزرگ احمد حسن هر	*khâje-ye bozorg, ahmad-e hasan, har*
روزی بسرای خویش بار دادی	*rôz-i be sarây-e khêsh bâr-dâdi-o tâ*
وتا نماز پیشین بنشستی و کار	*namâz-e pêshin bénshasti-o kâr bé-randi. man bâ pesarân-e u budami*

202

براندی . من با پسران او بودمی
و آنچه فرمودی نوشتمی .

o ânche farmudi neveshtami. The great lord Ahmad son of Hasan used to hold court every day at his house and sat until the noon prayer, seeing to administrative tasks. I was with his sons, and I would write down everything he said. —Nizami Aruzi

کسان که در رمضان چنگ میشکستندی
نسیم گل بشنیدند و توبه بشکستند

kasân-ke dar ramazân chang míshekastandi / nasim-e gol bésheni-dand-o tawbe bésh'kastand. Those who used to smash harps during Ramadan suddenly smelled the rose-breeze and broke their vows. — Sa'di

§88 The archaic present stem of *budan*. In addition to the present stem *bâsh-*, which survives in modern Persian, there was another present stem of *budan*, namely *bov-*, which gives the following present paradigm.

بوم	*bovam*	بویم	*bovim*
بوی	*bovi*	بوید	*bovid*
بود	*bovad*	بوند	*bovand*

The negative is regularly formed with the *ná-* prefix *(nábovam, ná-bovi, &c.)*.

§89 The archaic negative copula. In addition to the negative copula as in modern Persian (see §18), there was another negative copula formed by adding the present copulative endings to the negative particle *na*.

نیم	*náyam*	نئیم	*náim*
نئی	*nái*	نئید	*náid*
نیست	*(nist)*	نیند	*náyand*

§90 The archaic past narrative. The archaic past narrative tense is formed by adding the pronominal endings, not directly to the past participle, but to a form of the third-person singular past narrative where an elision of the -e of the participle to the -ast of the third person takes place (thus *oftâdé-ast > oftâdást*). The paradigm is as follows.

افتادستم	*oftâdástam*	افتادستیم	*oftâdástim*
افتادستی	*oftâdástid*	افتادستید	*oftâdástid*
افتادست	*oftâdást*	افتادستند	*oftâdástand*

The form also occurs in the past habitual-conditional:

افتادستمی	*oftâdástami*	افتادستیمی	*oftâdástimi*
	—		—
افتادستی	*oftâdásti*	افتادستندی	*oftâdástandi*

These forms occur with some frequency in poetry.

کاشکی آن شب و آن روز که ترسیدم از آن
نفتــادستـــی و شـــادی نشــدستــی تیمـــار

kâsh-ki ân shab-o ân rôz ke tarsidam az ân / náfotâdasti-o shâdi náshodasti timâr. Would that the night and day I feared had not befallen and joy had not turned to grief. —Khaqani

§91 The gnomic past. A special use of the past in classical Persian, extremely common in poetry, is equivalent to the Greek gnomic aorist, i.e., the simple past used for proverbial sayings and statements of general validity. The present is used in English.

فرق شاهی و بندگی بـرخـاست   چـون قضـای نبشتـه آمـد پیــش
farq-e shâhi-o bandegi bar-khâst / chon qazâ-ye nebeshte âmad pêsh. The distinction between king and slave disappears when "written fate" (death) comes forth. —Sa'di

بخش سوم Part Three

دستور زبان Colloquial

عامیانه Transformations

§92 Phonological transformations.

92.1 In almost all words in all environments *-ân-* becomes *-un-*.

tehrân > tehrun
âqâyân > âqâyun
ân khâne > un khune

Only a few words are not subject to the *ân > un* transformation (e.g., *dâstân* "story", *qor'ân* "Koran").

92.2 In a few words *-âm-* becomes *-um-*, like

âmadan > umadan
kodâm > kodum
tamâm > tamum

but these are isolated instances, and *âm> um* is not a general transformation in colloquial Persian.

92.3 *-st-* is generally pronounced *-ss-*, as in

dast-am hast > dass-am hass
ân kojâ-st? > un kojâ-ss?

92.4 Final *-ar* becomes *-e* in the following words:

digar > dige
ágar > áge
mágar > máge

92.5 Final *-é* followed by any enclitic becomes *-á-*.

bachche-ash > bachchá-sh
khaste-ast > khastá-ss
khâne-ham > khuná-m

92.6 In the narrative tense final *-é* drops when followed by enclitic -*i*.

rafté-i > raftí

didé-im > didím

92.7 The plural suffix *-hâ* tends to become *-â,* as indeed almost all intervocalic *h* tends to be elided. When *-hâ* is suffixed to words ending in *-é,* both *-é* and *-h-* are elided.

ketâbhâ > ketâbâ
bachchehâ > bachchâ

92.8 Most words ending in *-âh* and *-â'* drop the final consonant.

ertefâ'-e ân sâkhtemân > ertefâ-ye un sâkhtemun
hamrâh > hamrâ

§93 The copulas. The short copula has two forms, one used after consonants and *-í* and another used after vowels other than *-í.*

Following consonants and *-í* the present copulas are:

-am	*-im*
-i	*-in*
-e	*-an(d)*

Following vowels other than *-í,* the present copulas are:

-m	*-ym*
-y	*-yn*
-st	*-n*

Examples:

khub-am	I'm all right	*khub-im*	we're all right
khub-i	you're all right	*khub-in*	you're all right
khub-e	he/she/it's all right	*khub-an*	they're all right

kojâ-m	where am I?	*kojâ-ym*	where are we?
kojâ-y	where are you?	*kojâ-yn*	where are you?
kojâ-st	where is he/she/it?	*kojâ-n*	where are they?

The long copulas are as follows.

hástam	I am	*hástim*	we are
hásti	you are	*hástin*	you are
hást	he/she/it is	*hástan*	they are

In most environments the distinction in meaning in written Persian (see §22) between the long and short copulas has been lost altogether, and generally in spoken Persian the distinction between the long and short copulas is purely one of usage. The long copulas are used (1) for emphasis, as in written Persian *(khub hást!* "it *is* good"), (2) after the non-specific enclitic in all persons except the third singular *(bachchâ-ye khub-i-hastan* "they're good children," but *bachche-ye khub-i-e* "he's a good child"), (3) always after *-(a)m,* the colloquial reflex of enclitic *-ham (khúb-am-hast* "it's good too"), and (4) after any word ending in a vowel other than *-í* and *-é* (which becomes *-á-* before the short copulas, see §92.5).

§94 Verbal inflections.

94.1 The past stem of almost all verbs remains as in written Persian (the notable exception is *tunestan* for *tavânestan)*. Some of the personal endings, however, undergo slight changes and reductions:

-am	*-im*
-i	*-in*
(-esh)	*-an*

An example is the past absolute inflection of *raftan:*

ráftam	*ráftim*
ráfti	*ráftin*
ráft(esh)	*ráftan*

The third-person singular zero ending of written Persian is often replaced in spoken Persian by *-esh.* Its use is optional.

94.2 Present stems, with exceptions noted below in §95, remain as in written Persian, as does the *mi-* progressive marker. The personal endings for stems ending in consonants are:

-am	*-im*

-i	*-in*
-e[1]	*-an*

as in the inflection of *gereftan:*

mígiram	*mígirim*
mígiri	*mígirin*
mígire	*mígiran*

For stems ending in vowels, the personal endings are:

-m	*-ym*
-y	*-yn*
-d	*-n*

as in the inflection of *umad-/â- (âmadan):*

míâm	*míâym*
míây	*míâyn*
míâd	*míân*

94.3 The past narrative tense is inflected as follows (for the trans-formation *-éa-* > *-á-* and *-éi-* > *-í-* see §92.5 above).

raftám	*raftím*
raftí	*raftín*
rafté	*raftán*

Note that, except in the third person singular, the only distinction between the past absolute and past narrative is one of stress. In all negatives *(náraftam)*, progressives *(míraftam)* and compounds *(bár-dâshtam)*, i.e., where the primary stress is removed from the verb it-self, the past narrative and the past absolute differ only in the third per-son singular *(náraft–nárafte, míraft–mírafte, bárdâsht–bárdâshte)*.

94.4 The formation of the subjunctive of simple verbs is identical to that of written Persian (using the colloquial form of the present stems given below in §95, e.g., *bénvisam, béram, bíâram, bíâm, várdâram)*.

---

[1]With following enclitic object, *-at-*, as *mígire* but *mígiratesh.*

In compound verbs, however, the *bé-* prefix is becoming more and more prevalent in spoken Persian, and with the exception of truly close compounds like *vardâshtan,* the *bé-* prefix is as likely as not to occur with compounds of *-kardan* and *-shodan.*

§95 Reduced, altered and contracted verbal stems.

WRITTEN FORM	PAST STEM	PRES. STEM	PRESENT 1ST SING.	IMPERATIVE
آوردن	*âvord-*	*-âr-*	*míâram*	*bíâr(in)*
انداختن	*(a)ndâkht-*	*-ndâz-*	*míndâzam*	*bándâz(in)*
برداشتن	*var-dâsht-*	*var-dâr-*	*vár-midâram*	*vár-dâr(in)*
توانستن	*tunest-*	*tun-*	*mítunam*	*bétun(in)*
خواستن	*khâst-*	*khâ-*	*míkhâm*	*békhâ(yn)*
دادن	*dâd-*	*d-*	*mídam*	*bédeh, bédin*
دانستن	*dunest-*	*dun-*	*mídunam*	*bédun(in)*
رفتن	*raft-*	*r-*	*míram*	*bóraw, bérin*
شدن	*shod-*	*sh-*	*mísham*	*béshaw, béshin*
شستن	*shost-*	*shur-*	*míshuram*	*béshur(in)*
شکستن	*sh(e)kast-*	*shkan-*	*míshkanam*	*béshkan(in)*
شنیدن	*shenid-*	*shn(av)-*	*míshn(av)am*	*béshnaw, béshnin*
شناختن	*sh(e)nâkht-*	*shnâs-*	*míshnâsam*	*béshnâs(in)*
گذاشتن	*g(o)zâsht-*	*(g)zâr-*	*mí(g)zâram*	*.bézâr(in), bógzâr(in)*
گذشتن	*g(o)zasht-*	*(g)zar-*	*mí(g)zaram*	*bézar(in) bógzar(in)*
گفتن	*goft-*	*g-*	*mígam*	*bégu, bégin*
نشستن	*n(e)shast-*	*(n)shin-*	*mí(n)shinam*	*bé(n)shin(in)*
نوشتن	*n(e)vesht-*	*nvis-*	*mínvisam*	*bénvis(in)*

§96 The present and past progressive.
In written Persian the present and simple past tenses serve as both habitual and progressive (i.e., *míravam* is both "I go" and "I'm going"; *míraftam* is both "I used

to go" and "I was going"). In colloquial Persian *míram* means only "I go" and *míraftam* means only "I used to go." For the present and past progressive a compound tense formation has developed with *dâshtan* as auxiliary, and they occur only in the affirmative—no negative exists.

The present progressive ("I am going") of *raftan* is as follows:

dâram míram	*dârim mírim*
dâri míri	*dârin mírin*
dâre míre	*dâran míran*

The past progressive ("I was going") is as follows:

dâshtam míraftam	*dâshtim míraftim*
dâshti mírafti	*dâshtin míraftin*
dâsht míraft	*dâshtan míraftan*

Contrast the following:

chekâr-mikonin?	What do you do (for a living)?
dârid chekâr-mikonin?	What are you doing?
rezâ doruq-mige.	Reza tells lies.
rezâ dâre doruq-mige.	Reza is lying.

§97 The direct-object marker. The specific direct-object marker *(-râ)* becomes *-ro* or *-re*. Following consonants the *r* may be dropped, giving *-o/-e*. The literary *márâ* is regularized to *man-o*.

in-o didín?	Have you seen this?
kif-e man-o kojâ gzâshtan?	Where did they put my bag?
inâ-ro kojâ paydâ-kardan?	Where did they find these?
aynak-esh-o gom-karde.	He's lost his glasses.
dar-o vâ-kon!	Open the door!

When a direct object is followed by *-(a)m*, the reflex of *-ham*, the direct-object marker is omitted altogether.

un-am didam.	I saw that one too.
chizâ-ye shomâ-m âvordam.	I brought your things too.

As in the classical language, the reflex of *-râ* is often used in spoken Persian as a dative, especially with verbs of motion and expressions of time.

shirâz-(r)o náraftam.	I haven't gone to Shiraz.
tamâm-e shahr-o gashtim.	We went all about the city.
emshab-(r)o haminjâ békhâbin.	Sleep here tonight.

§98 The emphasizing particle -*ke*. The particle *ke,* not to be confused with the relative pronoun (§40) or the temporal conjunction (§57), serves to emphasize the word it follows. The same effect is achieved in English by voice intonation.

ín-ke dorost nist.	*This* is not right.
in doróst-ke nist.	This is not *right*.
in dorost níst-ke.	This is *not* right.
mán-ke némiram máge be zur-am bébarin!	*I'*m not going unless you take me by force!

§99 Pronominal enclitics. There are two sets of pronominal enclitics, one postconsonantal and the other postvocalic. Following consonants, the enclitics are:

-am	*-emun*	*pedáram*	*pedáremun*
-et	*-etun*	*pedáret*	*pedáretun*
-esh	*-eshun*	*pedáresh*	*pedáreshun*

Following vowels, the enclitics are:

-m	*-mun*	*khunám*	*khunámun*
-t	*-tun*	*khunát*	*khunátun*
-sh	*-shun*	*khunásh*	*khunáshun*

§100 Prepositions. Most prepositions remain as they are in written Persian. *Dar* "in, inside" is seldom used in spoken Persian, however; in its place *tu* (optionally *tu-ye*) is used. Prepositional phrases of location tend to follow the verb, unlike written Persian.

ráftan tu(-ye) un khune.	They went into that house.
gozâshtamesh tu(-ye) keshu.	I put it in the drawer.

212

bíâyn tu!   Come in!

In expressions of motion toward and location in, prepositions are generally dispensed with entirely in spoken Persian.

del-am míkhâst béram tehrun.	I wanted to go to Tehran.
man emruz némikhâm bémunam khune.	I don't want to stay at home today.
bâyad un daftar-e dige bâshe.	He should be in that other office.

Contrary to written usage, the pronominal enclitics can be added to all prepositions. With the enclitics *be* becomes *béh-* (*béham, béhet, béhesh,* etc.), *bâ* becomes *bâhâ-* (*bâhâm, bâhât, bâhâsh,* etc.) and *hamrâh* becomes *hamrâhâ-* (*hamrâhâm, hamrâhât, hamrâhâsh,* etc.). The only other simple preposition in common use is *az, bar* being obsolete and *dar* being either omitted or suppleted by *tu.*

béhesh nágoftin zud bíâd?	Didn't you tell him to come early?
ali bâhâm bude.	Ali was with me.
un hamrâhâsh kíe?	Who's that with her?
ázesh khosh-et némiâd?	Don't you like it?

Appendix A

The Uses of *T â*

I. The preposition *tâ* can mean "until," "up to," or "by" (with reference to time).

تا آن وقت اورا ندیده بودیم.	*tâ ân vaqt u-râ nádide-budim.*	We hadn't seen him **until** then.
این برنامه تا ساعت ۲۲ ادامه دارد.	*in barnâme tâ sâ'at-e bist-o do edâme-dârad.*	This program will continue **until** 10 PM.
تا بحال چنین چیزی‌را نشنیده ایم.	*tâ be hâl chonin chiz-i-râ náshenideim.*	**Up to** now we haven't heard of such a thing.
تا فردا باید تا صفحهٔ دویست این کتاب را بخوانیم.	*tâ fardâ bâyad tâ safhe-ye 200-e in ketâb-râ békhânim.*	**By** tomorrow we have to read **up to** page 200 in this book.
تا اندازه‌ای درست است.	*tâ andâze-i dorost-ast.*	**To** a certain extent it is right.

II. The conjunction *tâ* has a variety of meanings depending upon its usage.

(1) With the present indicative it usually means "(for) as long as" or "since."

215

تا آنجاست من نباید   *tâ ânjâ-st man nábâyad*   As long as (since)
بروم.   *bémiravam.*   he's there, I don't
   have to go.

(2) With the subjunctive *tâ* means:

(a) "so long as" or "insofar as" with reference to the future.

تا تو زنده باشی دیگر   *tâ to zende bâshi,*   Don't ever say any
از این حرفها نزن!   *digar az in harfhâ*   more of these things
   názan!   **so long as** you
   live!

تا توانی از وقتت   *tâ tavâni az vaqt-et*   **Insofar as** you are
استفاده کن.   *estefâde-kon.*   able, make use of
   your time.

(b) "until" (when the *tâ*-clause follows the main verb).

من همینجا میمانم تا شما   *man haminjâ mímâ-*   I'll stay here **until**
برگردید.   *nam tâ shomâ bar-*   you return.
   gardid.

(c) "by the time that" with reference to the future.

تا بیائید دیر شده   *tâ bíâid dir-shode-ast.*   **By the time** you
است.   come it'll be too
   late.

(d) "in order that" for a final purpose clause.

آمدم تا اورا ببینم.   *âmadam tâ u-râ*   I came **in order to**
   bébinam.   see him.

(3) With the negative present subjunctive it can mean:

(a) "until"

تا اورا نبینم نمیتوانم   *tâ u-râ nábinam némi-*   I can't go **until** I see
بروم.   *tavânam béravam.*   him.

(b) "before"

بايد تا دير نشود اورا   *bâyad tâ dir náshavad*   I have to see him
ببينم .   *u-râ bébinam.*   **before** it's too late.

(4) With the past absolute *tâ* means

(a) "by the time" with reference to the past:

تا على رسيد آنها رفته   *tâ ali resid, ânhâ rafte-*   **By the time** Ali
بودند .   *budand.*   arrived, they had
gone.

(b) "as soon as":

تا رسيديم اورا ديديم .   *tâ residim u-râ didim.*   **As soon as** we
arrived we saw him.

Appendix B
Telling Time, Days of the Week, Months of the Year

Telling Time

ساعت چند است؟	*sâ'at-e chand-ast?*	What time is it?
ساعت ده است.	*sâ'at-e dah-ast.*	It's ten o'clock.
ساعت ده و ربع است.	*sâ'at-e dah-o rob'-ast.*	It's ten fifteen.
ساعت ده و نیم است.	*sâ'at-e dah-o nim-ast.*	It's ten thirty.
ساعت یازده و ربع کم است.	*sâ'at-e yâzdah-o rob' kam-ast.*	It's quarter to eleven (ten forty-five).

Divisions of the Day

بامداد	*bâmdâd*	early morning (dawn)
صبح	*sobh*	morning (generally)
قبل از ظهر	*qabl az zohr*	before noon (AM)
ظهر	*zohr*	noon
بعد از ظهر	*ba'd az zohr*	after noon (PM)
عصر	*asr*	late afternoon, early evening
شب	*shab*	night
نیمه شب، نصف شب	*nimeshab, nesf-e shab*	midnight

218

ساعت شش قبل از ظهر امروز	sâ'at-e shesh-e qablaz-zohr-e emruz	6 AM today
ساعت شش بعد از ظهر فردا	sâ'at-e shesh-e ba'daz-zohr-e fardâ	6 PM tomorrow
ساعت نیم	sâ'at-e nim	12:30 PM

Days of the Week

| امروز چندشنبه است؟ | emruz chandshambe-ast? | What day of the week is it today? |
| امروز شنبه است. | emruz shambe-ast. | Today's Saturday. |

شنبه	shambe	Saturday
یکشنبه	yekshambe	Sunday
دوشنبه	doshambe	Monday
سه شنبه	seshambe	Tuesday
چهارشنبه	chahârshambe	Wednesday
پنجشنبه	panjshambe	Thursday
جمعه	jom'e	Friday

Since traditionally the day of the week starts at sundown, the night is generally called the "eve" of what we call the next day.

| شب جمعه | shab-e jom'e | Thursday night ("Friday eve") |
| شب یکشنبه | shab-e yekshambe | Saturday night ("Sunday eve") |

When *shab* is placed after the name of the day, it means the night following that day.

| جمعه شب | jom'e shab | Friday night |
| یکشنبه شب | yekshambe shab | Sunday night |

The plural is used for expressing "on Monday," etc.

پنجشنبه‌ها و جمعه‌ها   *panjshambehâ-o*   We don't work on
کار نمی‌کنیم.   *jom'ehâ kâr-*   Thursday or Friday.
   némikonim.

Months of the Year

The Iranian calendar begins each year at the vernal equinox *(nawruz = 1 Farvardin)*, which usually falls on March 21st. The first six months contain thirty-one days each; the second five months contain thirty days each; the last month contains twenty-nine days except in leap years, when it has thirty. The Iranian months correspond to the signs of the zodiac.

فصل بهار   *fasl-e bahâr* spring

فروردین   *farvardin* (March 21–April 20, Aries)

اردیبهشت   *ordibehesht* (April 21–May 21, Taurus)

خرداد   *khordâd* (May 22–June 21, Gemini)

فصل تابستان   *fasl-e tâbestân* summer

تیر   *tir* (June 22–July 22, Cancer)

مرداد   *mordâd* (July 23–August 22, Leo)

شهریور   *shahrivar* (August 23–September 22, Virgo)

فصل پائیز   *fasl-e pâiz* autumn

مهر   *mehr* (September 23–October 22, Libra)

آبان   *âbân* (October 23–November 21, Scorpio)

آذر   *âzar* (November 22–December 21, Sagittarius)

فصل زمستان   *fasl-e zemestân* winter

دی   *day* (December 22–January 20, Capricorn)

بهمن   *bahman* (January 21–February 19, Aquarius)

اسفند (یار)   *esfand(yâr)* (February 20–March 20, Pisces)

The Solar Hegira era *(hejri-e shamsi)* is used in Iran. On *nawruz,* the vernal equinox and Iranian New Year's Day, the Solar Hegira era is 621 years behind the Christian era.

On March 21, 1976 (1 Farvardin 2535) the Imperial *(shâhanshâhi)* era was proclaimed. On Nawruz the Imperial era was 559 years ahead of the Christian era. The Imperial era was cancelled after about two years, and Iran returned to the Solar Hegira calendar.

The other calendrical system in use in Iran is the Islamic lunar Hegira era (A.H., *anno hegirae),* which began in A.D. 622 with the migration of the Prophet Muhammad from Mecca to Medina. This calendar is used for determining religious holidays in Iran and, being lunar, it bears no readily discernable relation to the solar year of the Christian or Solar Hegira calendars. The lunar year falls $11^{1}/_{4}$ days short of the solar year annually. The formulae for conversion are:

$$A.D. = (A.H. \times 0.970225) + 621.54$$
$$A.H. = (A.D. - 621.54) \div 0.970225$$

The Islamic lunar months, which do not correspond with solar months in any way, are:

محرم	*moharram*	رجب	*rajab*
صفر	*safar*	شعبان	*sha'bân*
ربیع‌الاول	*rabi'ol'avval*	رمضان	*ramazân*
ربیع‌الثانی	*rabi'ossâni*	شوال	*shavvâl*
جمادی‌الاولی	*jomâdal'ulâ*	ذی‌القعده	*zelqa'de*
جمادی‌الاخری	*jomâdal'okhrâ*	ذی‌الحجه	*zelhejje*

The European-style months used in Persian, taken from French, are as follows:

ژانویه	*zhânvie* January	آوریل	*âvril* April
فوریه	*fevrie* February	مه	*me* May
مارس	*mârs* March	ژوئن	*zhuan* June

221

ژوئیه *zhuie* July   اکتبر *oktobr* October

اوت *ut* August   نوامبر *novâmbr* November

سپتامبر *septâmbr* September   دسامبر *desâmbr* December

Reading Dates

Dates are read in the following fashion. Note particularly where *ezâfe*s fall.

۱۱ اوت ۱۹۹۲ (م)	*yâzdahom-e ut (sâl)-e yek-hezâr-o nohsad-o navad-o do(-e milâdi)*	August 11, 1992 (A.D.)
۲۰ مرداد ۱۳۷۱ (ه ش)	*bistom-e mordâd (sâl)-e yek-hezâr-o sisad-o haftâd-o yek(-e hejri-e shamsi)*	20 Mordad 1371 (Solar Hegira)
۱۱ صفر ۱۴۱۳ (ه ق)	*yâzdahom-e safar (sâl)-e yek-hezâr-o chahârsad-o sizdah (-e hejri-e qamari)*	11 Safar 1413 (A.H., Lunar Hegira)

نمونه‌هائی چند   Examples of
از نثر معاصر   Contemporary
فارسی   Persian Prose

میگویند در زمانهای قدیم یك كاسب كم مایهٔ كاشی هرچه داشت فروخت
و دست زنش را گرفت و از كاشان خارج شد و رفت و رفت تا به تبریز
رسید . در آنجا یك دكان كباب پزی دایر كرد .

در اولین روزی كه دكان آب و جاروب شد ، كاسب كاشی به انتظار
5   مشتری نشست و پس از چند دقیقه‌ای چهار نفر از باباشمل‌های تبریز
وارد دكان شدند و از كباب مفصل طلب كردند و با نان خوردند. هنگام
خروج از دكان به صاحب دكان بطور آمرانه گفتند «آهای از پول خبری
نیست. صدایت هم در نیاید. اگر میخواهی در امان باشی باید هر روز
همینطور از ما پذیرائی كنی. آن هم مجانی. فهمیدی؟ در غیر اینصورت
10   پدرت را در می‌آوریم!»

این حرفها را زدند و رفتند. كاشی بینوا از ترس بلافاصله دكان را بست
و از تبریز با زنش خارج شد و آمد و آمد تا به شهر و دیار خود ، یعنی
كاشان ، رسید. به محض ورود به خانهٔ قبلی به زنش گفت «در خانه را
محكم ببند!» او هم بست. مرد كاشی بالای بام رفت ، رو به شهر تبریز
15   ایستاد و با فریاد عصبانیت دستها را مرتب بالا و پائین برد و به لوطی‌ها و
باباشمل‌های تبریز بد و بیراه گفت و با توپ و تشر افزود كه «من پدرتان
را درمیآورم! مرا میترسانید ؟!»

زنش از داخل حیاط فریاد زد «باباجان، بیا پائین! میخواهی خون راه
بیندازی؟»

---

1 *kâseb* tradesman; *kammâye* petty; *kâshi* native of Kashan (Kashanis have a reputation for timidity, while Tabrizis are noted for being "rough and tough")

2 *khârej-shodan* to go out

3 *dokkân-e kabâbpazi* kabob shop; *dâyer-kardan* to open, run

4 *âb-o-jârub-shodan* to be swept clean; *entezâr* expectation

5 *moshtari* customer; *bâbâshamal* ruffian, tough

6 *mofassal* elaborate; *talab-kardan* to order; *nân* bread (kabob is customarily ordered with either bread or rice); *hengâm-e* at the time of

7 *khoruj* going out, leaving; *sâheb-dokkân* shopkeeper; *âmerâne* imperious; *âhây* hey!; *khabar* news

8 *amân* safety

9 *pazirâi-kardan az* receive, take care of; *majâni* gratis; *dar qayr-e in surat* otherwise

10 *pedar-e kas-i-râ dar-âvordan* to "get" somebody

11 *binavâ* miserable; *belâfâsele* immediately

12 *diâr* region; *ya'ni* that is

224

13 *be mahz-e vorud* immediately upon entering
14 *bâm* roof; *ru be* facing
15 *istâd-/ist-* stand; *faryâd* shout; *asabâniyat* anger; *morattab* continuous(ly); *luti* ruffian
16 *bad-o birâh goftan* to curse at; *bâ tup-*

o tashar vindictively; *afzud-/afzâ-* to add
17 *tarsânidan* see §72
18 *hayât* courtyard; *faryâd-zadan* to shout; *bâbâ-jân* address of endearment; *khun râh-andâkhtan* to start a (blood) feud

٢

نیم کیلو گوشت گوسفند خریده بودم و از حاشیهٔ خیابان گلچین گلچین بطرف خانه میرفتم که دوستی به من رسید و بعد از خوش و بش و احوال پرسی ، دیدم عینک طبی و به اصطلاح «ذره‌بینی» به چشم دارد .

با تعجب گفتم «فلانی ، مگر چشمهایت عیب و علتی پیدا کرده؟»

5   گفت «نه ، یک چشمم کمی ضعیف شده بود و اشیاءرا درست نمی‌دید و روزنامه درست نمی‌توانستم بخوانم . بناچار به چشم‌پزشک مراجعه کردم و معلوم شد که چشم چپم ضعیف شده و دکتر این عینک‌را داد که به چشم بزنم.» خداحافظی کرد و رفت .

بعد از رفتن دوستم احساس کردم یک چشم من هم ضعیف است . یعنی
10   چه؟ تا چند لحظهٔ پیش که خوب بود . چطور ظرف چند ثانیه یکی‌اش ضعیف شد؟ کمی فکر کردم که بدانم کدام چشمم ضعیف است . نتوانستم چیزی بفهم . لاعلاج همانجا کنار پیاده‌رو ایستادم و پاکت گوشت‌را روی زمین گذاشتم . چشم چپم را بستم و با چشم راست کلاغی‌را که (روی آنتن

1 *gusht* meat; *gusfand* sheep; *hâshie* edge; *khiâbân* avenue; *golchin* gingerly, carefully
2 *khosh-o besh* chit-chat; *ahvâlporsi* asking one's condition
3 *aynak-e tebbi* prescription glasses; *be estelâh* idiomatically, "as they say"; *zarrebin* magnifying glass
4 *ta'ajjob* astonishment; *folâni* "so-and-so," dummy name; *ayb* defect, fault; *ellat* malady
5 *za'if* weak; *shay'* pl *ashyâ'* thing
6 *be nâchâr* "there was nothing to be done but"; *cheshmpezeshk* eye doctor;

morâje'e-kardan to consult
7 *ma'lum-shodan* become apparent, be learned; *chap* left
9 *ehsâs-kardan* to feel; *ya'ni che?* what does it mean?
10 *lahze* moment; *zarf-e* within; *sânie* second
12 *lâ'elâj* = *be nâchâr*, see line 6 above; *kenâr* edge; *piâderaw* sidewalk; *pâket* package
13 *râst* right; *kalâq* crow; *ânten* antenna

رادیوی پشت بام خانهٔ مقابل نشسته بود، نشانه گرفتم. دیدم درست است.
کلاغ را کاملاً می‌بینم. رنگش سیاه است. نوکش بقاعده است و پاهایش را
هم خوب می‌بینم. خاطرم جمع شد که چشم راستم معیوب نیست و هر
عیبی هست در چشم چپ است.

5   کف دستم را گذاشتم روی چشم راست و با چشم چپ کلاغ را نشانه
گرفتم. بی‌اختیار دلم فرو ریخت. سرم درد گرفت و شقیقه‌هایم شروع کرد
به زدن. گردن کلاغ کوتاه شده بود، نوک‌ش را درست نمی‌دیدم، پاهایش
محو بود و رنگش خاکستری. یعنی چه؟ دستپاچه شدم. فوری دستم را از
روی چشم راستم برداشتم و چشم چپم را بستم. دیدم درست می‌بینم.

10 کلاغ همان کلاغ اولی است، ولی مگر به این زودی امکان داشت که من
دست از این آزمایش طبی بردارم؟

   پاکت گوشت را روی زمین گذاشتم و به دیوار پیاده‌رو و خیابان تکیه
دادم و دیگر بدون اینکه از کف دستهایم کمک بگیرم، با بستن و باز
کردن پلکهای چشمم شروع کردم به آزمایش کردن. از بد حادثه نمی‌دانم

15 کلاغ مورد نشانه و آزمایش من از چه چیز ترسید که رم کرد و پرید و من
ماندم بی‌نشانه. برای پیدا کردن هدف تازه‌ای به تکاپو افتادم ولی از بس
هول شده بودم چشم راستم هم دیگر کار نمیکرد. بالاخره گنجشکی را که
بفاصلهٔ سیصد متری روی سیم برق خیابان نشسته بود پیدا کردم و
بلافاصله با چشم راست امتحان کردم. دیدم در گنجشک بودنش حرفی

20 نیست ولی کمی ریزتر شد، و با چشم چپم که نگاه کردم روی سیم فقط

---

1 *posht-e bâm* roof; *moqâbel* opposite;
   neshâne-gereftan to take aim at

2 *nuk* beak; *be qâ'ede* as it should be

3 *khâter jam'-shodan* to be relieved;
   ma'yub faulty

5 *kaff-e dast* palm of the hand

6 *biekhtiâr* involuntarily; *del foru-*
   rikhtan for the heart to sink; *shaqiqe*
   temple

7 *gardan* neck; *pâ* foot

8 *mahv* blurred; *khâkestari* grey; *dast-*
   pâche-shodan to get nervous; *fawri*
   immediately

11 *âzmâyesh-e tebbi* medical experiment

12 *takye-dâdan be* to lean against

13 *komak* help

14 *pelk* eyelid; *az bad-e hâdese* as bad
   luck would have it

15 *mawred-e neshâne* that was the object
   of my aim; *ram-kardan* to shy; *paridan*
   to fly off

16 *hadaf* target; *takâpu* search

17 *hawl-shodan* to be terrified; *gonjeshk*
   sparrow

18 *sim* wire

19 *emtehân-kardan* to test; *harf-i nist dar*
   there's no question about

20 *riz* tiny

یك نقطهٔ سیاه دیدم. اصلاً و ابداً شباهتی به گنجشك نداشت. مردی را كه
از كنارم میگذشت صدا كردم و گفتم «داداش، بیزحمت یك چشمت را
ببند!»

مردك از همه جا بیخبر نگاه معنیداری به من كرد و قبل از اینكه به
دستور من عمل كند و یك چشمش را ببندد، با كمك دستهایش در
جیبهایش را محكم گرفت و بعد پرسید «چرا؟»

گفتم «تو چكار داری؟ ببند!»

مردك كه به خیالش میخواهم یا جیبش را بزنم یا یك چشمه از
چشمبندیهای پروفسور شاندو و میرزا ملكم خان را نشانش بدهم، روبروی
من ایستاد و یك چشمش را بست. گفتم «حالا پشتت را به من بكن و ببین
آنطرف خیابان روی سیم چه میبینی؟» باز یكی دیگر از همان نگاههای
معنیدار به من كرد و سرش را بطرفی كه من نشان داده بودم گرداند و
گفت «هیچی!»

دیدم این مادرمرده از من كورتر است. پرسیدم «روی سیم چیزی
نیست؟» گفت «نه» گفتم «كور خدا! من با یك چشم سالم می بینم. تو
چطور نمیبینی؟»

گفت «كور پدرت است! كور مادرت است! خوب، نمیبینم. مگر زور
است؟»

یك چشمم را بستم و با چشم دیگرم روی سیم را نگاه كردم. دیدم من
هم چیزی نمیبینم. چشم معیوبم را بستم و با چشم سالم نگاه كردم. باز
هم چیزی ندیدم. دستپاچه شدم كه نكند هر دو چشم معیوب شده.

1 *noqte* point, dot; *aslan o abadan* (not)
in the least; *shebâhat* resemblance

2 *kenâr* side; *dâdâsh* brother (colloq.);
bizahmat "if it's no bother," please

3 *az hame jâ bikhabar* "with no idea
what's going on"; *ma' nidâr* meaning-
ful

4 *dastur* order; *amal-kardan be* to act on;
dar-e jib pocket flap; *mohkam* tight

8 *be khiâl-esh* "as he thought"; *jib-zadan*
to pickpocket; *yek cheshme az
cheshmbandihâ* a sleight-of-hand trick

9 Prof. Shandou, a famous magician in

Iran; Mirza Malkom Khan, infamous
for deceit and trickery

10 *posht* back(side)

12 *sar gardândan* to turn the head

14 *mâdarmorde* "poor fellow"; *kur* blind

15 *kur-e khodâ* blind fool; *sâlem* sound,
good

17 *kur pedar-et ast...* an impolite rejoin-
der to the author's having called him a
blind fool; *magar zur-ast?* "Do I have
to?"

مردك با عصبانیت گفت «آخر، مقصودت چیست؟ چه چیزرا میخواهی

ببینی؟»

گفتم «گنجشکی روی آن سیم بود . حالا نمی‌بینمش .»

خودش‌را کنار کشید و گفت «حتماً پریده. گنجشك مال شما بود؟»

5   گفتم «نه ، من گنجشکم کجا بود؟» انگشت ایمایش را کلنگی کرد و چند

بار به بالای شقیقه‌اش کوبید و گفت «تو هم اگر عقل درستی داشتی،

روزگارت بهتر از این بود» و راه افتاد .

از عینك طبی، اثر خسرو شاهانی

1 *asabâniyat* anger; *maqsud* intent	6 *kubidan* to tap; *aql* mind
5 *gonjeshk-am kojâ bud?* Where would I get a sparrow from?; *angosht-e imâ* index finger; *kolangi-kardan* to crook	7 *ruzgâr-et behtar bud* "you'd be better off"

۳

من یك روز گرم تابستان، دقیقاً یك سیزده مرداد ، حدود ساعت سه و

ربع کم بعد از ظهر عاشق شدم. تلخی‌ها و زهر هجری که چشیدم بارها

مرا به این فکر انداخت که اگر یك دوازدهم یا یك چهاردهم مرداد بود ،

شاید اینطور نمی‌شد .

5   آن روز هم مثل هر روز، با فشار و زور و تهدید و کمی وعده های

طلائی برای عصر، مارا ، یعنی من و خواهرم‌را ، توی زیرزمین کرده بودند

که بخوابیم. در گرمای شدید تهران خواب بعد از ظهر برای همۀ بچه‌ها

اجباری بود . ولی آنروز هم ما مثل هر بعد از ظهر دیگر در انتظار این

بودیم که آقاجان خوابش ببرد و برای بازی به باغ برویم. وقتی صدای

10   خورخور آقاجان بلند شد ، من سررا از زیر شمد بیرون آوردم و نگاهی به

1 *daqiqan* exactly; *hodud-e* about	6 *asr* late afternoon; *zirzamin* basement
2 *âsheq-shodan* to fall in love; *talkh* bitter; *zahr-e hajr* pangs of separation; *cheshidan* to taste	7 *garmâ* heat; *shadid* severe
	8 *ejbâri* obligatory; *entezâr* expectation
3 *kas-i-râ be fekr andâkhtan* to make s.o. think	9 *âqâ-jân* "daddy"; *bâzi* play
	10 *khorkhor* snoring; *shamad* sheet
5 *feshâr* pressure; *zur* force; *tahdid* threat; *va'de-ye talâ'i* promise of something nice	

ساعت دیواری انداختم. ساعت دو و نیم بعد از ظهر بود. طفلک خواهرم

در انتظار بخواب رفتن آقاجان خوابش برده بود. ناچار گذاشتم و تنها

پاورچین بیرون آمدم.

لیلی دختر دائی‌جان و برادر کوچکش نیم ساعتی بود در باغ انتظار

مارا می‌کشیدند. بین خانه‌های ما که در یک باغ بزرگ ساخته شده بود،

دیواری وجود نداشت. مثل هر روز زیر سایهٔ درخت گردوی بزرگ بدون

سر و صدا مشغول صحبت و بازی شدیم. یکوقت نگاه من به نگاه لیلی

افتاد. یک جفت چشم سیاه درشت به من نگاه میکرد. نتوانستم نگاهم را از

نگاه او جدا کنم. هیچ نمیدانم چه مدت ما چشم در چشم هم دوخته

بودیم که ناگهان مادرم با شلاق چندشاخه‌ای بالای سر ما ظاهر شد. لیلی و

برادرش به خانهٔ خود فرار کردند و مادر تهدید کنان مرا به زیرزمین زیر

شمد برگرداند. قبل از اینکه سرم بکلی زیر شمد پنهان شود چشمم به

ساعت دیواری افتاد. سه و ده دقیقه کم بعد از ظهر بود. مادرم قبل از

اینکه بنوبت خود سرش را زیر شمد کند، گفت «خدا رحمت کرد دائیت

بیدار نشد وگرنه همه‌تان را تکه تکه میکرد.»

مادرم حق داشت. دائی‌جان نسبت به دستوراتی که میداد خیلی تعصب

داشت. دستور داده بود که بچه‌ها قبل از ساعت پنج بعد از ظهر حتی

نفس نباید بکشند. داخل چهار دیواری باغ نه تنها ما بچه‌ها مزهٔ نخوابیدن

بعد از ظهر و سر و صدا کردن در موقع خواب دائی‌جان را چشیده

1 *teflak* poor kid

2 *gozâshtam-o…âmadan* "I set out and came"

3 *pâvarchin* on tiptoes

4 *dâi-jân* "dear uncle"; *entezâr-e kas-i-râ keshidan* to wait for s.o.

6 *vojud-dâshtan* to exist; *sâye* shade; *derakht* tree; *gerdu* walnut; *bedun-e* without

7 *sar-o sedâ* noise; *bâzi* play

8 *joft* pair; *dorosht* huge

9 *jodâ-kardan* to separate; *che moddat* how long; *cheshm dar chashm-e ham dukhte* staring at each other

10 *nâgahân* suddenly; *shallâq* switch; *chandshâkhei* made of several

branches; *zâher-shodan* to appear

11 *farâr-kardan* to run away; *tahdid-kardan* to threaten

12 *penhân-shodan* to disappear

14 *nawbat* turn; *rahmat-kardan* to have mercy

15 *teketeke-kardan* to chop to pieces

16 *haqq-dâshtan* to be right; *nesbat be* in relation to; *dastur -ât* order; *ta'assob* fanaticism

18 *nafas-keshidan* to breathe; *dâkhel-e* within; *maze-ye chiz-i-râ cheshidan* to have a taste of s.th.

19 *sarosedâ-kardan* to make a racket

229

بودیم ، بلکه کلاغها و کبوترها هم کمتر در آن محدودده پیدایشان میشد ۱

چون دائیجان چند بار با تفنگ شکاری آنهارا قلع و قمع کرده بود . ۲

فروشندگان دوره‌گرد هم تا حدود ساعت پنج از کوچهٔ ما که به اسم دائی ۳

جان موسوم بود عبور نمی‌کردند زیرا دو سه دفعه الاغی طالبی‌فروش و ۴

پیازی از دائیجان سیلی خورده بودند . ۵

اما آنروز خاطر من سخت مشغول بود و اسم دائیجان خاطرات دعواها
و اوقات تلخی‌های اورا به یادم نیاورد . حتی یک لحظه از یاد چشمهای لیلی
و نگاه او نمی‌توانستم فارغ شوم و به هر طرف می‌غلطیدم و به هر چیزی
سعی می‌کردم فکر کنم چشمهای سیاه اورا روشن‌تر از آنکه واقعاً در برابرم
باشد می‌دیدم . ۱۰

شب باز توی پشه‌بند چشمهای لیلی به سراغم آمدند . عصر دیگر اورا
ندیده بودم ولی چشمها و نگاه نوازشگرش آنجا بودند . نمیدانم چه مدت
گذشت . ناگهان فکر عجیبی تمام مغزمرا فرا گرفت : خدایا ، نکند عاشق
لیلی شده باشم! سعی کردم به این فکرم بخندم ولی هیچ خنده‌ام نیامد .
ممکن است آدم از یک فکر احمقانه خنده‌اش نگیرد ولی دلیل نمیشود که ۱۵
احمقانه نباشد . مگر ممکن است آدم اینطور بدون مقدمه عاشق شود ؟
سعی کردم کلیهٔ اطلاعاتمرا دربارهٔ عشق بررسی کنم . متأسفانه این
اطلاعات وسیع نبود . با اینکه بیش از سیزده سال از عمرم میگذشت ، تا

1 *kabutar* pigeon; *mahdude* limited (period); *paydâ-yeshân mishod* "they were to be found"

2 *tofang-e shekâri* shotgun; *qal'oqam'-kardan* to exterminate

3 *forushande-ye dawregard* peddler; *kuche* lane

4 *mawsum be* named for; *obur-kardan* to cross, come through; *zirâ* because; *olâqi* donkey driver; *tâlebi* melon

5 *piâzi* onion seller; *sili-khordan* to get slapped

6 *khâter* mind; *khâterât* memories; *da'vâ* fight

7 *awqâttalkhi* bad mood; *lahze* moment

8 *fâregh-shodan az* to be free of; *qaltidan* to toss

9 *vâqe'an* really, actually; *dar barâbar-e* opposite, in front of

11 *tu-ye* inside of; *pasheband* mosquito net; *be sorâq-e kas-i âmadan* to come in search of s.o.

12 *navâzeshgar* caressing

13 *ajib* amazing; *maqz* brain; *farâ-gereftan* to seize; *âsheq-e kas-i-râ shodan* to fall in love with s.o.

14 *khandidan be* to laugh at

15 *ahmaqâne* stupid; *dalil némishavad ke* "that doesn't mean that"

16 *moqaddeme* preliminaries

17 *kolliye* totality; *ettelâ'* information; *eshq* love; *barresi-kardan* to inventory; *mota'assefâne* regrettably

18 *vasi'* vast; *omr* life

آن موقع یك عاشق ندیده بودم. کتابهای عاشقانه و شرح حال عشاق هم
آنموقع خیلی کم چاپ شده بود. تازه نمی‌گذاشتند همهٔ آنها را ما بخوانیم.
پدر و مادر و بستگان مخصوصاً دائی‌جان که سایهٔ وجودش و افکار و
عقایدش روی سر همهٔ افراد خانواده بود) هر نوع خروج بدون محافظ از
خانه را برای ما بچه‌ها منع میکردند و جرئت نزدیك شدن به بچه‌های کوچه
را نداشتیم. رادیو هم که خیلی وقت نبود افتتاح شده بود در دو سه
ساعت برنامهٔ روزانهٔ خود مطلب مهمی نداشت که به روشن شدن ذهن کمك
کند.

در مرور اطلاعاتم راجع به عشق، در وهلهٔ اول به لیلی و مجنون
برخوردم که قصه‌اش را بارها شنیده بودم. ولی هرچه زوایای مغزم را کاوش
کردم، دیدم چیزی راجع به طرز عاشق شدن مجنون به لیلی نشنیده‌ام.
فقط میگفتند مجنون عاشق لیلی شد.

اصلاً شاید بهتر بود در این بررسی پای لیلی و مجنون را به میان نمی
کشیدم زیرا هماسم بودن لیلی و دختر دائی‌جان احتمالاً بدون اینکه خودم
بدانم در استنتاجهای بعدیم مؤثر بود. اما چاره ای نداشتم. مهمترین
عشاق آشنایم همین لیلی و مجنون بودند. غیر از آنها از شیرین و فرهاد
هم، مخصوصاً از طرز عاشق شدن آنها، چیزی زیادی نمی‌دانستم. یك
داستان عاشقانه هم که در پاورقی یك روزنامه چاپ شده بود خوانده بودم

1 *âsheq* pl *oshshâq* lover; *âsheqâne* romantic; *sharh-e hâl* biography
2 *châp-shodan* to be printed; *tâze* more-
over
3 *baste -gân* relative; *makhsusan* especially; *fekr* pl *afkâr* thought, idea
4 *aqide* pl *aqâyed* belief; *fard* pl *afrâd* individual; *khânevâde* family; *khoruj*
going out; *bedun-e* without; *mohâfez*
guardian
5 *man'-kardan* to forbid; *jor'at-dâshtan* to
dare
6 *eftetâh-shodan* to be inaugurated
7 *barnâme* program; *zehn* mind; *komak-
kardan* to help
9 *morur* review; *râje' be* about; *dar
vahle-ye avval* in the first instance
10 *bar-khordan be* to come across; *qesse*
story; *zâvie* pl *zavâyâ* corner, recess;
kâvesh-kardan to scrape
11 *tarz* manner
13 *aslan* actually; *pâ-ye kas-i-râ be miân
keshidan* to get s.o. involved
14 *zírâ* because; *ham-esm* namesake;
ehtemâlan probably
15 *estentâj* conclusion; *ba'di* later (adj.);
mo'asser influential; *châre* remedy
16 *qayr az* other than, aside from
18 *dâstân* story; *pâvaraqi* the bottom of a
page of newsprint, where serialized
novels were often printed

ولی چند شمارهٔ اولش را نخوانده بودم و یکی از همکلاسی هایم برایم
تعریف کرده بود . در نتیجه شروع ماجرا را نمی دانستم .

صدای دوازده ضربهٔ زنگ ساعت دیواری زیرزمین را شنیدم . خدایا ،
نصف شب شده بود و من هنوز نخوابیده بودم . این ساعت تا یادم می آمد

5 در خانهٔ ما بود و اولین بار بود که صدای زنگ ساعت ۱۲ شب را میشنیدم .
شاید این بی خوابی هم دلیلی بر عاشق شدنم بود . در نیمه تاریکی حیاط
که از پشت توری پشه بند سایه های درختها و بته های گل را بصورت اشباح
عجیب و غریبی میدیدم وحشت برم داشته بود چون قبل از اینکه دربارهٔ
عاشق شدن یا نشدنم به نتیجه برسم از سرنوشت عشاقی که مرور کرده

10 بودم وحشت کردم . تقریباً همهٔ آنها سرنوشت غم انگیزی داشتند و ماجرا به
مرگ و میر تمام شده بود .

لیلی و مجنون مرگ و میر ، شیرین و فرهاد مرگ و میر ، رومئو و ژولیت
مرگ و میر ، پل و ورژینی مرگ و میر ، آن پاورقی عاشقانه مرگ و میر .
خدایا نکند واقعاً عاشق شده باشم و من هم بمیرم !

15 از دائی جان ناپلئون ، اثر ایرج پزشکزاد

---

1 *hamkelâsi* classmate
2 *dar natije* as a result
3 *zarbe* strike; *zang* bell
6 *bikhâbi* sleeplessness; *dalil bar* indication of; *târik* dark; *hayât* courtyard
7 *turi* netting; *bote* bush; *be surat-e* in the shape of; *ashbâh* ghosts
8 *ajib-o qarib* strange, fantastic; *vahshat bar-dâshtan* to terrify

9 *be natije residan* to come to a conclusion; *sarnevesht* fate
10 *vahshat-kardan az* to be terrified by; *qam-angiz* tragic
11 *marg-o mir* death and dying
13 Paul and Virginie, a pair of youthful lovers in a story by St. Pierre
15 *nâpole' on* (colloquially *nâpel' on*) Napoleon

to be situated → قرار داس ←

to make an agreement → قرار گذاشتن ←

٤

یک روز صبح که از خواب بیدار شدم، وضع اطاق و خانه‌ام را غیر از
هر روز دیدم. شهری که من قبلاً در آن زندگی میکردم در منطقه‌ای بود
که درخت خرما فقط در گلدانها نگهداری میشد و در زمستان هم حتماً
لازم بود آنها را با گلدانهای دیگر به گلخانه‌ های سر پوشیده و اطاقهای
محفوظ انتقال داد. ولی آنروز صبح وقتی بعادت مرسوم که قبل از بیرون
آمدن از رختخواب، قدری به اینطرف و آنطرف غلت میزنم و خمیازه
میکشم و به اطراف نگاه میکنم، از پنجره به بیرون نگاه کردم، چشمم بر
نخلهای بلندی افتاد که در داخل حیاط، شاخه‌هایش از باد تندی تکان
میخورد و باز دورتر، سرهای درختان خرمای بسیار دیده میشد. نه،
خواب نمی‌دیدم. مشغول تماشای فیلمی هم نبودم. من خودم بودم که از
خواب بیدار شده بودم و با دو چشم در عالم بیداری درختان نخل را در
خارج می‌دیدم که شاخه‌هایشان از وزش باد میلرزید و صدای خش و
خش آن به گوش من میرسید.

خانه‌ام محوطهٔ بزرگی بود که بیشتر به یک باغ متروک و فراموش شده
شباهت داشت که یک ساختمان پهن با یک ردیف ستون چهارگوش و کوتاه
در وسط آن قرار داشت که کف اطاقهای آن با زمین حیاط برابر بود.
زمینی که دور تا دور آن ساختمان بود شاید در چندین سال قبل باغچه
بندی شده بود که تنها درختان قابل ذکر آن همین نخلها بودند که بدنهای

---

1 *vaz'* situation; *qayr az* other than
2 *manteqe* region
3 *khormâ* date; *goldân* flower pot; *negahdâri-shodan* to be kept
4 *golkhâne* greenhouse; *sarpushide* cov-
   ered
5 *mahfuz* protected; *enteqâl-dâdan* to
   move, transfer; *be âdat-e marsum* as
   usual
6 *qalt-zadan* to toss and turn; *khamyâze-
   keshidan* to yawn
8 *nakhl* date palm; *dâkhel-e* inside;
   shâkhe branch; *bâd* wind; *tond* fast;
   takân-khordan to shake
10 *khâb-didan* to dream
11 *bidâr* awake; *âlam* world

12 *khârej* outside; *vazesh-e bâd* blowing
   of the wind; *larzidan* to tremble;
   khesh-o khesh rustle
14 *mohavvate* enclosure; *matruk* abandoned
15 *shebâhat-dâshtan be* to resemble;
   pahn wide, low; *radif* row; *sotun* column; *chahârgush* square
16 *vasat* middle; *qarâr-dâshtan* to be situated; *kaff-e otâq* floor; *barâbar* level
17 *dawr tâ dawr-e* all around; *bâqche-
   bandi-shodan* to be divided into garden
   plots
18 *qâbel-e zekr* worth mentioning; *badan*
   body, trunk

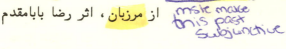

۱ کلفت و گرهدارشان با الیاف قهوه‌ای‌رنگ ، مانند ستون‌هائی ، اینجا و آنجا

۲ دیده میشد . در گوشهٔ باغ هم نزدیك سوراخی که در پای دیوار قرار

۳ داشت و شاید محل ورود یا خروج آب بود چند درخت کج و معوج که

۴ شاخه‌هایشان بطرف زمین خم شده بود خودنمائی میکرد . در باغچه‌ها

۵ علفهای خودرو بسیار روئیده بود و مثل بیابانی بود که علف‌های بهاریش

از تابش آفتاب سوزان تابستان خشکیده باشد .

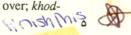

از مرزبان ، اثر رضا بابامقدم

---

1 *koloft* thick; *gerehdâr* knotted; *alyâf* fibers; *qahveirang* coffee-colored; *mânand-e* like

2 *gushe* corner; *surâkh* hole

3 *mahall* place; *vorud* entrance; *khoruj* exit; *kaj-o mo'avvaj* crooked

4 *kham-shodan* to be bent over; *khod-* *nomâi-kardan* to display oneself

5 *alaf* weed; *khodru* wild; *ruidan* to grow; *biâbân* wilderness; *bahâr* spring

6 *tâbesh* heat; *âftâb* sun; *suzân* burning; *khoshkidan* to dry out

7 *marzbân* border guard

او توی رختخواب که افتاد و به عادت همیشه روزنامه و مدادرا دست

گرفت ، دید که نمی‌تواند جدول را حل کند . توی گوشش زنگ میزد و

جدول با خانه‌های سفید و سیاهش که هر دو براق بود و با نور آزار

دهنده ای میدرخشید چشمش‌را میزد . نگاهش روی روزنامه بود ، اما

۵ قیافه‌های تهرانی‌ها و مرتضی خان و خنده ها و حرفهای مسخره‌شان‌را

میدید و میشنید . میدانست که این کارش به نظر آنها چه اندازه بی

معنی و پوچ و ابلهانه است و باز میدانست که جز این ، کار دیگری از

دستش بر نمی‌آید . مثل اینکه به آنها یا خودش لج کرده باشد ، تصمیم

گرفت جدول‌را تا خانهٔ آخر حل کند . از همهٔ کارهای دنیا تنها این کار از

۱۰ دست او بر می‌آمد و او میخواست به خودش ثابت کند که دست کم از

عهدهٔ این کار بر می‌آید .

---

1 *rakhtekhâb* bed(sheets); *be âdat-e hamishe* as usual; *medâd* pencil

2 *jadval* puzzle; *hall-kardan* to solve; *zang-zadan* to ring, buzz

3 *barrâq* glittering; *nur* light; *âzâr-dâdan* to annoy

4 *derakhshidan* to shine

5 *qiâfe* face; *mortazâ khân* proper name; *khande* laughter; *maskhare* derisive

6 *nazar* view, opinion; *bima'ni* meaningless

7 *puch* silly; *ablahâne* stupid

8 *kâr az dast bar-âmadan* to be capable of doing s.th.; *lajj-kardan* to be obstinate; *tasmim-gereftan* to decide

10 *sâbet-kardan* to prove; *dast-e kam* at least

11 *az ohde bar-âmadan* to accomplish

با سماجت شرح خانه هارا میخواند و به مغزش فشار میآورد . میخواست
کلمهٔ صحیح‌را حدس بزند و جدول‌را با اشتباههای خودش کثیف و سیاه
نکند . اما کلمه‌های گوناگون مثل اخگرهائی که از ذغال افروخته می‌جهد ، از
گوشه و کنار ذهنش می‌پرید و پیش از آنکه او بتواند آنهارا بگیرد یا
ببیند خاموش میشد . سرش گیج میرفت . زنگ گوشش زننده و آزار دهنده
شده بود . پلکهایش سنگین میشد و بهم میرفت . و او که میکوشید آنهارا
باز نگهدارد ، درد تحمل‌ناپذیری تخم چشمش‌را بیرون میکشید . تمام
تنش سست شده بود و نزدیک بود رویهم وا برود . دستهایش که روزنامه
و مدادرا گرفته بود تیر میکشید . میخواست روزنامه و مدادرا ول کند و
خودش‌را شل و بیحال زمین بیندازد .

گیج و بی‌تاب و کلافه شده بود . مثل اینکه اورا با زنجیر بسته بودند و
از همه طرف می‌کشیدند . یکباره با بیچارگی به گریه افتاد . هق و هق گریه
میکرد . روی خودش خم شده بود و شانه هایش میلرزید و دانه‌های اشك
از زیر عینکش راه می‌افتاد و روی خانه‌های جدول می‌چکید و پخش
میشد و رنگ جوهررا ظاهر میکرد .

حس میکرد که در این دنیا به درد هیچ کاری نمی‌خورد و باطل و
بیهوده است . هیچ کاری بلد نبود و کارهای پیش پا افتاده‌ای هم که
میدانست تازه نمی‌توانست از عهده‌اش برآید ، یا از آن استفاده‌ای کند که
زندگیش اندکی راحت‌تر یا دلپذیرتر بشود . دلش میخواست یك نفر بود

1 *samâjat* obstinacy; *sharh* explanation; *maqz* brain; *feshâr-âvordan* to apply pressure
2 *kalime* word; *sahih* correct; *eshtebâh* mistake
3 *ammâ* but; *gunâgun* various; *akhgar* spark; *zoqâl* coal; *afrukhtan* to light; *jast-/jeh-* to jump
4 *kenâr* edge; *zehn* mind; *paridan* to fly
5 *gij-raftan* to spin; *pelk* eyelid; *sangin* heavy; *beham-raftan* to go together, close; *kushidan* to try
7 *tahammolnâpazir* unendurable; *tokhm-e cheshm* eyeball
8 *tan* body; *sost* weak; *ruyeham vâ-raftan* to collapse
9 *tir-keshidan* to tingle; *vel-kardan* to let go of
10 *shol* loose; *bihâl* listless
11 *bitâb* weak; *kalâfe* impatient; *zanjir* chain
12 *heq-o heq gerye-kardan* to sob
13 *kham-shodan* to bend over; *shâne* shoulder; *dâne-ye ashk* teardrop
14 *chekidan* to drip; *pakhsh-shodan* to spread
15 *jawhar* ink; *zâher-kardan* to make dark
16 *hess-kardan* to feel; *bâtel* useless
17 *bihude* futile; *pish-e pâ oftâde* trivial
19 *andak-i* a little bit; *râhat* comfortable; *delpazir* pleasant

که سر بر شانه‌اش بگذارد و تا آنجا که میتواند گریه کند ، و او نوازشش
کند و دلداریش بدهد . اما هیچکس را نداشت .

زنش هم که کمی آنطرف‌تر با دهان باز خوابیده بود و نفسهای بلند
پرصدا میکشید چنان غرق خواب بود که از صدای گریهٔ او هم بیدار
نشد . تنها بود ، نشسته بود و تنها و بیچاره زار می گریست . در آخر
روزنامه و مداد از دستش افتاد و پلکهای او با خستگی و سنگینی بهم
رفت . و پیش از آنکه کاملاً بخواب برود فقط توانست عینکش را از
چشمش بردارد .

از جدول کلمات متقاطع ، اثر فریدون تنکابنی

1 *navâzesh-kardan* to comfort
2 *deldâri-dâdan* to console
3 *nafas* breath
4 *qarq-e khâb* fast asleep

5 *zâr geristan* to weep bitterly
9 *jadval-e kalemât-e motaqâte'* crossword
puzzle

مرد پس از اینکه نماز ظهر را در مسجد بزرگ بازار خواند بیرون آمد و
راهی را گرفت و به یکی از محله‌های شهر رفت . بچه‌ها از اینکه موجود
ناشناس و عجیبی را می‌دیدند که همه چیزش برایشان تازگی داشت
خوشحال شدند و دنبالش راه افتادند . و چند دلقک و معرکه‌گیر هم که
کارشان به کسادی کشیده بود به خیال آنکه میتوانند از وجود او و برای
گرمی بازار خودشان استفاده‌ای ببرند به آنها پیوستند . آدمهای کنجکاو هم
طبیعةً از روی کنجکاوی و گداها ، شاید به علت احساسی که از مشترک
بودن سرنوشت خودشان و این فقیر تازه‌وارد که اندکی هم دیوانه می‌نمود
می‌کردند ، به حلقهٔ این جمع درآمدند . مرد جوان نمیدانست با آنها چه

1 *namâz-khândan* to perform prayer; *masjed* mosque
2 *mahalle* quarter; *mawjud* being
3 *nâshenâs* unfamiliar; *ajib* strange
4 *dombâl-e* after, on the heels of; *dalqak* clown, buffoon; *ma'rekegir* acrobat
5 *kasâdi* slump; *be khiâl-e ânke* thinking, imagining that; *vojud* existence
6 *garmi-e bâzâr* briskness of market;

payvast-/payvand- be to join; *konjkâv* curious
7 *tabi' atan* naturally; *gedâ* beggar; *ellat* reason; *ehsâs* feeling; *moshtarek* in common
8 *sarnevesht* fate; *faqir* poor; *tâzevâred* newcomer
9 *halqe* ring; *jam'* group

236

کند . با خودش میگفت «مسلم است که یکتنه از پس آنها برنمیآیم و هرچه
بگویم جریتر خواهند شد .» این بود که تصمیم گرفت پررویی و ایستادگی
کند و به کارشان کاری نداشته باشد . باز به هرکس میرسید سراغ شیخ
بهائی و خانهٔ اورا میگرفت و میگفت کار واجبی با او دارد .

چند جا یکی دو نفر به خیال افتادند که اورا گول بزنند . خودشان یا
دیگریرا «شیخ بهائی» نامیدند ، اما خنده و هیاهوی خیل بیکارهها و
تماشاگران کاررا خراب کرد ، و مرد جوان باز با سماجت و خونسردی در
هر خانهرا میکوفت و جلو هرکسرا میگرفت و سؤالش را تکرار میکرد .

یک جا به کوچهٔ تنگ و باریکی رسید که چند دهاتی فقیر و لاغر میوه
هایشانرا که روی خرهای لاغرتر از خودشان گذاشته بودند برای فروش
عرضه میداشتند ، راه بند آمده بود . همه ایستادند . مرد جوان به پیر
مردی که میوه میخرید نزدیک شد . از او خواهش کرد که به سؤالش
جواب بدهد . بچهها و بیکارهها از پشت سر او به جلو خیره شدند . چند
نفر سرک کشیدند . در یکی دو خانه باز و بسته شد و بعد جمعیت ، مثل
برفی که آب شود ، به پراکندگی رفت . بچهها که دیگر قضیه برایشان
شیرینی و لطفی نداشت به خرهای دهاتیها هجوم آوردند و به غارت میوه
ها مشغول شدند . معرکهگیرها از فرصت استفاده کردند و در یک گوشهٔ
فراخ و وسیع کوچه بساط خودرا بر پا کردند که تا دیر نشده و مردم به
خانههایشان نرفتهاند کاری انجام بدهند .

از اذان غروب ، اثر بهرام صادقی

1 *mosallam* certain; *yektane* in one
~~piece~~; *bar-âmadan* to come through
2 *jari* bold; *porrui-kardan* to be bold;
istâdegi-kardan to stand one's ground
3 *sorâq-e kas-i-râ gereftan* to ask the
whereabouts of someone
4 *vâjeb* urgent; *gul-zadan* to fool
6 *nâmidan* to name, call; *hayâhu* uproar;
khayl crowd
7 *tamâshâgar* onlooker; *khunsardi* calm
8 *kuft-/kub-* to pound, knock; *jelaw-e
kas-i-râ gereftan* to stop someone;
tekrâr-kardan to repeat
9 *kuche* lane; *tang* narrow, tight; *bârik*
narrow, thin; *lâqar* skinny

10 *khar* donkey; *arze-dâshtan* to display;
band-âmadan to come to a standstill
12 *khâhesh-kardan az* to beg, entreat
13 *jelaw* front, forward; *khire-shodan* to
stare
14 *sarak-keshidan* to poke one's head
out; *jam'iyat* group
15 *parâkande* scattered; *qaziye* affair
16 *lotf* interest; *hojum-âvordan* to attack; *qârat* plunder; *forsat* opportunity
18 *farâkh* broad; *vasi'* wide; *besât bar pâ
kardan* to spread one's carpet, "to set
up shop"
20 *azân-e qorub* evening call to prayer

237

۷

گنبد طلائی باشکوهی با مناره‌های قشنگش پدیدار شد و گنبد آبی
دیگری قرینهٔ آن نمایان گردید که میان خانه‌های گلی مثل وصلهٔ ناجور بود .
نزدیك غروب بود که کاروان وارد خیابانی شد که دو طرفش دیوارهای
خراب و دکانهای کوچك بود . در اینجا ازدحام مهیبی بر پا شد : عربهای
پاچه‌ورمالیده ، صورتهای احمق فینه‌بسر ، قیافه‌های آب زیر که عمامه‌ای با
ریشها و ناخنهای حنابسته و سرهای تراشیده تسبیح میگردانیدند و با
نعلین و عبا و زیرشلواری قدم میزدند . زبان فارسی حرف میزدند ، یا
ترکی بلغور میکردند ، یا عربی از بیخ گلو و از توی روده‌هایشان در میآمد
و در هوا غلغل میزد . زنهای عرب با صورتهای خال کوبیدهٔ چرك چشمهای
واسوخته ، حلقه از پرهٔ بینی‌شان گذرانده بودند . یکی از آنها پستان
سیاهش را تا نصفه در دهن بچهٔ کثیفی که در بغلش بود فرو کرده بود .
این جمعیت به انواع گوناگون جلب مشتری میکرد : یکی نوحه میخواند ،
یکی سینه میزد ، یکی مهر و تسبیح و کفن متبرك میفروخت ، یکی جن
میگرفت ، یکی دعا مینوشت ، یکی هم خانه کرایه میداد .
جهودهای قبا دراز از مسافران طلا و جواهر میخریدند . جلو قهوه‌خانه‌ای
عربی نشسته بود ، انگشت در بینیش کرده بود و با دست دیگرش چرك

5
10
15

1 *gombad* dome; *talâi* golden; *bâshokuh* splendid; *menâre* minaret; *qashang* beautiful; *padidâr-shodan* to come into view; *âbi* blue
2 *qarine* twin; *geli* made of mud; *vasle* patch; *nâjur* inappropriate, wrong
3 *qorub* sunset; *kâravân* caravan
4 *ezdehâm* crowd; *mohib* frightful; *bar pâ shodan* to arise
5 *pâchevarmâlide* impudent; *surat* face; *ahmaq* stupid; *fine* fez; *âb zir-e kâh* sly, sneaky; *amâmei* beturbaned
6 *rishe* beard; *nâkhon* fingernail; *hanâbaste* hennaed; *tarâshidan* to shave; *tasbih* worry beads
7 *na'layn* sandals; *abâ* cloak; *qadamzadan* to walk about
8 *balqur-kardan* to gobble; *bikh-e golu* depths of the throat; *rude* bowel
9 *qolqol-zadan* to make a racket; *khâlkubidan* to tattoo; *cherk* filth(y)
10 *vâsukhte* bleary; *halqe* ring; *pare-ye bini* nostril; *pestân* breast
11 *tâ nesfe* half way; *baqal* lap; *forukardan* to shove down
12 *jam'iyat* group, crowd; *jalb-kardan* to attract; *moshtari* customer; *nawhekhândan* to wail (professionally)
13 *sine* breast; *mohr* seal; *kafan* shroud; *motabarrek* blessed; *jenn-gereftan* to exorcise demons
14 *do'â* prayer; *kerâye-dâdan* to rent out
15 *jahud* Jew; *qabâ* coat; *mosâfer* traveler; *talâ* gold; *javâher* jewel; *qahvekhâne* coffeehouse
16 *angosht* finger; *bini* nose

لای انگشتهای پایش را در میآورد و صورتش از مگس پوشیده شده بود و
شپش از سرش بالا میرفت.

کاروان که ایستاد ، مشدی رمضان و حسین آقا جلو دویدند ، کمك
کردند ، خانم گلین و عزیز آقارا از کجاوه پائین آوردند . جمعیت زیادی به
5   مسافران هجوم آوردند . هر تکه از چیزهایشان بدست یکنفر بود و آنهارا
بخانه خودشان دعوت میکردند . ولی درین میان عزیز آقا گم شد . هرچه
دنبالش گشتند ، از هرکه پرسیدند بیفایده بود .

بالاخره ، بعد از آنکه خانم گلین و حسین آقا و مشدی رمضان یك اطاق
کثیف گلی از قرار شبی هفت روپیه کرایه کردند ، دوباره به جستجوی عزیز
10   آقا رفتند . تمام شهررا زیر پا کردند . از کفشدار و از زیارتنامه‌خوانها یکی
یکی سراغ عزیز آقارا بنام و نشانی گرفتند . اثری از او بدست نیامد . آخر
وقت بود ، صحن کمی خلوت شد . خانم گلین برای نهمین بار داخل حرم
شد و دید که دسته‌ای زن و آخوند دور زنی گرد آمده‌اند که بقفل ضریح
چسبیده آنرا میبوسد و فریاد میزند .

15   هرچه از او میپرسیدند مگر چه شده ، جواب نمیداد . بالاخره پس از
اصرار زیاد گفت :

«من یك کاری کرده‌ام ، میترسم سید الشهدا مرا نبخشد .»

همین جمله‌را تکرار میکرد و سیل اشك از چشمانش سرازیر بود . خانم
گلین صدای عزیز آقارا شناخت ، جلو رفت . دست اورا کشید ، برد در
20   صحن و بکمك حسین آقا اورا بخانه بردند ، دورش جمع شدند . بعد از

1 *lâ-ye* in between; *magas* fly
2 *shepesh* lice
3 *mashdi ramazân* masc. proper name; *davidan* to run
4 *khânom gelin* fem. proper name; *aziz-âqâ* fem. proper name; *kajâve* camel-litter in which women ride
5 *hojum-âvordan be* to attack; *tekke* piece
9 *az qarâr-e* at the rate of; *rupie* rupee (unit of currency formerly used in Iraq; this story is set at the shrine of Imam Husayn in Kerbela)
10 *kafshdâr* mosque attendant who guards shoes; *ziâratnâmekhân* a cleric

hired to recite the ritual at a shrine
11 *neshâni* description; *asar* trace
12 *sahn* courtyard; *haram* sanctuary
13 *âkhond* cleric, mulla; *gerd-âmadan dawr-e* to gather around; *qofl* lock; *zarih* grate that surrounds a saint's tomb
14 *chasbidan be* to cling to; *busidan* to kiss; *faryâd-zadan* to cry out
16 *esrâr* insistence
17 *sayyedoshshohadâ* "lord of martyrs," title of Imam Husayn.
18 *jomle* sentence; *sayl* flood; *ashk* tear; *sarâzir* rolling down

آنکه دو تا چائی شیرین باو دادند و یک قلیان برایش چاق کردند ، عزیز

آقا شرط کرد که حسین آقا از اطاق بیرون برود تا سرگذشت خودش را

نقل کند. حسین آقا که از در بیرون رفت، عزیز آقا قلیان را جلو کشید و

اینجور شروع کرد .

از طلب آمرزش، اثر صادق هدایت

1 *qalyân* water pipe, hookah; *châq-kardan*
to get a water pipe going
2 *shart-kardan* to stipulate; *sargozasht*
adventure
3 *naql-kardan* to relate
4 *injur = intawr*

Examples of Classical Persian Prose

نمونه‌هائی چند از نثر کلاسیك فارسی

۱

در شهری مردی درزی بر دروازهٔ شهر دوکان داشتی بر در گورستان ،
و کوزهٔ در میخی آویخته بود و هوسش آن بودی که هر جنازه که از در
شهر بیرون بردندی وی سنگی در آن کوزه افکندی و هر ماهی حساب آن
سنگها کردی که چند کس بیرون بردند و آن کوزه‌را تهی کردی و باز
سنگ در همی افکندی. تا روزگاری برآمد ، درزی نیز بمرد . مردی بطلب
درزی آمد و خبر مرگ او نداشت. در دوکانش بسته دید . همسایهٔ اورا
پرسید که این درزی کجاست که حاضر نیست؟ همسایه گفت که درزی نیز
در کوزه افتاد .

(از قابوسنامه ، تألیف امیر عنصر المعالی کیکاوس در سال ٤٧٥ هجری)

1 *darzi* tailor; *darvâze* gate; *dukân* variant
of *dokkân* shop; *dâshti* see §87; *gures-
tân* graveyard

2 *kuze* jug, pitcher; *mikh* nail, peg;
âvikht-/âviz- to hang; *havas* passion,
fancy; *janâze* funeral

3 *vay = u; sang* stone; *afkand-/afkan-* to
toss; *hesâb-kardan* to count

4 *tahi-kardan* to empty

5 *ruzgâr bar-âmadan* for time to pass; *niz*
too, also; *talab* search

6 *khabar* news

7 *hâzer* present

9 *Qâbusnâme*, a book of counsel written
in 1082 by Amir Onsorolma'âli Kay-
kâus for his son; *ta'lif* composition

۲

گویند روزی نوشروان عادل برنشسته بود و با خاصگیان بشکار میرفت
و بر کنار دیهی گذر کرد . پیری‌را دید نودساله که گوز در زمین مینشاند .
نوشروان‌را عجب آمد زیرا که بیست سال گوز کشته بر میدهد . گفت «ای
پیر، گوز میکاری؟» گفت «آری.» خدایگان گفت «چندان بخواهی زیست که
برش بخوری؟» پیر گفت «کشتند و خوردیم و کاریم و خورند.»
نوشروان را خوش آمد . گفت «زه!» در وقت خزینه‌دار‌را گفت تا هزار

1 *nushervân* Anosharvan, title of the
Sassanian king Chosroës I, r. A.D.
531–579; *âdel* just; *bar-neshastan* to
mount; *khâssegân* elite; *shekâr* hunt

2 *gozar-kardan bar* to pass by; *gawz*
walnut

3 *kas-i-râ ajab-âmadan* to be astonished;
zírâ-ke because; *kesht-/kâr-* to plant;

bar-dâdan to yield fruit; *ay* O
(vocative)

4 *âre* yes; *khodâyegân* great lord;
chandân how long; *zist-/zi-* to live

6 *zeh* bravo; *dar vaqt* immediately;
khazinedâr treasurer

درم به پیر داد. پیر گفت «ای خداوند، هیچکس زودتر از بنده بر این
گوز نخورد.» گفت «چگونه؟» پیر گفت «اگر من گوز نکشتمی و خدایگان
اینجا گذر نکردی، آنچ ببنده رسید نرسیدی و بنده آن جواب ندادی.
من این هزار درم از کجا یافتمی؟» نوشروان گفت «زهازه!» خزینه‌دار در
وقت دو هزار درم دیگر بدو داد بهر آنکه دو بار «زه» بر زبان نوشروان
رفت.

(از سیاستنامهٔ خواجه نظام‌الملك)

1 *deram* drachma; *bande* slave, for "I"
2 *chegune* how?
3 *ânch* an archaic spelling for *ânche*
5 *bahr-e ânke* because; *zabân* tongue

7 *Siâsatnâme*, a book of counsel for
princes written by Khâje Nezâmol-
molk (d. 1092)

۲

آورده‌اند که بازرگانی بود اندک‌مایه، و میخواست که سفری کند. صد
من آهن داشت. در خانهٔ دوستی بر سبیل ودیعت نهاد و برفت. چون آمد
امین ودیعت‌را بفروخته بود و بها خرج کرده. بازرگان روزی بطلب آهن
بنزدیك او رفت. مرد گفت «آهن تو در بیغولهٔ خانه بنهاده بودم و احتیاطی
تمام بکرده. آنجا سوراخ موش بود. تا من واقف شدم تمام بخورده بود.»
بازرگان جواب داد که «راست می‌گوئی، موش آهن سخت دوست دارد و
دندان او بر خائیدن آهن قادر باشد.» امین «راستکار» شاد شد، یعنی
پنداشت که بازرگان نرم گشت و دل از آن برداشت. گفت «امروز بخانهٔ من
مهمان باش.» گفت «فردا باز آیم.» رفت و چون بسر کوی رسید پسری‌را
از آن او ببرد و پنهان کرد. چون بجستند و ندا در شهر دادند، بازرگان

1 *bâzargân* merchant; *andakmâye* of little
capital, petty; *safar-kardan* to take a
trip
2 *man* maund (weight); *âhan* iron; *bar
sabil-e* in the way of, for; *vadi'at* safe-
keeping; *nehâd-/neh-* to place
3 *amin* trustee; *bahâ* price; *kharj-kardan*
to spend
4 *biqule* pit; *ehtiât-kardan* to take precaution

5 *surâkh* hole; *mush* mouse; *vâqef* aware
6 *sakht* very much, extremely
7 *dandân* tooth; *khâidan* to gnaw; *qâder
bar* capable of; *râstkâr* honest; *shâd*
happy; *yá'ni* that is
8 *pendâsht-/pendâr-* to think; *narm* soft;
del bar-dâshtan az to give up hope of
9 *mehmân* guest; *sar* head; *kuy* lane
10 *penhân-kardan* to hide; *jost-/ju-* to
search; *nedâ-dâdan* to herald

243

گفت «من بازی دیدم که کودك میبرد.» امین فریاد برداشت که «دروغ و
محال چرا میگوئی؟ باز کودکیرا چون برگیرد؟» بازرگان بخندید و گفت
«در شهری که موش صد من آهن بتواند خورد ، بازی کودکیرا بمقدار ده
من بر تواند گرفت.» امین دانست که حال چیست. گفت «موش آهن نخورده
است. پسر باز ده و آهن بستان!»

5

از کلیله و دمنهٔ بهرامشاهی (در حدود ۵۳۸ه‍/۱۱٤۳م،
ترجمهٔ ابوالمعالی نصرالله بن محمد)

1 *bâz* hawk; *kudak* child; *faryâd bar-dâshtan* to cry out
2 *mohâl* absurd; *bar-gereftan* to pick up
3 *meqdâr* amount
5 *setad-/setân-* to take away
6 *Kalile-o Demne-ye Bahrâmshâhi*, a Persian translation of Ibn al-Muqaf-

fa''s Arabic *Kalila wa-Dimna*, made by Abolma'âli Nasrollâh ebn-e Mohammad ca. 1143. The 8th-century Arabic version was made from a Middle Persian translation of the Sanskrit original of the famous Bidpai fables.
8 *tarjome* translation

٤

پادشاهیرا شنیدم که به کشتن اسیری اشارت کرد . بیچاره در حالت
نومیدی ملكرا دشنام دادن گرفت و سقط گفتن که گفتهاند «هرکه دست از
جان بشوید ، هرچه در دل دارد بگوید .»

اذا یَئِسَ الإنسانُ طالَ لسانُهُ   کَسِنَّورِ مَغلوبٍ یَصولُ عَلی الکَلبِ
وقتِ ضرورت چو نمانَد گریز   دستَ بگیرد سرِ شمشیرِ تیز

5

ملك پرسید که «چه میگوید؟» یکی از وزرای نیکمحضر گفت «ای
خداوند ، میگوید وَالکاظمینَ الغَیظَ وَالعافینَ عَنِ الناس.» ملكرا بر وی
رحمت آمد و از سر خون او درگذشت.

1 *pâdeshâh* king; *asir* prisoner; *eshârat-kardan be* to indicate; *bichâre* helpless; *hâlat* state
2 *nawmidi* desperation; *doshnâm-dâdan* to curse; *saqat-goftan* to revile; *dast az jân shostan* to give up hope of life
4 (Arabic) "When man despairs his tongue grows long, like a cornered cat attacking a dog."

5 *zarurat* necessity; *cho = chon; goriz* (means of) escape; *sar* tip; *shamshir* sword; *tiz* sharp
6 *vazir* pl *vozarâ* vizier; *nikmahzar* of good counsel
7 *khodâvand* lord; *valkâzemin...nâs* "and those who bridle their anger and forgive people" (Koran 3:134)
8 *rahmat* mercy; *az sar-e khun-e kas-i dar-gozashtan* to spare one's life

وزیر دیگر که ضد او بود گفت «ابنای جنس مارا نشاید در حضرت
پادشاهان جز به راستی سخن گفتن. این، ملکرا دشنام داد و ناسزا گفت.»
ملک روی از این سخن درهم کشید و گفت «مرا آن دروغ پسندیده‌تر
آمد از این راست که تو گفتی که آن‌را روی در مصلحتی بود و این‌را بنا
بر خبثی.» و خردمندان گفته‌اند «دروغی مصلحت‌آمیز بهْ از راستی فتنه
انگیز.»

هرکه شاه آن کند که او گوید   حیف باشد که جز نکو گوید

بر طاق ایوان فریدون نبشته بود

جهــــان ای بـــرادر نمـــانَـد بکس

دل اندر جهان آفریـن بنـد و بس

مکـن تکیـه بـر ملک دنیـا و پشت

که بسیار کس چون تو پرورد وکشت

چو آهنگِ رفتن کنـــد جـــانِ پاك

چه بر تختِ مردن چه بر رویِ خاك

یکی از ملوك خراسان، محمودِ سَبُکتگین‌را بخواب دید بعد از وفات

---

1 *zedd* opposite; *abnâ-ye jens* peers; *nâshâyad* it is not fitting; *hazrat* presence

2 *râsti* truth; *sokhan* speech; *nâsazâ* improper

3 *ruy darham keshidan* to frown; *doruq* lie; *pasandidan* to approve

4 *maslahat* prudence; *benâ* basis, foundation

5 *khobs* vileness; *kheradmand* wise; *maslahatâmiz* prudent; *beh = behtar*; *fetneangiz* seditious

7 *hayf* pity; *neku* (for *niku*) good, beautiful

8 *tâq* arch; *ayvân* portico; *feridun* Freidoun, mythical king of Iran; *nebeshte = neveshte*

10 *andar = dar*; *del dar chiz-i bastan* to set one's heart on s.th.; *jahân-âfarin* world-creator

11 *takye-kardan bar* to rely on; *posht-kardan bar* to lean on; *molk* kingdom; *donyâ* this world

12 *parvard-/parvar-* to nourish

13 *âhang-e kâr-i kardan* to be about to do s.th.; *jân* soul; *pâk* pure

14 *che...che* [what difference does it make] whether...or; *takht* throne; *khâk* dust

15 *malek* pl *moluk* king; *khorâsân* Khurasan, northeastern province of modern Iran, formerly extended to the Oxus and included much of modern Afghanistan; *mahmud-e saboktegin* Sultan Mahmud of Ghazna (r. 998–1030), known for his rapacious appetite for conquest; *vafât* death

او به صد سال که جملهٔ وجود او ریخته بود و خاک شده مگر چشمانش که
در چشمخانه همی گردید و نظر همی کرد . سایر حکما از تعبیر آن فرو
ماندند مگر درویشی که خدمت بجای آورد و گفت «هنوز نگران است که
ملکش با دگران است.»

5   بس نامور بزیـر زمین دفن کـــرده اند
     کز هستیَش بروی زمین بر نشـان نماند
     آن پیـر لاشه را کـه سپـردنـد زیـر خـاک
     خاکش چنان بخورد کزو استخوان نماند
     زنده است نـام فـرّخ نـوشیـروان بعـدل
10   گرچه بسی گذشت که نوشین روان نماند
     خیری کـن ای فلان و غنیمت شمار عمر
     زان پیشتر که بانگ بر آید «فلان نماند»

از گلستان سعدی (٦٥٦هـ/١٢٥٨م)

1 *jomle-ye* all of; *vojud* body; *rikht-/ riz-* to decompose; *mágar* except for

2 *nazar-kardan* to gaze; *sâyer-e* all of; *hakim* pl *hokamâ* philosopher; *ta'bir* interpretation; *foru-mândan az* to be incapable of

3 *darvish* dervish, poor man; *khedmat be jây âvordan* to perform an obeisance; *negarân* worried

4 *degar* abbreviated form of *digar*

5 *bas* many a; *nâmvar* renowned; *dafn-kardan* to bury

6 *hasti* existence; *be ru-ye zamin bar* see §83; *neshân* trace

7 *lâshe* corpse; *sepord-/sepâr-* to entrust;

khâk dust, earth

8 *kazu = ke az u; ostakhân* bone

9 *zende* alive; *nâm* renown; *farrokh* splendid; *nushirvân* Chosroës I Anosharvan the Just, see p. 242; *adl* justice

10 *nushin* sweet; *ravân* soul (*nushin-ravân* is a popular—and false—etymology for Nushirvan)

11 *khayr-kardan* to be charitable, do good; *qanimat-shomordan* to make the most of; *omr* life

12 *zân pishtar ke = pish(tar) az ân-ke; bâng* cry, shout; *bar-âmadan* to go up; *folân* So-and-so

٥

مالیخولیا علتی است که اطبا در معالجت او فرو مانند . اگرچه امراض

سوداوی همه مزمن است ، لیکن مالیخولیا خاصیتی دارد بدیر زائل شدن .

و ابو الحسن بن یحیی اندر کتاب معالجت بقراطی که اندر طب کس چنان

کتابی نکرده است برشمرد از ائمه و حکما و فضلا و فلاسفه که چند از

5   ایشان بدان علت معلول گشته‌اند . اما حکایت کرد مرا استاد من از الشیخ

الامام محمد بن عقیل القزوینی از امیر فخرالدوله باکالیجار البویی که یکی را

از آل بویه مالیخولیا پدید آمد و اورا درین علت چنان صورت بست که او

گاوی شده است . همه روز بانگ همی کرد و این و آن را همی گفت که «مرا

بکشید که از گوشت من هریسه نیکو آید» تا کار بدرجه‌ای بکشید که نیز

10   هیچ نخورد و روزها برآمد و نهار کرد . و اطبا در معالجت او عاجز آمدند .

و خواجه ابو علی اندرین حالت وزیر بود ، و شاهنشاه علاء الدوله محمد بن

دشمنزیار بر وی اقبالی داشت و جملهٔ ملک در دست او نهاده بود و کلی

شغل برای و تدبیر او باز گذاشته . و الحق بعد اسکندر که ارسطاطالیس

وزیر او بود ، هیچ پادشاه چون ابو علی وزیر نداشته بود ، و درین حال که

15   خواجه ابو علی وزیر بود ، هر روز پیش از صبحدم برخاستی و از کتاب

---

1 *mâlikhulyâ* melancholia; *ellat* malady;
tabib pl *atebbâ* doctor; *mo'âlejat* treat-
ment; *foru-mândan* to fail; *maraz* pl
amrâz disease

2 *sawdâvi* melancholic; *mozmen* chron-
ic; *likan* but; *khâssiyat* characteristic;
zâ'el-shodan to pass away

3 *boqrâti* Hippocratic; *tebb* medicine

4 *bar-shomordan az* to recount; *emâm* pl
a'emme leader; *hakim* pl *hokamâ*
physician; *fâzel* pl *fozalâ* learned man;
faylasuf pl *falâsefe* philosopher

5 *ma'lul* afflicted; *hekâyat-kardan* to
relate; *ostâd* master

7 *âl-e buye* the Buyid dynasty, r. 932–
1062; *padid-âmadan* to appear; *surat-
bastan* to seem, be imagined

8 *gâv* cow; *bâng-kardan* to shout (here,
to moo)

9 *harise* porridge; *niku* good; *kâr be
daraje-i keshid ke* it went so far that;
niz too, also

10 *ruzhâ bar-âmad* days passed; *nahâr-
kardan* to waste away; *âjez* incapable

11 *khâje abu-ali* Avicenna; *alâ'oddawle
mohammad ebn-e doshmanziâr* ruler of
central and western Persia, r. 1008–
1041

12 *eqbâl-dâshtan bar* to hold in high es-
teem; *jomle-ye* all of; *molk* kingdom;
kolli all

13 *shoql* work; *ra'y-o tadbir* manage-
ment; *bâz-gozâshtan* to turn over;
álhaqq in truth; *eskandar* Alexander
(the Great); *arestâtâlis* Aristotle

15 *sobhdam* dawn; *ketâb-e shefâ* Avicenna's great work on philosophy

شفا دو كاغذ تصنيف كردى. چون صبح صادق بدميدى شاگردان را بار
دادى چون كيا رئيس بهمنيار و ابو منصور بن زيله و عبد الواحد جوزجانى
و سليمان دمشقى و من كه باكاليجارم. تا بوقت اسفار سبقها بخوانديمى و
در پى او نماز كرديمى و تا بيرون آمدمانى هزار سوار از مشاهير و معارف
و ارباب حوائج و اصحاب عرائض بر در سراى او گرد آمده بودى. و
خواجه برنشستى و آن جماعت در خدمت او برفتندى. چون بديوان
رسيدى سوار دوهزار شده بودى. پس بديوان تا نماز پيشين بماندى و
چون باز گشتى بخوان آمدى. جماعتى با او نان بخوردندى. پس بقيلوله
مشغول شدى و چون برخاستى نماز بكردى و پيش شاهنشاه شدى و تا
نماز ديگر پيش او مفاوضه و محاوره بودى. ميان ايشان در مهمات ملك دو
تن بودند كه هرگز ثالثى نبودى. و مقصود ازين حكايت آنست كه خواجه را
هيچ فراغت نبودى.

پس چون اطبا از معالجت آن جوان عاجز آمدند، پيش شاهنشاه ملك
معظم علاء الدوله آن حال بگفتند و اورا شفيع بر انگيختند كه خواجه را
بگويد تا آن جوان را علاج كند. علاء الدوله اشارت كرد و خواجه قبول
كرد. پس گفت "آن جوان را بشارت دهيد كه قصاب همى آيد تا ترا
بكشد" و با آن جوان گفتند. او شادى همى كرد. پس خواجه برنشست و

5

10

15

1 *kâqaz* page; *tasnif-kardan* to compose; *sobh-e sâdeq* true dawn; *damidan* to break (dawn); *shâgerd* pupil; *bâr-dâdan* to hold court, receive

3 *esfâr* bright morning; *sabaq* lesson

4 *dar pay-e* after, behind; *âmademâni* archaic 1st plural habitual past of *âmadan; savâr* mounted (on horse-back); *mashhur* pl *mashâhir* famous; *ma' âref* nobles

5 *arbâb-e havâ' ej* people in need; *ashâb-e arâ' ez* petitioners; *sarâ* residence; *gerd-âmadan* to gather around

6 *bar-neshastan* to mount; *jamâ' at* group; *khedmat* service; *divân* divan, place where administration was conducted

7 *namâz-e pishin* midday prayer

8 *bâz-gashtan* to come back; *khân* dining table; *nân-khordan* to dine; *qaylule* nap

9 *shodan* to go

10 *namâz-e digar* afternoon prayer; *mofâveze* deliberation; *mohâvere* discussion; *mohemmât-e molk* affairs of state

11 *hargez* (+ neg.) never

12 *farâqat* leisure

13 *malek-e mo' azzam* magnificent king

14 *shafi' bar-angikhtan* to pursuade someone to intercede

15 *elâj-kardan* to treat; *eshârat-kardan* to make a motion, allude; *qabul-kardan* to accept

16 *beshârat* good news; *qassâb* butcher

17 *shâdi-kardan* to rejoice

همچنان با کوکبه بر در سرای بیمار آمد و با تنی دو دررفت، و کاردی
بدست گرفته گفت «این گاو کجاست تا اورا بکشم؟»

آن جوان همچو گاو بانگی کرد، یعنی اینجاست. خواجه گفت «بمیان
سرای آریدش و دست و پای او ببندید و فرو افکنید!»

بیمار چون آن شنید بدوید و به میان سرای آمد و بر پهلوی راست
خفت، و پای او سخت ببستند. پس خواجه ابو علی بیامد و کارد بر کارد
مالید و فرو نشست و دست بر پهلوی او نهاد چنانکه عادت قصابان بود.
پس گفت «وه! این چه گاو لاغریست! اینرا نشاید کشتن. علف دهیدش تا
فربه شود!» و برخاست و بیرون آمد و مردمرا گفت که «دست و پای او
بگشائید و خوردنی آنچه فرمایم پیش او برید و اورا گوئید بخور تا زود
فربه شود.»

چنان کردند که خواجه گفت. خوردنی پیش او بردند و او همی خورد.
و بعد از آن، هرچه از اشربه و ادویه خواجه فرمودی بدو دادندی و
گفتند که «نیک بخور که این گاورا نیک فربه کند.» او بشنودی و بخوردی
بر آن امید که فربه شود تا اورا بکشند.

پس اطبا دست بمعالجت او برگشادند چنانکه خواجه ابو علی میفرمود.
یک ماهرا بصلاح آمد و صحت یافت، و همه اهل خرد دانند که این چنین
معالجت نتوان کرد الا بفضلی کامل و علمی تمام و حدسی راست.

از چهار مقاله، تالیف نظامی عروضی سمرقندی
در حدود ۵۵۰هـ/۱۱۵۵م

---

1 *kawkabe* entourage; *bimâr* patient; *tan*
person; *dar-raftan* to go in
3 *hamcho* like; *miân* middle
4 *âr-* for *âvor-*; *foru-afkandan* to throw
down
5 *pahlu* side
6 *khoft-/khâb-* to lie down
7 *mâlidan* to rub; *foru-neshastan* to sit
down; *âdat* custom
8 *vah* bah; *lâqar* skinny; *alaf* fodder
9 *farbeh* fat

10 *goshâd-/goshâ-* to open, untie
13 *sharbat* pl *ashrebe* potion; *davâ* pl
advie medicine
14 *shenudan = shenidan*
16 *dast bar-goshâdan be* to undertake
17 *be salâh âmadan* to be cured; *sehhat-
yâftan* to recover; *ahl-e kherad* the
wise
18 *ellâ* except; *fazl* learning; *kâmel*
perfect; *elm* knowledge

English-Persian Vocabulary

able, be توانستن
about (prep.) دربارهٔ
about to خواستن
about, nearly تقریباً ، در حدود
adventure ماجرا
afraid, be ترسیدن
ago قبل ، پیش
airplane هواپیما
airport فرودگاه
Ali علی
all همه
all, in جمعاً
almost تقریباً
always همیشه
American آمریکائی
amount مقدار
announcer گوینده
answer (n.) جواب
answer (vb.) جواب دادن
anymore, not دیگر...نه

arrive رسیدن
ask پرسیدن
ask questions سؤال کردن
at all اصلاً

bad بد
be بودن
because برای اینکه ، چونکه
bed تختخواب
bed, go to خوابیدن
before (adv.) قبلا ، پیش
before (conj.) قبل/پیش از اینکه
before (prep.) قبل از ، پیش از
better بهتر
big بزرگ
black سیاه
blouse بلوز
book کتاب
both...and هم...هم
box جعبه

boy پسر	continue ادامه دادن به
break شکستن	correct درست
bring همراه آوردن ، آوردن	count شمردن
broken شکسته ، خراب	country کشور
brother برادر	crowded شلوغ
build ساختن	
building ساختمان	daughter دختر
buy خریدن	day روز
	deliver رساندن
car ماشین	dentistry دندانپزشکی
carry بردن	department store فروشگاه
caught, get گیر افتادن	desk میز
chair صندلی	die مردن
chalk گچ	difference, make a فرق کردن
chance, by اتفاقاً	difficult مشکل ، سخت
cheap ارزان	difficulty, have اشکال داشتن
child بچه	dinner شام
childish بچگانه	direction طرف
city شهر	dirty کثیف
class کلاس	dish ظرف
clean تمیز	dishwashing ظرفشوئی
clever زرنگ	distance فاصله
clock ساعت	do کارکردن
close (adj.) نزدیک	doctor پزشک ، دکتر
close (vb.) بستن	door در
clothes لباس	doubt شك
coffee قهوه	drink خوردن
cold سرد	
come آمدن	each هرکدام ، هر
come back بازآمدن ، برگشتن	early زود
come out درآمدن	easy آسان

eat خوردن

else دیگر

English انگلیسی

enter وارد شدن

eraser پاک کن

even حتی

event اتفاق ، واقعه

every همه ، هر

evil بد

example نمونه

except جز

expensive گران

extinguish خاموش کردن

far دور

father پدر

few چند

film فیلم

finally بالاخره

find یافتن ، پیدا کردن

finish تمام کردن

fire آتش

first اولین ، اول

food غذا

for برای

forget فراموش کردن

forgive بخشیدن

forward پیش

friend دوست

fruit میوه

garden باغ

gentleman آقا

get out (of vehicle) پیاده شدن

get under way راه افتادن

get up برخاستن ، پا شدن

give دادن

glass لیوان

go رفتن

good خوب

green سبز

grow up بزرگ شدن

guess حدس زدن

half نصف ، نیم

hand دست

happen اتفاق افتادن

happy خوشحال

hard سخت

have داشتن

have a good time خوش گذشتن

hear شنیدن

heavy سنگین

hello, say سلام کردن

here اینجا

home خانه

hour ساعت

house خانه

how چطور

how many چند

important مهم

درآمد income

جالب interesting

ایران Iran

ایرانی Iranian

کار job

نزدیک بودن just about to

نگهداشتن keep

کیلو (گرم) kilogram

مهربان kind

نوع kind, sort

شناختن (know (somebody

دانستن (know (something

خانم lady

آخر last

گذشته last, past

دیشب last night

پارسال last year

دیر late

دیرکردن late, be

بعداً (later (adv.

یادگرفتن learn

اقلاً least, at

ترک کردن ، رفتن leave

چپ left

درس lesson

گذاشتن let

نامه letter

کتابخانه library

زندگانی ، زندگی life

چراغ light

مثل (like (prep.

خوش آمدن ، دوست داشتن like

مایع liquid

گوش کردن listen

کوچک little

کم little bit

زندگی کردن live

نگاه کردن look

دنبال گشتن look for

گم کردن lose

گم شدن lost, get

بسیار ، زیاد ، خیلی lot

بلندگو loudspeaker

دوست داشتن love

ناهار lunch

دیوانه mad

مرد man

هرچند ، هرچه matter, no

دقیقه minute

پول money

ماه month

بیشتر more

صبح morning

امروز صبح morning, this

مادر mother

کوه mountain

زیاد ، بسیار ، خیلی much

name نام ، اسم

near نزدیك

nearly تقریباً; not nearly so بهیچوجه

neighbor همسایه

never هرگز ، هیچوقت

new جدید ، تازه ، نو

newspaper روزنامه

nothing هیچ ، هیچ چیز

now حالا

offer تقدیم کردن

old پیر ، کهنه ، قدیمی

on روی

one (adj.) یك

one (pron.) یکی

only فقط ، تنها ، جز

other دیگر

otherwise گرنه

out بیرون

own خود

past گذشته

pay پرداختن ، قیمت دادن ، دادن

pen قلم

people مردم

perfectly کاملاً

Persian فارسی

person کس ، نفر

pick up برداشتن

plane هواپیما

polite مؤدب

possible ممکن

possible, be امکان داشتن

price قیمت

probable, be احتمال داشتن

provided that بشرطی که

put نهادن ، گزاردن ، گذاشتن

put on (clothes) پوشیدن

pyjamas پیژامه

quarter ربع

question سؤال

quiet آرام

rain باران باریدن ، باران آمدن

raincoat بارانی

reach رسیدن

read خواندن

reformatory دارالتادیب

relatively نسبةً

return (v. int.) برگشتن

return (v. trs.) برگرداندن

right راست ، درست

right here همینجا

room اطاق

salesperson فروشنده

same همان

sample نمونه

say گفتن

say, have s.th. to حرفها داشتن

scarcely نه...هنوز

255

school مدرسه	stay ماندن
see دیدن	stop (v. trs.) جلوگرفتن ، نگهداشتن
seem نمودن ، بنظر آمدن	stretch out درازکشیدن
select انتخاب کردن	stroll, take a گردش کردن
sell فروختن	student دانشجو
send فرستادن	study درس خواندن ، خواندن
sentence محاکمه کردن	summer تابستان
set out راه افتادن	surgeon جراح
several چند	sweater پولور
shoes کفش	
show نشان دادن	table میز
shut بستن	take گرفتن ، بردن
sick مریض	take back برگرداندن
simple ساده	take off (airplane) پروازکردن
sister خواهر	take off (clothes) درآوردن
six شش	tea چای
skirt دامن	teacher معلم
sleep خوابیدن	Tehran تهران
small کوچک	tell گفتن ، تعریف کردن
smart زرنگ	that (adj., pron.) آن
socks جوراب	that (conj.) که
something کاری ، چیزی	there آنجا
somewhere جائی	thing کار ، چیز
soon زود	think فکرکردن
sooner, no هنوز...نه	think about فکر چیزی بودن
speak صحبت کردن ، حرف زدن	third سوم
spend (money) خرج کردن	this این
spend (time) گذراندن	this year امسال
stand up پا شدن	throw away دور انداختن
start شروع کردن/شدن	time بار، دفعه، مدت ، ساعت
	time, have a good خوش گذشتن

to برای ، به
today امروز
tomorrow فردا
too نیز ، هم
too much زیاد ، خیلی
town شهر
try سعی‌کردن
turn around برگشتن
turn on روشن‌کردن

unbelievable باورنکردنی
undershirt زیرپیراهن
understand فهمیدن
university دانشگاه
unless بجز اینکه
unlucky بدبخت
use of, make استفاده‌کردن
use, be of به‌درد خوردن
usually معمولاً

very بسیار ، خیلی
vicinity نزدیکیها
village ده

want خواستن
wash شستن
water آب
way راه
wear پوشیدن

weather هوا
week هفته
what چه
whatever هرچه
when کی
when (conj.) که ، وقتی‌که
where کجا
wherever هرکجا
which کدام
who کی
whoever هرکه
why چرا
wife زن
window پنجره
winter زمستان
wish, I کاش ، کاشکی
with به ، با
woman زن
word حرف
work (n.) کار
work (vb.) کارکردن
write نوشتن

year سال
year, last پارسال
year, this امسال
yesterday دیروز

Persian-English Vocabulary

آ *â-* pres. stem of *âmadan*

آب *âb* water; ~ *zir-e kâh* sly, sneaky; ~*i* blue; ~*yâri-kardan* to irrigate

آتش *âtesh* fire

آخر *âkhar* pl *avâkher* last, end; *avâkher-e mâh* the latter part of the month

آخوند *âkhond* cleric, molla

آدم *âdam* one, human being, person

آرام *ârâm* calm, quiet

آری *âre* indeed, yes

آزار *âzâr* annoyance; ~-*dâdan* to annoy

آزمایش *âzmâyesh* experiment

آزمودن *âzmud-/âzmâ-* to try, test

آسان *âsân* easy; ~*i* ease

آسیا *âsyâ* Asia

آشنا *âshnâ bâ* acquainted with

آغاز *âqâz* beginning

آفریدن *âfarid-/âfarin-* to create

آفتاب *âftâb* sun

آقا *âqâ* gentleman, sir, Mr.; ~-*jân* common respectful address to fathers

آماده *âmâde* ready

آمدن *âmad-/â-* to come

آمرانه *âmerâne* imperious

آمرزیدن *âmorzidan* to have mercy on

آمریکا *âmrikâ* America; ~*i* American

آموختن *âmukht-/âmuz-* to learn

آموزش *âmuzesh* learning; *vezârat-e ~ o parvaresh* Ministry of Education

آمیختن *âmikht-/âmiz-* to mix

آن *ân* that; ~*jâ* there; ~*che* that which, what; ~*tawr* thus, like that; ~*qadr* that much, so much

آنتن *ânten* antenna

آواز *âvâz* voice, song, singing; ~*khân* singer; ~-*khândan* to sing

258

آوردن   *âvord-/âvor-* to bring

آهای   *âhây* hey

آینده   *âyande* coming, next, future

آئین   *âin, âyin* custom

ابداً   *abadan* (+ neg.) never, not at all

ابزار   *abzâr* tool, instrument

ابله   *ablah* stupid, fool; ~*âne* foolish

اتفاق   *ettefâq* chance, occurrence; ~ *oftâdan* to occur, happen; ~*an* by chance

اثر   *asar* pl *âsâr* trace

اجباری   *ejbâri* obligatory

احتمال   *ehtemâl* probability; ~*dâshtan* to be probable; ~*an* probably

احتیاط   *ehtiât* precaution; ~*kardan* to take precaution

احساس   *ehsâs* pl *-ât* feeling; ~*kardan* to feel

احمق   *ahmaq* stupid, fool; ~*âne* stupid, silly

اختیار   *ekhtiâr* choice; ~*kardan* to choose; *bi*~ involuntarily

اخگر   *akhgar* spark

ادامه   *edâme-dâdan be* to continue (trs.); ~*dâshtan* to continue (intrs.)

اذان   *azân* call to prayer

اذیت   *aziyat* annoyance; ~*kardan* to annoy, vex

ارزان   *arzân* cheap

از   *az* from, among, of (partitive); ~ *in-ke* because, since

ازدحام   *ezdehâm* crowd

اسب   *asb* horse

استاد   *ostâd* master, professor

استراحت   *esterâhat* rest; ~*kardan* to rest

استفاده   *estefâde-kardan az* to make use of

استنتاج   *estentâj* conclusion

اسم   *esm* pl *asâmi* name; *ham*~ namesake

اشباح   *ashbâh* ghosts, phantoms

اشتباه   *eshtebâh* mistake; ~*kardan* to make a mistake

اشک   *ashk* tears

اشکال   *eshkâl -ât* difficulty, problem

اصرار   *esrâr* insistence; ~*kardan* to insist

اصطلاح   *estelâh* idiom, technical expression; *be* ~ idiomatically

اصفهان   *esfahân* Isfahan

اصلا   *aslan* actually; (+ neg.) not at all

اصلی   *asli* original

اطاق   *otâq* room

اطبا   *atebbâ* pl of *tabib*

اطلاع   *ettelâ' -ât* information

اعلام   *e' lâm-kardan* to make known

اعلان   *e' lân-kardan* to announce

افتادن *oftâd-/oft-* to fall, befall

افتتاح *eftetâh* inauguration; ~-*shodan* to be opened

افروختن *afrukht-/afruz-* to light, kindle

افزودن *afzud-/afzâ-* to add

افسرده *afsorde* dejected

افکندن *afkand-/afkan-* to throw, cast

اقلاً *aqallan* at least

اکنون *aknun* now

اگر *ágar* if; ~-*ham* although, even though; ~*che* although

الاغ *olâq* donkey; ~*i* donkey driver

الآن *al' ân* now

الیاف *alyâf* fibers

اما *ámmâ* but, nonetheless

امان *amân* safety

امتحان *emtehân* examination, test; ~-*kardan* to test

امروز *emruz* today

امسال *emsâl* this year

امشب *emshab* tonight

امضا *emzâ* signature; ~-*kardan* to sign

امکان *emkân* possibility; ~-*dâshtan* to be possible

امن *amn* safety, security

امید *omid* hope; ~*vâr* hopeful

انتخاب *entekhâb -ât* election; ~-*kardan* to elect, choose

انتظار *entezâr* expectation; ~-*e kas-i-râ keshidan* to wait for someone

انتقال *enteqâl* transfer; ~-*dâdan* to transfer, move

انجام *anjâm-dâdan* to accomplish

اند *-and* they are

انداختن *andâkht-/andâz-* to throw, cast

اندازه *andâze* measure, extent

اندك *andak* little (bit)

انقلاب *enqelâb -ât* revolution; ~*i -un* revolutionary

انگشت *angosht* finger; ~*ar* ring

انگلیس *englis* English, British; ~*i* English (language)

انگیختن *angikht-/angiz-* to stir up

او *u* he, she

اوقات *awqât* pl of *vaqt*; ~*talkh* irritated, in a bad mood

اول *avval* first

ایران *irân* Iran, Persia; ~*i* Iranian, Persian

ایستادگی *istâdegi-kardan* to stand one's ground

ایستادن *istâd-/ist-* to stop, stand still

ایشان *ishân* they

ایل *il -ât* tribe

این *in* this; ~*jâ* here; ~*tawr* thus, like this; ~*qadr* so much, this much

اینك *inak* here is

با *bâ* with, despite

باآنكه *bâ ân-ke* although

بابا *bâbâ* daddy; *~-shamal* ruffian, thug

باختن *bâkht-/bâz-* to gamble, lose (game, bet)

باد *bâd* wind

بار *bâr* time; load; *~-bordan* to carry a load; *~bar* porter; *do~e* again, another time

باران *bârân* rain

باريدن *bâridan* to rain down

باريك *bârik* thin, narrow

باز *bâz* again; yet, still; open; *~ âmadan* to come again; *~-kardan* to open; *~-mândan* to lag behind; *~-ham* still, nonetheless; pres. stem of *bâkhtan*

بازار *bâzâr* bazaar, market

بازى *bâzi* play; *~-kardan* to play

باش *bâsh* pres. stem of *budan*

باطل *bâtel* useless, invalid, void

باغ *bâq -ât* garden, orchard; *~che* garden plot; *~che-bandi-shodan* to be divided up into plots

باقى *bâqi* remaining, left

بالا *bâlâ* up; *~-ye* over, on top of

بالاخره *bel' akhare* finally, at last

بام *bâm* roof

بانگ *bâng* cry; *~-kardan* to shout

باور *bâvar* belief; *~-kardan* to believe

باهم *bâham* together

باهوش *bâhush* intelligent

بايد *bâyad* must

بايست *bâyest* (past of *bâyad*) must

بته *bote* bush, shrub

بچه *bachche* child; *~gâne* childish

بخت *bakht* luck, fortune

بخشودن *bakhshud-/bakhshâ-* to forgive

بخشيدن *bakhshidan* to give, bestow, forgive

بد *bad* bad, evil, ill; *~-o birâh goftan be* to curse

بدن *badan* pl *abdân* body

بدون *bedun-e* without

بر *bar-* pres. stem of *bordan; bor-* pres. stem of *boridan; bar* over, upon, at, against; *bar* fruit

برابر *barâbar* level, equal; opposite

برادر *barâdar* brother

براق *barrâq* glittering

برآمدن *bar-âmadan* to turn out, come through

براى *barâ-ye* for; *~ in-ke* because

برتر *bartar* superior; *~i* superiority

برخاستن *bar-khâstan* to rise up, stand up

برخوردن *bar-khordan be* to meet, come across

261

برداشتن *bar-dâshtan* to pick up

بردن *bord-/bar-* to carry, take, win

بررسی *barresi* inventory

برف *barf* snow

برق *barq* electricity

برگشتن *bar-gashtan* to return

برنامه *barnâme* program

برومند *borumand* worthy, prosperous

بریدن *boridan* to cut

بزرگ *bozorg* big; ~-*shodan* to grow up; ~*vâr* great

بس *bas* enough, plenty, many a

بساط *besât* carpet; ~ *bar pâ kardan* to set up shop

بستن *bast-/band-* to shut, fasten, tie

بسته *baste -gân* relative

بسیار *besyâr* very, much

بشقاب *boshqâb* plate

بطری *botri* bottle

بعد *ba'd* after; ~*an* afterward; ~ *az* after (prep.); ~ *az ân-ke* after (conj.)

بعضی *ba'z-i* some

بعید *ba'id* unlikely

بغل *baqal* lap

بقچه *boqche* sack, bundle

بقیه *baqiye* the rest

بلافاصله *belâfâsele* immediately

بلد *balad-budan* to know, know how (+ subj.)

بلغور *balqur-kardan* to gobble, chatter

بلند *boland* tall, loud

بله *bále* yes

بند *band-* pres. stem of *bastan;* ~-*âmadan* to come to an end, be blocked

بودن *bud-/bâsh-* to be

بوسیدن *busidan* to kiss

به *be* to, with, by; *beh* better

بهار *bahâr* spring

به به *bah bah* exclamation of delight

بهتر *behtar* better

بهم *beham* together

بهیچوجه *behichvajh* in no way, (+ neg.) not nearly so

بی *bi* without; ~ *ân-ke* unless, without

بیابان *biâbân* wilderness

بیچاره *bichâre* helpless, poor

بیخ *bikh* bottom, root

بیدار *bidâr* awake; ~-*shodan* to wake up

بیرون *birun* outside

بیشتر *bish(tar)* more

بین *bin-* pres. stem of *didan; bayn-e* between, among

بینوا *binavâ* miserable

بینی *bini* nose

بیهوده *bihude* futile

پا *pâ* foot; ~-*khordan* to be trod on; ~-*shodan* to stand up; *bar* ~ standing, erect; ~*varaqi* bottom of a page, footnote; ~*varchin* on tiptoes

پاچه *pâche* cuff; ~*varmâlide* impudent

پارچه *pârche* cloth

پارسال *pârsâl* last year

پاك *pâk* clean, pure; ~-*kardan* to clean, erase; ~*kon* eraser

پاكت *pâket* package, parcel, envelope

پائین *pâin* down, downstairs

پختن *pokht-/paz-* to cook

پخش *pakhsh-shodan* to spread; ~*idan* to spread

پدر *pedar* father

پدیدار *padidâr* visible; ~-*shodan* to come into view

پذیرائی *pazirâi* reception; ~-*kardan az* to receive, entertain

پذیرفتن *paziroft-/pazir-* to accept, receive

پر *por* full

پراکنده *parâkande* scattered

پرداختن *pardâkht-/pardâz-* to pay

پررو *porru* bold, insolent; ~*i-kardan* to be bold

پرستیدن *parastidan* to serve, worship

پرسیدن *porsidan* ask (*az* a person)

پرنده *parande -gân* bird

پرواز *parvâz* flight; ~-*kardan* to fly, take off

پروردن *parvard-/parvar-* to train, nourish

پره *pare-ye bini* nostril

پریدن *paridan* to fly away, soar

پریشان *parishân* upset, confused

پز *paz-* pres. stem of *pokhtan*

پزشك *pezeshk* physician

پس *pas* then, therefore; *pas-e* through; ~ *az* after (prep.); ~ *az ân-ke* after (conj.)

پستان *pestân* breast

پسته *peste* pistachio

پسر *pesar* boy, son

پشت *posht* back; ~-*e* behind; ~-*e bâm* roof

پشه *pashe* mosquito; ~*band* mosquito net

پلك *pelk* eyelid

پلنگ *palang* leopard

پنجره *panjare* window

پندار *pendâr* notion

پنداشتن *pendâsht-/pendâr-* to think, consider

پنهان *penhân* hidden; ~-*kardan* to hide; ~-*shodan* to disappear

پوچ *puch* silly, nonsense

پوشیدن *pushidan* to put on, wear

پول *pul* money; ~-*dâr* wealthy, rich

263

پهلو *pahlu* side

پهن *pahn* wide, stretched out

پی *pay-e* after

پیاده *piâde* on foot, by foot; ~-*shodan* to get out/off (of a vehicle); ~*raw* sidewalk, pedestrian

پیاز *piâz* onion

پیچیدن *pichidan* to wrap, turn, twist

پیدا *paydâ-kardan* to find

پیر *pir* old

پیرامون *pirâmun* environ

پیش *pish* forward; ~-*e* before, in front of; -*e* ~ ago; ~-*âmadan* to come up, happen; ~ *az* before (prep.); ~ *az in-ke* before (conj.); ~-*e pâ oftâde* trivial; ~-*raftan* to progress, advance; ~*nehâd* suggestion; ~*vâ* leader

پیوستن *payvast-/payvand- be* to join

تا *tâ* unit; to, up to; so long as, until; in order that; ~ *ânjâ-ke* insofar as

تابستان *tâbestân* summer

تابش *tâbesh* heat, warmth

تاریخ *târikh* pl *tavârikh* date, history

تاریک *târik* dark; ~*i* darkness

تازه *tâze* fresh, novel, recent(ly); furthermore; ~*vâred* newcomer

تبریز *tabriz* Tabriz

تحدید *tahdid* threat; ~-*kardan* to threaten

تحمل *tahammol* endurance; ~*nâpazir* unendurable

تحویل *tahvil* consignment

تختخواب *takhtekhâb* bed

تخم *tokhm* seed; ~-*e cheshm* eyeball; ~-*e morq* egg

تر *tar* wet

تراشیدن *tarâshidan* to shave

ترجیح *tarjih-dâdan* to prefer

تردامن *tardâman* scandalous

ترس *tars* fear; ~*ândan* to scare; ~*idan az* to fear, be afraid of

ترک *tark-kardan* to leave

ترمز *tormoz* brake

تسبیح *tasbih* rosary, worry beads

تشر *tashar* battle ax

تشنه *teshne* thirsty

تصمیم *tasmim* decision; ~-*gereftan* to decide

تعجب *ta'ajjob* astonishment

تعداد *te'dâd* number

تعریف *ta'rif* definition; ~-*kardan az* to tell about, relate; *ta'rif-kardan* to define

تعصب *ta'assob* fanaticism

تعمیر *ta'mir* repair; ~-*kardan* to repair

تغییر *taqyir* change; ~-*dâdan* to change (trs.); ~-*kardan* to change (intrs.)

تفنگ *tofang* gun, rifle; ~-*e shekâri* shotgun

تقدیم *taqdim* presentation; ~-*kardan* to present, offer

تقریباً *taqriban* almost, nearly

تقسیم *taqsim* division; ~-*kardan* to divide

تکاپو *takâpu* search, quest

تکان *takân-khordan* to shake, move (intrs.); ~-*dâdan* to shake, move (trs.)

تکرار *tekrâr-kardan* to repeat

تکه *teke* piece; ~~-*kardan* to chop to pieces

تکیه *takye-dâdan be* to lean against

تلخ *talkh* bitter; ~*i* bitterness

تماشا *tamâshâ* show; ~-*kardan* to watch; ~*gar* onlooker

تمام *tamâm-e* all of; ~-*shodan* to be finished; ~-*kardan* to finish

تمبر *tambr* stamp

تن *tan* body, person

تنبل *tambal* lazy

تند *tond* fast, quick

تنگ *tang* narrow, tight

تنها *tanhâ* alone, only

تو *to* you (sing.); *tu(-ye)* in, inside

توانا *tavânâ* capable

توانستن *tavânest-/tavân-* to be able

توبه *tawbe* repentance

توپ *tup* ball, cannonball; *bâ ~ o tashar* vindictively

توجه *tavajjoh* attention; ~-*dâshtan be* to pay attention to

توری *turi* net, screen

توقف *tavaqqof* stop, halt; ~-*kardan* to make a stop

تومان *tomân* 10 rials, toman

توی *tu-ye* in, inside

تهران *tehrân* Tehran

تیر *tir* arrow, bullet; ~-*keshidan* to tingle

ثابت *sâbet* proven; ~-*kardan* to prove

ثالث *sâles* third

ثانی *sâni* second (adj.)

ثانیه *sânie* pl *savâni* second (time)

جا *jâ* place

جاروب *jârub* broom; ~-*shodan* to be swept

جالب *jâleb* interesting

جان *jân* soul, life; dear

جدا *jodâ* separate; ~*i* separation; ~-*kardan* to separate

جدول *jadval* table, crisscross; ~-*e kalemât-e motaqâte'* crossword puzzle

جدید *jadid* new

جراح *jarrâh* surgeon; ~*i* surgery

جری *jari* bold

جریان *jarayân* flow

جرئت *jor'at* courage; ~-*dâshtan* to dare

جز *joz* except; *(be)* ~ *in-ke* unless, except that

جزیره *jazire* pl *jazâyer* island

جستجو *jostoju* search, hunt

جستن *jost-/ju-* to search for, seek; *jast-/jeh-* to leap, jump

جعبه *ja'be* box

جفت *joft* pair, mate

جلب *jalb-kardan* to attract

جلسه *jalese* session

جلو *jelaw-e* in front of; ~-*e chiz-i-râ gereftan* to stop (trs.)

جمع *jam'* group; ~-*kardan* to collect, gather; ~*iyat* group

جمله *jomle* sentence; totality

جن *jenn* the djinn, demons; ~-*gereftan* to exorcise demons

جنوب *jonub* south

جو *ju-* pres. stem of *jostan*

جواب *javâb -ât* answer, response; ~-*dâdan* to answer

جوان *javân* young, youth; ~*mard* chivalrous, noble

جواهر *javâher -ât* jewel

جور *jur* (colloq.) = *tawr; ân~ = ântawr; in~ = intawr; che~ = chetawr*

جوراب *jurâb* socks

جوهر *jawhar* ink

جهان *jahân* world

جهود *jahud* Jew

جیب *jib* pocket; ~-*boridan* to pickpocket

چاپ *châp-shodan* to be printed; ~-*kardan* to print

چاره *châre* remedy, alternative

چاق *châq-kardan* to puff on a waterpipe to get it going

چای *chây* tea

چپ *chap* left

چرا *chérâ* why; yes

چراغ *cherâq* light, lamp, flashlight

چرک *cherk* filth(y)

چسبیدن *chasbidan be* to stick to, cling to

چشم *cheshm* eye; ~*bandi* sleight-of-hand; ~*pezeshk* eye doctor

چشیدن *cheshidan* to taste

چطور *chetawr* how

چقدر *cheqadr* how much

چکیدن *chekidan* to drip

چگونه *chegune* how, in what manner

چمدان *chamedân* suitcase

چنان *chonân* so, so much, such; ~*che* in case that

چند *chand* how many, how much

چنگال *changâl* fork

چنین *chonin* so, so much, such

چو *cho* apocopated form of *chon*

چون *chon* because, since; when, if; like; ~-*ke* because, since

چه *che* what; *che...che* whether...or

چهار *chahâr* four; ~*gush* square

چیز *chiz* thing

حادثه *hâdese* pl *havâdes* event, incident; *az bad-e ~* as bad luck would have it

حاشیه *hâshie* edge, margin

حال *hâl* pl *ahvâl* state, condition

حالا *hâlâ* now, at present

حالت *hâlat* pl *hâlât* state, condition

حتماً *hatman* certainly, surely

حتی *háttâ* even, until

حدس *hads* guess; ~-*zadan* to guess

حدود *hodud-e* about, ca.

حرف *harf* -*hâ* word; pl *horuf* letter; ~-*zadan* to speak

حرکت *harakat* -*kât* motion, movement; ~-*kardan* to move

حرم *haram* sanctuary

حس *hess-kardan* to feel

حسرت *hasrat* regret

حق *haqq* pl *hoquq* right; ~-*dâshtan* to be right, be in the right

حقیقت *haqiqat* pl *haqâyeq* truth

حل *hall-kardan* to solve

حلقه *halqe* ring

حماسه *hamâse* epic

حمام *hammâm* bath(house)

حمله *hamle-kardan* to attack

حنا *hanâ* henna; ~-*bastan* to apply henna

حوصله *hawsele* patience

حیاط *hayât* courtyard

خارج *khârej* exterior, outside; *~ az* outside of; ~-*shodan az* to go out of, leave; ~*e* foreign: *vezârat-e ~e* Ministry of Foreign Affairs

خاستن *khâst-/khiz-* to rise

خاطر *khâter* mind; ~*jam'* relieved; *be ~-e* for the sake of; ~*e* pl -*rât* memory

خاك *khâk* earth, dust

خاکستر *khâkestar* ash; ~*i* grey

خال *khâl* tattoo; ~-*kubidan* to tattoo

خاله *khâle* maternal aunt

خالی *khâli* empty, void

خاموش *khâmush-kardan* to turn out/off, silence

خاندان *khânedân* family

خانم *khânom* lady, Miss, Mrs., Ms.

خانواده *khânevâde* family

خانه *khâne* house, home

خبر *khabar* pl *akhbâr* news

خدا *khodâ* God

خداحافظ *khodâhâfez* goodbye; ~*i-kardan bâ* to say goodbye to

خر *khar* donkey, ass

خراب *kharâb* broken, ruined; ~*e* pl -*bât* ruin

خرج *kharj-kardan* to spend (money)

خرد *kherad* wisdom; ~*mand* wise

خرگوش *khargush* rabbit

خرما *khormâ* date

خروج *khoruj* exit, going out

خریدن *kharidan* to buy

خسته *khaste* tired

خشك *khoshk* dry; ~*idan* to dry out

خصوصی *khosusi* private

خط *khatt* pl *khotut* line, handwriting

خلوت *khalvat* empty

خم *kham* bent, bent over

خمیازه *khamyâze* yawn; ~-*keshidan* to yawn

خنده *khande* laughter

خندیدن *khandidan* to laugh

خواب *khâb* sleep; ~*ândan* to put to sleep, lay down; ~*idan* to sleep, go to sleep; ~-*didan* to dream

خواستن *khâst-/khâh-* to want

خواندن *khând-/khân-* to read, recite, sing

خواه *khâh-* pres. stem of *khâstan*

خواهر *khâhar* sister

خواهش *khâhesh-kardan* to request

خوب *khub* good, well

خود *khod* self; ~*ru* wild

خودنمائی *khodnomâi-kardan* to display oneself

خوردن *khord-/khor-* to eat, drink; ~ *be* to hit, collide with

خوش *khosh* good; ~ *o besh* chit-chat

خوشحال *khoshhâl* happy

خوشگل *khoshgel* pretty, handsome

خوشمزه *khoshmaze* delicious

خون *khun* blood; ~ *râh-andâkhtan* to start a blood feud; ~*sard* calm

خویش *khish* self

خیابان *khiâbân* avenue

خیال *khiâl* thought, notion

خیر *khayr* good(ness), charity

خیره *khire* transfixed; ~-*shodan* to stare blankly

خیز *khiz-* pres. stem of *khâstan*

خیلی *kháyli* very, much, many

داخل *dâkhel* inside, interior

داداش *dâdâsh* brother, friend

دادن *dâd-/deh-* to give

دار *dâr-* pres. stem of *dâsh-tan*

دارا *dârâ* having, possessing

دارالتادیب *dârotta' dib* reformatory

داستان *dâstân* story

داشتن *dâsht-/dâr-* to have, hold, keep

دانا *dânâ -yân* learned, wise

دانستن *dânest-/dân-* to know, realize

دانش *dânesh* knowledge; ~*ju* student; ~*gâh* university

دانه *dâne* seed, unit

دایر *dâyer-kardan* to run (a shop)

دائی *dâi* maternal uncle

دبیرستان *dabirestân* high school

دختر *dokhtar* girl, daughter

در *dar* in; door

دراز *darâz* long; ~*-keshidan* to stretch out

درآمد *darâmad* income

درآمدن *dar-âmadan* to come out, come in

درباره *darbâre-ye* about, concerning

درخت *derakht -ân* tree

درخشیدن *derakhshidan* to shine

درد *dard* pain; *be ~-e kási khordan* to be of use to s.o.

دررفتن *dar-raftan* to run away

درس *dars* lesson; ~*-khândan* to study

درست *dorost* correct

درشت *dorosht* huge, rough

در میان *dar miân-e* amidst

دروغ *doruq* lie

درهم *darham* confused, jumbled

دریا *daryâ* sea; ~*che* lake

دریافتن *dar-yâftan* to comprehend

دزد *dozd* thief; ~*idan* to rob, steal

دست *dast* hand; *az ~ dâdan* to lose; *~ bar-dâshtan az* to stop, cease; ~*-keshidan az* to stop, cease; ~*-e kam* at least; ~*pâche* nervous, confused

دستور *dastur -ât* order, rule

دسته *daste* group, set

دعا *do' â* prayer

دعوا *da' vâ* fight

دعوت *da' vat* invitation; ~*-kardan* to invite

دفتر *daftar* office

دفعه *daf' e* pl *dafa' ât* time, instance

دقیق *daqiq* precise; ~*an* precisely; ~*e* pl *daqâyeq* minute

دکان *dokkân* pl *dakâkin* shop

دکتر *doktor* doctor

دم *dam* moment, breath

دل *del* heart, stomach; ~*pazir* pleasant

دلاور *delâvar* warrior, brave

دلداری *deldâri* consolation; ~*dâdan* to console

دلیل *dalil* reason

دنبال *dombâl-e* after, on the heels of; ~*-e chiz-i gashtan* to look for something

دندان *dandân* tooth; ~*pezeshk* dentist

دنیا *donyâ* this world; *be* ~ *âmadan* to be born

دوختن *dukht-/duz-* to stitch, sew

دور *dur* far; ~ *andâkhtan* to throw away

دوره *dawre* turn; ~*gard* street seller

دوست *dust* friend; ~*-dâshtan* to love

دویدن *davidan, dawidan* to run

ده *deh-* pres. stem of *dâdan*

ده *deh -ât* village

دهاتی *dehâti* villager

دهان *dahân* mouth

دیار *diâr* region

دیدن *did-/bin-* to see

دیده *dide -gân* eye

دیر *dir* late; ~*-shodan* to get late; ~*-kardan* to be late

دیروز *diruz* yesterday

دیشب *dishab* last night

دیگر *digar* other; (+ neg.) no more

دیوار *divâr* wall

دیوانه *divâne* mad, crazy

ذره *zarre* atom; ~*bin* magnifying glass

ذغال *zoqâl* coal, charcoal

ذهن *zehn* mind

رابع *râbe'* fourth

راجع به *râje' be* about, concerning

راحت *râhat* comfortable

رادیو *râdyo* radio

راست *râst* right, true; ~*i* truth

راندن *rând-/rân-* to drive

راه *râh* way, road; *(be)* ~*oftâdan* to get under way, set out; ~*-raftan* to walk, go, proceed; ~*nemudan* to guide; ~*nemâ* guide

ربع *rob'* quarter

رحمت *rahmat* mercy; ~*-kardan* to have mercy

رخت *rakht* clothes, clothing

رختخواب *rakhtekhâb* bedclothes

ردیف *radif* row

رساندن *resân(i)dan* to deliver

رستن *rost-/ru-* to grow; *rast-/rah-* to escape

رسیدن *residan be* to arrive at, reach

270

رشد *roshd* growth, maturity;
~-*kardan* to grow,
mature

رشید *rashid* eldest

رغبت *raqbat* delight, desirous-
ness

رفتار *raftâr* conduct

رفتن *raft-/raw-* to go; *roft-
/rub-* to sweep

رقصیدن *raqsidan* to dance

رم *ram* skittish, not tame; ~-
kardan to shy off

رنگ *rang* color

رو *ru* face, aspect; *ru-* pres.
stem of *rostan; raw-*
pres. stem of *raftan*

روان *ravân* soul

روبرو *ruberu-ye* in front of,
facing

روح *ruh* pl *arvâh* spirit; ~*âni -
un* cleric

روده *rude* bowel

روز *ruz* day; ~*gâr* time;
~*nâme* newspaper

روستا *rustâ* village

روشن *rawshan* light, bright,
clear; ~-*kardan* to turn
on (lights)

روی *ru-ye* on

رویهم *ruyeham* jumbled; ~ *vâ-
raftan* to collapse; ~*rafte*
generally

روئیدن *ruidan* to grow

ریختن *rikht-/riz-* to pour; to fall
to pieces

ریز *riz* tiny; pres. stem of
rikhtan

ریش *rish* beard

زار *zâr* bitter(ly)

زان *zân = az ân* (poet.)

زانو *zânu -ân* knee

زاویه *zâvie* pl *zavâyâ* corner,
angle, recess

زبان *zabân* tongue

زحمت *zahmat* bother, trouble;
~-*keshidan* to go to
trouble; *bi* ~ "if it's no
bother," please

زدن *zad-/zan-* to hit, strike

زرنگ *zerang* clever

زمان *zamân* time, era

زمستان *zemestân* winter

زمین *zamin* land, earth, floor

زن *zan* woman, wife

زن *zan-* pres. stem of *zadan*

زنجیر *zanjir* chain

زندگانی *zendegâni* life

زندگی *zendegi* life; ~-*kardan* to
live

زنده *zende* alive

زنگ *zang* bell; ~-*zadan* to ring

زوبین *zubin* javelin

زود *zud* early; quick, fast

زور *zur* force

زهر *zahr* poison; ~-*e hajr*
pangs of separation

زیاد *ziâd* much

زیبا *zibâ* beautiful

زیر *zir-e* under; *~zamin* basement

زیرا *zírâ* because

زیستن *zist-/zi-* to live

زیلو *zilu* coarse type of rug

ساختمان *sâkhtemân* building

ساختن *sâkht-/sâz-* to build, make

ساده *sâde* simple

ساعت *sâ'at* pl *sâ'ât* hour; clock

سال *sâl* year

سالم *sâlem* sound, healthy

سایه *sâye* shadow, shade

سبز *sabz* green

ستون *sotun* column

سخت *sakht* hard, very

سر *sar* head; beginning, end; *~ dar-âvordan az* to understand; *~dard* headache

سرا *sarâ* public building, official residence, palace

سرازیر *sarâzir* headed down, rolling down

سراغ *sorâq-e kas-i-râ gereftan* to look for, search for someone; *be ~-e kas-i âmadan* to come looking for someone

سرد *sard* cold (adj.)

سرشناس *sarshenâs* well-known

سرك *sarak-keshidan* to poke the head out

سرگرم *sargarm* busy; *~i* hobby, amusement

سرما *sarmâ* cold (n.); *~-khordan* to catch cold

سرگذشت *sargozasht* adventure

سرنوشت *sarnevesht* fate

سروصدا *sarosedâ* noise; *~-kardan* to make noise

سروکار *sarokâr-dâshtan bâ* to associate with

سعی *sa'y-kardan* to try

سفر *safar* journey

سفید *sefid* white

سلام *salâm* greeting; *~-kardan be* to greet

سلامت *salâmat* healthy; *~i* health

سلطان *soltân* pl *salâtin* sultan

سماجت *samâjat* obstinacy

سنگ *sang* stone, rock; *~in* heavy

سوار *savâr* horseman, riding (vehicle); *~-shodan* to mount, get in/on (vehicle)

سؤال *so'al -ât* question; *~-kardan* to ask questions

سوختن *sukht-/suz-* to burn

سود *sud* profit

سوراخ *surâkh* hole

سوز *suz-* pres. stem of *sukhtan*

سیاه *siâh* black

سیل *sayl* flood, torrent

سیلی *sili* slap; *~-khordan* to get slapped; *~-zadan* to slap

272

سیم *sim* wire

سینه *sine* breast, chest

شاخه *shâkhe* branch

شاد *shâd* joyful, happy

شاعر *shâ'er* pl *sho'arâ* poet

شام *shâm* evening, evening meal

شانه *shâne* shoulder

شاه *shâh -ân* king; *shâhanshâh* king of kings, emperor

شاهنامه *Shâhnâme-ye Ferdawsi* the Book of Kings by Abu'l-Qasim Firdawsi (completed A.D. 1010)

شاید *shâyad* maybe

شایستن *shâyest-/shây-* to be proper

شب *shab* night

شبانه‌روز *shabâneruz* day, 24 hours

شباهت *shebâhat* resemblance; ~-*dâshtan be* to resemble

شپش *shepesh* lice

شخص *shakhs* pl *ashkhâs* person

شدت *sheddat* intensity

شدن *shod-/shaw-* to become, be possible

شدید *shadid* severe, intense

شراب *sharâb* wine

شرح *sharh* explanation; ~-*e hâl* biography

شرط *shart* pl *sharâyet* condition, qualification; ~-*bastan* to make a bet; ~-*kardan* to stipulate; *be ~ike* provided that

شرق *sharq* east, orient

شروع *shoru'-kardan be* (+ inf.) to begin, start

شستن *shost-/shu-* to wash

شعار *sho'âr* motto, slogan, emblem

شقیقه *shaqiqe* temple

شك *shakk* doubt

شكر *shekar* sugar; *shokr* thanks

شكستن *shekast-/shekan-* to break

شكوه *shokuh* splendor; *bâ~* splendid

شل *shol* loose, flabby

شلاق *shallâq* switch, crop

شلوغ *sholuq* crowded

شما *shomâ* you (pl.)

شماره *shomâre* number

شمال *shemâl* north

شمد *shamad* thin white sheet

شمردن *shomord-/shomâr-* to count

شمشیر *shamshir* sword

شناختن *shenâkht-/shenâs-* to know, recognize

شنیدن *shenid-/shenaw-* to hear

شو *shaw-* pres. stem of *shodan; shu-* pres. stem of *shostan*

شوهر *shawhar* husband

273

شهر *shahr* city; ~*bâni* police headquarters; ~*dâr* mayor

شیء *shay'* pl *ashyâ'* thing, article

شیر *shir* milk; lion

شیراز *shirâz* Shiraz

شیرین *shirin* sweet

صاحب *sâheb* owner, master

صبح *sobh* morning; ~*âne* breakfast

صحبت *sohbat-kardan* talk

صحن *sahn* mosque courtyard

صحیح *sahih* correct

صدا *sedâ* sound, voice; ~*kardan* to call out to

صندلی *sandali* chair

صورت *surat* face; case: *dar ân* ~ in that case; *dar qayr-e in* ~ otherwise; ~*bastan* to appear, seem; to be possible

ضرب *zarb* beat, beating; ~*e* stroke (of a clock)

ضریح *zarih* grating around a saint's tomb

ضعف *za'f* weakness

ضعیف *za'if* thin, skinny, weak

طالبی *tâlebi* melon, canteloupe

طب *tebb* medicine; ~*i* medical

طبقه *tabaqe* -*qât* class, stratum

طبیب *tabib* pl *atebbâ* doctor

طبیعت *tabi'at* nature; ~*an* naturally

طبیعی *tabi'i* natural

طرز *tarz* manner

طرف *taraf* direction; ~-*e* toward

طشت *tasht* tub

طفل *tefl* pl *atfâl* child; ~*ak* poor kid

طلا *talâ* gold; ~*i* golden

طلب *talab* request; ~-*kardan* to demand, ask for

طور *tawr* pl *atvâr* manner

طوع *taw'* willingness

ظاهر *zâher* apparent; ~-*shodan* to appear; ~-*kardan* to make apparent

ظرف *zarf* dish, container; ~-*e* within

ظهر *zohr* noon

عادت *âdat* -*dât* custom, habit

عاشق *âsheq* pl *oshshâq* lover, in love; ~-*e kas-i shodan* to fall in love with s.o.

عالم *âlam* world

عامیانه *âmmiâne* common

عبا *abâ* sleeveless cloak

عبور *obur-kardan* to cross, traverse

عجیب *ajib* strange

عدد *adad* number, unit

عذر *ozr* pardon; ~-*khâstan* to beg pardon

274

عرض *arz* petition; ~-*kardan* to say humbly

عرضه *arze* display; ~-*dâshtan* to display (wares)

عشق *eshq* love

عصبانی *asabâni* angry; ~*yat* anger

عصر *asr* late afternoon

عقیده *aqide* pl *aqâyed* belief

علت *ellat* pl *elal* malady

علف *alaf* fodder, grass, weed

علی *ali* Ali; ~*zâde* Alizadeh

عمامه *amâme* turban

عمر *omr* life, age

عمل *amal* pl *a'mâl* act, deed, job; ~-*kardan be* to act on

عمله *amale -jât* worker

عمو *amu* paternal uncle

عمه *amme* paternal aunt

عوض *avaz-kardan* to change (trs.)

عهده *ohde* responsibility; *az* ~ *bar-âmadan* to accomplish

عیب *ayb* pl *oyub* fault, flaw

عینك *aynak* eyeglasses

غارت *qârat* plunder

غذا *qazâ* food

غرب *qarb* west

غریب *qarib* strange, stranger

غرق *qarq-shodan* to sink, drown; ~-*e khâb* sound asleep

غروب *qorub* sunset

غلت *qalt* toss; ~-*zadan* to toss

غلطیدن *qaltidan* to toss and turn

غم *qam* grief; ~-*khordan* to grieve; ~*angiz* tragic

غیر *qayr* other (-*e, az* than)

فارسی *fârsi* Persian (language)

فارغ *fâreq* free, unencumbered; ~-*shodan az* to get free of

فاصله *fâsele* distance; ~-*dâshtan bâ* to be distant from

فایده *fâyede* pl *favâyed* advantage, benefit

فراخ *farâkh* broad

فرار *farâr-kardan* to run away

فراگرفتن *farâ-gereftan* to seize, overtake

فراموش *farâmush* forgetting; ~-*kardan* to forget; ~*kâr* forgetful

فربه *farbeh* fat, fatted

فرد *fard* pl *afrâd* individual

فردا *fardâ* tomorrow, next day

فرستادن *ferestâd-/ferest-* to send, dispatch

فرسنگ *farsang* league, ca. 6 km.

فرش *farsh-kardan* to furnish

فرصت *forsat* opportunity

فرق *farq* difference; ~-*kardan* to make a difference; ~-*dâshtan bâ* to be different from

فرمان *farmân* order; *~bardâr* obedience

فرمایش *farmâyesh -ât* order, command

فرمودن *farmud-/farmâ-* to order, command

فرو *foru* down; *~-rikhtan* to sink; *~-kardan* to shove down

فروختن *forukht-/forush-* to sell

فرودگاه *forudgâh* airport

فروشگاه *forushgâh* department store

فروشنده *forushande* seller, salesperson

فریاد *faryâd* shout, cry; *~-zadan* to shout

فشار *feshâr* pressure; *~-âvordan be* to apply pressure to

فشردن *feshord-/feshâr-* to press

فعلاً *fe'lan* at present

فقط *faqat* only

فقیر *faqir* pl *foqarâ* poor

فکر *fekr* pl *afkâr* thought, idea; *~-kardan* to think

فلان *folân* so-and-so

فن *fann* pl *fonun* skill, art

فنجان *fenjân* cup

فور *fawr: ~an* immediately; *~i* immediate, urgent

فوق *fawq-e* above; *~-esh* at most

فهم *fahm* understanding; *~idan* to understand

فینه *fine* fez

قابل ذکر *qâbel-e zekr* worthy of mention

قاشق *qâshoq* spoon

قاعده *qâ'ede* pl *qavâ'ed* rule; *be ~* according to rule, as it should be

قبا *qabâ* coat, greatcoat; *~darâz* wearing a long coat

قبل *qabl* before; *~an* before (adv.); *~ az* before (prep.); *~ az in-ke* before (conj.); *-e ~* ago

قبول *qabul-kardan* to accept

قدر *qadr* amount, extent

قدم *qadam* pace; *~-zadan* to walk about

قدیم *qadim* ancient; *~i* old

قرار *qarâr-dâshtan* to be situated; *~-gereftan* to settle, be stable; *~-gozâshtan* to fix on a time, make a date; *az ~-e* at the rate of

قربان *qorbân* sacrifice

قرینه *qarine* twin, matching

قرمز *qermez* red

قشنگ *qashang* pretty, beautiful

قصه *qesse* pl *qesas* story

قضیه *qaziye* pl *qazâyâ* affair

قطار *qatâr* train

قفل *qofl* lock

قلب *qalb* heart

قلع وقمع *qal'oqam'-kardan* to exterminate, wipe out

قلم *qalam* pl *aqlâm* pen

قلیان *qalyân* water pipe, hookah

قنات *qanât* canal

قوی *qavi* strong

قهوه *qahve* coffee; ~*irang* coffee-colored; ~*khâne* coffeehouse

قیافه *qiâfe* face, mien

قیمت *qaymat* price, value

کار *kâr* work, job; thing; ~-*kardan* to work, to do something; *be* ~ *bordan* to use; ~*khâne* -*jât* factory; ~*gar* worker

کارد *kârd* knife

کاروان *kâravân* caravan

کاسب *kâseb* tradesman

کاش *kâsh(ki)* would that

کاغذ *kâqaz* paper; ~*bâzi* paper-shuffling

کامل *kâmel* complete, perfect; ~*an* completely, perfectly

کان *kân* = *ke ân* (poet.)

کاوش *kâvesh-kardan* to scrape

کاه *kâh* straw

کباب *kabâb* grilled meat; *dokkân-e* ~*pazi* grill shop

کبوتر *kabutar* pigeon

کت *kot* jacket

کتاب *ketâb* book; ~*khâne* library

کثافت *kesâfat* dirt, filth; ~*kâr* messy

کثیف *kasif* dirty

کج *kaj* crooked

کجا *kojâ* where

کجاوه *kajâve* camel litter

کدام *kodâm* which

کرایه *kerâye* rent; ~-*dâdan* to rent out; ~-*kardan* to rent

کردن -*kard*-/-*kon*- compound verb

کس *kas* person, one

کساد *kasâd* slow (market); ~*i* slump (in market)

کشت *kesht-shodan* to be cultivated

کشتن *kesht*-/*kâr*- to plant; *kosht*-/*kosh*- to kill

کشتی *keshti* boat, ship

کشور *keshvar* country

کشیدن *keshidan* to draw, pull

کف *kaff* palm; ~-*e zamin* floor

کفش *kafsh* shoe

کفن *kafan* shroud

کلاس *kelâs* class; *sar-e* ~ in class, to class

کلاغ *kalâq* crow

کلافه *kalâfe* impatient, out of sorts

کلانتری *kalântari* police station

کلفت *koloft* thick

کلمه *kaleme* pl -*mât* word

کلنگی *kolangi-kardan* to crook

کلید *kelid* key, switch

کلیه *kolliye* totality

کم *kam* little

کمک *komak* help; *~-kardan* to help

کم‌مایه *kammâye* petty, with little capital

کمند *kamand* lasso

کن *kon-* pres. stem of *kar-dan*

کنار *kenâr* side, edge

کنج *konj* corner; *~kâv* curious

کنیه *konye* nickname, patro-nymic

کوبیدن *kubidan* to tap, pound

کوتاه *kutâh* short

کوچک *kuchek* little, small

کوچه *kuche* lane

کودک *kudak* child

کور *kur* blind

کوشش *kushesh* attempt; *~-kar-dan* to make an effort

کوشیدن *kushidan* to strive

کوفتن *kuft-/kub-* to pound

کوه *kuh* mountain

که *ke* that; when; for

کهنه *kohne* old

کی *kay* when; *ki* who

کیلو *kilo* kilogram

گاو *gâv* cow

گاه *gâh* time; *gâh gâh* from time to time; *~-i* occa-sionally, once

گچ *gach* chalk

گدا *gedâ* beggar

گذاشتن *gozâsht-/gozâr-* to put, place; let

گذراندن *gozarândan* to spend (time)

گذشتن *gozasht-/gozar- az* to pass by, go beyond

گذشته *gozashte* past, last

گران *gerân* expensive

گربه *gorbe* cat

گرد *gard-* pres. stem of *gash-tan; gerd* round, *~-e* around (prep.), *~-âma-dan* to gather round

گرداندن *gardândan* to turn (trs.)

گردن *gardan* neck

گردو *gerdu* walnut

گردیدن *gardidan* to turn (int.); substitutes for *shodan* in cmpds.

گرسنه *gorosne* hungry

گرفتار *gereftâr* taken, seized, busy

گرفتن *gereft-/gir-* to take, seize

گرم *garm* warm, hot

گرما *garmâ* warmth, heat

گره *gereh* knot; *~-zadan* to tie a knot; *~-dâr* knotted

گریستن *gerist-/gery-* to cry

گریه *gerye-kardan* to cry

گزاردن *gozârdan* to put, place, submit

گشاد *goshâd* wide

گشتن *gasht-/gard-* to turn (int.)

گشودن *goshud-/goshâ-* to open, widen

گفتگو *goftogu* talk, dialogue

گفتن *goft-/gu-* to say

گل *gol* flower, rose; ~*chin* carefully, gingerly; ~*dân* flowerpot; ~*khâne* greenhouse; *gel* mud

گلو *golu* throat

گلیم *gelim* woven rug

گمان *gomân* thought, notion; ~*-kardan* to think, consider

گم *gom* lost; ~*-shodan* to get lost; ~*-kardan* to lose

گناه *gonâh* crime, sin

گنبد *gombad* dome

گنجشك *gonjeshk* sparrow

گو *gu-* pres. stem of *goftan*

گوسفند *gusfand* sheep

گوش *gush* ear; ~*-dâdan* to listen; ~*-kardan be* to listen to

گوشت *gusht* meat

گوشه *gushe* corner

گول *gul-khordan* to be deceived; *gul-zadan* to deceive, fool

گوناگون *gunâgun* various

گیج *gij* dizzy, spinning

گیر *gir-* pres. stem of *gereftan*

گیرافتادن *gir-oftâdan* to get caught

لازم *lâzem* necessary

لاعلاج *lâ' elâj* with no alternative

لاغر *lâqar* thin, skinny

لای *lâ-ye* in between

لباس *lebâs* clothes

لج *lajj* obstinacy; -*kardan* to be obstinate

لحظه *lahze* pl *lahazât* moment

لرزیدن *larzidan* to tremble, shake

لطف *lotf* kindness; interest

لودادن *law-dâdan* to inform on

لوطی *luti* tough, ruffian

لیتر *litr* liter

لیوان *livân* glass, tumbler

ما *mâ* we, us

ماجرا *mâjarâ* adventure

مادر *mâdar* mother

ماشین *mâshin* car, automobile

مال *mâl* pl *amvâl* possession

مامور *ma' mur -in* agent

ماندن *mând-/mân-* to remain, stay; (neg.) to cease to exist

مانستن *mânest-/mân- be* to resemble

مانند *mânand-e* like (prep.)

ماه *mâh* moon, month

مایع *mâye'* liquid

مایه *mâye* capital, base

متاسف *mota' assef* sorry; ~*âne* regrettably

متبرك *motabarrek* blessed

متر *metr* meter

متروك *matruk* abandoned

متقاطع *motaqâte'* intersecting

مثل *masal* pl *amsâl* likeness; ~an for example; *mesl-e* like (prep.); ~-e in-ke as though

مجال *majâl* opportunity

مجانى *majâni* free, gratis

مجبور *majbur* obliged

مجله *majalle -lât* magazine

محافظ *mohâfez* guardian

محاكمه *mohâkeme-kardan* to sentence

محال *mohâl* absurd, impossible

محبت *mahabbat* affection, kindness

محدود *mahdud* limited, delineated; ~e defined period

محض *be mahz-e* as soon as

محل *mahall* place; ~e quarter of a city

محفوظ *mahfuz* protected

محكم *mohkam* tight, fast, hard

محو *mahv-shodan* to be obliterated

محوطه *mohavvate* enclosure

محيط *mohit* milieu

مخصوصاً *makhsusan* especially

مداد *medâd* pencil

مدت *moddat* period of time

مدرسه *madrase* school

مراجعه *morâje'e-kardan be* to consult

مرام *marâm* goal

مرتب *morattab* constant, continual

مرتبه *martabe* pl *marâteb* degree; *be marâteb* much (with comparatives)

مرتكب *mortakeb-shodan* to commit (crime, sin)

مرد *mard* man

مرداد *mordâd* midsummer month

مردك *mardak* fellow

مردم *mardom* people

مردن *mord-/mir-* to die

مرز *marz* border; ~bân border guard

مرسوم *marsum* customary

مرغ *morq* chicken

مرگ *marg* death; ~ o mir death and dying

مرور *morur* review

مريض *mariz* sick

مريم *maryam* Maryam

مزرعه *mazra'e* pl *mazâre'* farm

مزه *maze* taste

مسافر *mosâfer* traveler

مساله *mas'ale* pl *masâ'el* problem

مسجد *masjed* mosque

مسخره *maskhare* derisive; ~-kardan az to mock

مسلك *maslak* career

مسلم *mosallam* certain

مشت *mosht* fist, fistful; ~-zadan to box

مشترک *moshtarek* in common

مشتری *moshtari* customer

مشغول *mashqul* busy, occupied

مشکل *moshkel* difficult, problematic

مشهور *mashhur* famous, well-known

مطلب *matlab* pl *matâleb* matter

مطمئن *motma'enn* sure, certain

مطیع *moti'* obedient

معاصر *moâser* contemporary

معذرت *ma'zarat* apology; ~-khâstan to apologize

معرکه‌گیر *ma'rekegir* acrobat

معروف *ma'ruf be* known as/for

معلم *mo'allem* -in teacher

معلوم *ma'lum* known, of course; ~-shodan to become known, be found out

معمولاً *ma'mulan* usually

معنی *ma'nâ* or *ma'ni* pl *ma'âni* meaning

معوج *moavvaj* crooked

معیوب *ma'yub* faulty

مغز *maqz* brain

مفصل *mofassal* elaborate

مفید *mofid* useful

مقابل *moqâbel* opposite, facing

مقام *maqâm* -ât position

مقایسه *moqâyese* comparison; ~-kardan to compare

مقدار *meqdâr* amount

مقدمه *moqaddeme* pl -mât preliminaries

مقصود *maqsud* intention

مگر *mâgar* interrogative particle; except; perhaps; ~ in-ke unless

مگس *magas* fly; ~kosh fly-swatter

ملک *malek* pl *moluk* king; *molk* kingdom

ملی *melli* national

ممکن *momken* possible

مملکت *mamlakat* pl *mamâlek* country

من *man* I, me

مناره *menâre* minaret

منتظر *montazer* waiting, expecting

منزل *manzel* pl *manâzel* station, residence

منطقه *manteqe* pl *manâteq* region

منع *man'-kardan* to forbid

مؤثر *mo'asser* influential

موجود *mawjud* existent, being

مؤدب *mo'addab* polite

موفق *movaffaq* successful; ~iyat success

موقع *mawqe'* pl *mavâqe'* time, opportunity

مهر *mohr* seal

مهربان *mehrbân* kind

مهم *mohemm* important

مهمان *mehmân* guest

مهیب *mohib* frightful

281

میان *miân* middle; *~e* midst

میر *mir-* pres. stem of *mordan*

میز *miz* table, desk

میل *mayl* inclination; *~-dâshtan* to be inclined

میوه *mive -jât* fruit

ناامید *nâomid* desperate, hopeless

ناپدید *nâpadid* invisible; *~-shodan* to disappear

ناجور *nâjur* inappropriate, wrong, out of place

ناچار *nâchâr* helpless; *be ~* there was nothing to do but

ناخن *nâkhon* fingernail

ناشناس *nâshenâs* unfamiliar

ناگهان *nâgahân* suddenly

نام *nâm* name

نامه *nâme* letter

نامیدن *nâmidan* to name

نان *nân* bread

ناهار *nâhâr* midday meal

نتیجه *natije* pl *natâyej* result, conclusion; *be ~ residan* to come to a conclusion

نثر *nasr* prose

نخ *nakh* thread; *~nomâ* threadbare

نخست *nakhost* first, prime; *~ vazir* prime minister

نخل *nakhl* date palm

نخیر *nákhayr* no

نزدیك *nazdik* close, near; *~i* vicinity

نسبت *nesbat* relationship; *~ be* relative to

نسبة *nesbatan* relatively

نشان *neshân-dâdan* to show; *~i* description, address

نشاندن *neshândan* to make sit down; quench; quell

نشانه *neshâne* target; *~-gereftan* to take aim at

نشستن *neshast-/neshin-* to sit, be seated

نشیمن *neshiman* home, nest

نصف *nesf* half

نظر *nazar* sight, view; *be ~ âmadan* to seem; *~-kardan* to gaze; *be ~-e* in the opinion of

نعره *na're* shout; *~-zadan* to cry out

نعلین *na'layn* sandals

نفر *nafar* person

نفس *nafas* breath; *~-keshidan* to breathe

نقطه *noqte* pl *noqat* dot, point

نقل *naql* narration; *~-kardan* to relate, narrate

نگاه *negâh* gaze, look; *~-kardan* to look (at)

نگهداری *negahdâri-shodan* to be kept

نگهداشتن *negah-dâshtan* to stop, hold, keep

نماز *namâz* prayer; *~-khândan* to pray

نمایان *nomâyân* apparent, visible

نمودن *nemud-/nemâ-* to seem, appear; to represent

نمونه *nemune* example, sample

نو *naw* new

نوازش *navâzesh* caress; ~-*kardan* to caress; ~*gar* caressing

نوبت *nawbat* turn

نوحه *nawhe* wailing; ~-*khândan* to wail

نور *nur* light

نوشتن *nevesht-/nevis-* to write

نوع *naw'* pl *anvâ'* sort, kind

نوك *nuk* beak

نه *na* no; ~...~ neither... nor; *neh-* pres. stem of *nehâdan*

نهادن *nehâd-/neh-* to place, put

نیز -*niz* too, also

نیزه *nize* spear

نیك *nik* = *niku*

نیکو *niku* good, well

نیم *nim* half

و -*o/va-* and

واجب *vâjeb* urgent

وارد *vâred-shodan be* to come in, enter

وارفتن *vâ-raftan* to collapse

واسوختن *vâ-sukhtan* to burn out

واقعاً *vâqe'an* really, actually

واقعه *vâqe'e* pl *vaqâye'* event, occurrence

وجود *vojud* existence; body; ~-*dâshtan* to exist

وحشت *vahshat* terror; ~ *bar-am dâsht* I was gripped by terror; ~-*kardan az* to be terrified by

وررفتن *var-raftan be* to tinker, fiddle with

ورود *vorud* entrance

وزارت *vezârat* ministry; ~*khâne* ministry

وزش *vazesh* blowing (of the wind)

وزیدن *vazidan* to blow (wind)

وزیر *vazir* pl *vozarâ* minister, vizier

وسط *vasat* middle

وسیع *vasi'* wide, broad, expansive

وسیله *vasile* pl *vasâyel* means

وصله *vasle* patch

وضع *vaz'* pl *awzâ'* situation

وعده *va'de* promise

وقت *vaqt* pl *awqât* time; ~-*ike* when

ول *vel* loose; ~-*kardan* to let go, turn loose

ولی *vâli* but

وهله *vahle* instance

وی *vay* he, she (archaic and literary)

هجری *hejri* of the Hegira

هجوم *hojum* attack; *~-âvordan be* to attack

هدف *hadaf* goal, target

هر *har* every; *~chand* however much; *~che* whatever; *~kojâ* wherever; *~ke* whoever; *~vaqt* whenever

هرگز *hargez* (+ neg.) never

هفته *hafte* week

هم *ham* each other; *-ham* too, also; *ham-* same; *~ân* that very, that same; *~ânjâ* right there; *~ântawr* just like that; *~ântawrke* just as; *~chonân* nonetheless

همديگر *hamdigar* each other

همراه *hamrâh* companion; *~-e* along with

همسال *hamsâl* contemporary, of the same age

همسايه *hamsâye -gân* neighbor

همشيره *hamshire* sister

همكلاسى *hamkelâsi* classmate

همه *hame* all, every

هميشگى *hamishegi* never-ending

هميشه *hamishe* always

همين *hamin* this very, this same; *~jâ* right here; *~tawr* just so

هنر *honar* art, skill; *~mand* artful, skillful, artisan

هنگام *hangâm* time, moment; *~-e* at the time of

هنوز *hanuz* still, yet

هوا *havâ* air, atmosphere, weather

هواپيما *havâpaymâ* airplane

هول *hawl-shodan* to be terrified, flustered

هياهو *hayâhu* uproar, ado

هيچ *hich* no, nothing; *~vaqt* ever, (+ neg.) never

يا *yâ* or

ياب *yâb-* pres. stem of *yâftan*

ياد *yâd* memory; *be ~ âvordan* to recall; *~-am âmad* I remembered; *~-am raft* I forgot; *~-dâdan* to teach; *~-gereftan* to learn

يارب *yârabb* O Lord!

يافتن *yâft-/yâb-* to find

يخ *yakh* ice; *~châl* refrigerator

يعنى *ya'ni* i.e., that is, that means

يك *yek* one (adj.); *~-i* one (pron.); *~bâre* all at once; *~digar* each other

Index

Numbers refer to paragraphs unless otherwise indicated.

TITLES OF INTEREST FROM IBEX PUBLISHERS

A Literary History of Persia
by Edward G. Browne
The classic history of Persian literature.
4 volumes / 2,323 pages / cloth / isbn 0-936347-66-X

The Divan-i-Hafiz
Translated and annotated by H. Wilberforce Clarke
1,180 pages / cloth / isbn 0-936347-80-5

A Millennium of Persian Poetry
by Wheeler M. Thackston
A guide to the reading and understanding of Persian Poetry
from the tenth to the twentieth century. In English and
Persian. Includes a glossary.
226 pages / softcover / isbn 0-936347-50-3

A Persian Reader by Lily Ayman (Ahy)
First grade reader specifically tailored for Persian language
children studying the language outside of Iran by the author of
the standard readers in Iran.
104 pages / softcover / reader: isbn 0-936347-34-1
96 pages / softcover / manual: isbn 0-936347-36-8

Persian Studies in North America
edited by Mehdi Marashi
Thirty-two articles on the state of the art of research and
teaching in Persian linguistics and literature.
560 pages / cloth / isbn 0-936347-31-8

An Introduction to Koranic and Classical Arabic
by Wheeler M. Thackston
360 pages / softcover / isbn 0-936347-40-6

To order the above books or receive our catalog, contact:
IBEX Publishers
Post Office Box 30087 / Bethesda, Maryland 20824 USA
Telephone (301) 718-8188 / Facsimile (301) 907-8707
www.ibexpub.com